Tadej POGAČAR: UNSTOPPABLE

Tadej Pogačar has spent a lot of time on the top step of the podium, with over 100 race wins in his professional career and more than 50 days in the Tour de France's famous leader's yellow jersey.

A biography of
the modern era's
greatest cyclist

Tadej
POGAČAR:
UNSTOPPABLE

Andy McGrath

BLOOMSBURY SPORT

LONDON • OXFORD • NEW YORK • NEW DELHI • SYDNEY

BLOOMSBURY SPORT
Bloomsbury Publishing Plc
50 Bedford Square, London, WC1B 3DP, UK
Bloomsbury Publishing Ireland Limited,
29 Earlsfort Terrace, Dublin 2, D02 AY28, Ireland

BLOOMSBURY, BLOOMSBURY SPORT and the Diana logo are trademarks of Bloomsbury Publishing Plc

First published in Great Britain, 2025

A catalogue record for this book is available from the British Library.

Library of Congress Cataloguing-in-Publication data has been applied for

ISBN: HB: 978-1-3994-2654-1; TPB: 978-1-3994-3185-9; ePDF: 978-1-3994-2651-0;
eBook: 978-1-3994-2653-4

2 4 6 8 10 9 7 5 3 1

Typeset in Adobe Garamond Pro by D.R. INK
Printed and bound in Great Britain by Clays Ltd, Elcograf S.p.A.

MIX
Paper | Supporting
responsible forestry
FSC® C018072
www.fsc.org

To find out more about our authors and books visit www.bloomsbury.com and sign up for our newsletters
For product safety related questions contact productsafety@bloomsbury.com

Contents

Pogačar's runaway success has helped to take UAE Team Emirates–XRG from a mid-table team in pro cycling's WorldTour top division to number one.

Winners are grinners: Pogačar celebrates time trial success on Peyragudes in the 2025 Tour de France, well on his way to a fourth victory in road cycling's flagship event.

Everyone loves 'Pogi': cycling fans wait expectantly for a glimpse of one of the sport's most popular racers ahead of a 2024 Tour de France stage.

AUTHOR'S NOTE

'I did not expect such a good start,' Tadej Pogačar said with a smile.

The shy, unassuming youngster was chatting to me in his team tracksuit in a sun-dappled courtyard at the 2019 Volta ao Algarve (Tour of the Algarve), a few days after his first win as a professional cyclist.

To be honest, I didn't think much of our first encounter and didn't leave the race believing he'd be a world-beater. No, he was a bright talent all right, but one in a crowded field of WorldTour wunderkinds, popping up at the top of the results sheet and probably set to recede into the pack again for months.

Well, it turns out that he is not like the others. For five years, Pogačar has been the fresh-faced but dominant force of professional cycling. In the modern sport, a contender tends to stick to his specialism – sprinter, *puncheur*, climber, stage racer, time triallist or *baroudeur*. Not Pogačar: he invades all domains and challenges all comers, seemingly improving with every season.

With four Tour de France triumphs, two world titles, a Giro d'Italia success and ten Monument victories among more than 100 wins achieved by the age of 27, comparisons to the great Eddy Merckx are, and will probably always be, inescapable.

Pogačar is a lot more than just awe-inspiring statistics and results, though. In this book, I want to give a comprehensive portrait of a champion, charting his journey from riding a unicycle around the quiet lanes of Komenda to becoming the barnstorming, perfectionist bike racer.

While his pedalling style appears effortless and hindsight makes his ascension seem inexorable, make no mistake, it has been far from straightforward.

I explore all the elements that went into creating this one-off: the character-building training sessions in Slovenia; the tactical lessons learned; the races where he redefined cycling; the setbacks he overcame; the components of both mind and body that have made him so prolific.

Travelling around Europe and to the United Arab Emirates, I conducted around 50 interviews with those who have been part of Pogačar's life: friends, teammates, ex-teammates, rivals, *directeurs sportifs*, mentors, coaches, biomechanists, mechanics, fans, school teachers and journalists.

There were many encounters with cycling's central figure in my old day job as the editor of *Rouleur*, helping to give me a head start. Let me thank my former employers, because it's through them that I interviewed Pogačar, his parents Mirko and Marjeta, his agent Alex Carera and Allan Peiper in 2021. Some of the quotes in the book's opening chapters are from that project.

Thanks also to GCN+. I journeyed to Slovenia in 2023 to make a documentary for them on the rise of Slovenian cycling, talking to Pogačar's parents again and several other key figures, helping with important background information. Sadly, it never saw the light of day, because the channel closed.

Pogačar and his inner circle declined to be interviewed for this book, but his voice runs through it, collected from our interactions over the years, as well as his innumerable press conferences and media dealings.

As his star has risen, Pogačar has gained in confidence and candour, while keeping the same humility and love of spectacular racing. He is still the chill 'Cannibal', Hinault with the bonhomie. Cycling has always just been a game to him, albeit one that he wins a lot more often than his peers.

It started in earnest at the Volta ao Algarve, but who knows where or when it will end? This will no doubt be the first of many books to be penned about this transcendent champion.

Andy McGrath
October 2025

Lean, green winning machine: wearing the eye-catching Slovenian national team kit, Pogačar pulled off one of his career's most daring breakaways at the 2025 World Championships road race in Rwanda.

The effort shows after sprinting to victory in stage 17 of the 2021 Tour de France atop the Col du Portet.

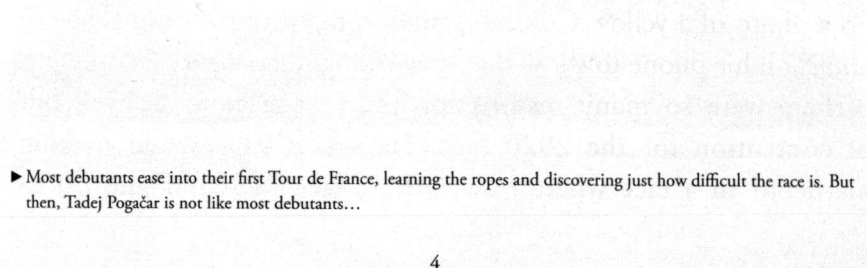
▶ Most debutants ease into their first Tour de France, learning the ropes and discovering just how difficult the race is. But then, Tadej Pogačar is not like most debutants…

1

THE HEIST

Lure, Tour de France 2020, Stage 20

Tadej Pogačar could see into the mechanics' truck from the team bus. A hive of activity, where the UAE Team Emirates staff were assembling his Colnago for the final day's stage in Paris in the white livery of best young rider.

'Why? So they don't have confidence [in me]?' he said to his team manager, with a smile, half-serious, half-joking. The implication was clear: he thought what many did not – Tour de France victory was still in play.

Joxean Fernández, a shaven-headed, Spanish live wire known universally in the sport as Matxin, told him to not worry. He pulled up a photo of a yellow Colnago frame, sprayed in the Tour shade of *jaune*, on his phone to show that they thought the same.

There were so many reasons for Tadej Pogačar to be well out of contention for the 2020 race. He was a 21-year-old making his debut in a race where only one rookie, Laurent Fignon, had won in the previous 40 years. The challenge was like a university freshman trying to complete his university course in a year with first-class honours.

He had only made his debut in a three-week Grand Tour 12 months earlier, finishing third at the 2019 Vuelta a España. But the Tour is a tougher challenge, physically and mentally. The rhythm of racing is different to other races, the fight for positioning is even more intense and starts earlier every stage, with the world's best riders in attendance, zeroed in on a stage win or a top-10 finish. Then there is heightened pressure from the hundreds of media, scrutinising gains, losses and drama daily.

Pogačar discovered this on stage 7, losing 81 seconds in crosswinds to his rivals, out of position and left behind after a puncture. It was characterised at the time as a typical *erreur de jeunesse*.

However, Pogačar was a fast learner, up to the challenge. By the penultimate stage of the Tour, he was sitting in second place, already the breakout star from the race after sprinting to two stage wins. He was 57 seconds behind the pre-race favourite and race leader, Primož Roglič. Such deficits have been overturned before on the race's final weekend, but only once in the 21st century and rarely between such evenly matched contenders.

A duel between two Slovenians would decide victory. Way out east on the bucolic, beech tree-filled edge of France's Vosges mountain range, the stage 20 time trial was 36.2 km long with a sting in its tail, the steep, arrhythmic 6 km of the final climb of La Planche des Belles Filles, where several sectors have gradients of double digits.

There was one more climb to go and Tadej Pogačar was going to throw everything at it. Second place on debut was already a dream, but he had a long shot at the ultimate fantasy.

· · · ·

The aim ahead of the Tour had been a top-5 place for Pogačar. UAE Team Emirates were weaker, lacking the firepower of star-studded rival squads Jumbo–Visma and Ineos Grenadiers, and left bereft of anticipated support riders in the Alps and Pyrenees, where the race is perennially decided.

They lost Pogačar's supposed joint leader Fabio Aru after he abandoned mid-race. His fellow Italian Davide Formolo also had to bid *arrivederci* after breaking his collarbone in a crash on stage 10. Key helper David de la Cruz battled on with a broken sacrum sustained on the opening day, while road captain Marco Marcato had a bladder infection. Jan Polanc was one of the few who could offer unaffected help. It built a problem-solving and backs-against-the-wall mentality within the team.

Ahead of the race's crucial final week, team *directeur sportif* Allan Peiper urged his skeleton crew not to settle for second best and to push for glory. Talking to Pogačar and his five remaining teammates, he used the example of the 2012 Giro d'Italia, when he was a team manager at Garmin-Sharp, a hotchpotch, underpowered team. Ryder Hesjedal, their Canadian outsider, took a memorable overall victory on the last-day time trial, moving ahead of long-time race leader Joaquim Rodríguez by just 16 seconds.

However, there was less cause for hope. Hesjedal had the edge over Rodríguez against the clock, whereas Roglič and Pogačar were closely matched. In fact, the race leader had beaten Pogačar comfortably in their only previous Grand Tour head-to-head at the 2019 Vuelta.

Roglič's team Jumbo–Visma had taken the Tour by the collar of the cycling jersey and squashed any attacking moves by rivals, showing their impressive strength in depth. The depleted UAE Team Emirates could offer little in the way of resistance, letting the Dutch squad do the controlling work of race leaders.

Little suggested Pogačar could claw the deficit back. In that year's Tour, he had not been able to distance Roglič since stage 8, almost two weeks earlier.

Three days before the time trial, the older Slovenian had put 17 seconds into Pogačar on the Col de la Loze, the race's highpoint. When Pogačar sought to crack him and make inroads, he was the one left watching the *maillot jaune* disappear up the road in the closing moments.

It was a blow to the youngster's morale and his challenge, though it underpinned the going trend: Roglič appeared to be the strongest rider with the strongest team, the surefire, deserved winner of the 2020 Tour de France. 'Before the time trial, it was over in my head,' Pogačar told *L'Équipe*. 'I was going to finish second and I was happy with that place and the best young rider's jersey.'

All Roglič had to do was not fall apart in the time trial – or be eclipsed by a spectacular performance.

. . . .

UAE Team Emirates had a secret weapon: meticulous preparation. 'I know every team reconned that Planche des Belles Filles time trial, but no one reconned it like we did,' the team's then-trainer and performance-coordinator John Wakefield says.

That was chiefly down to one of Pogačar's mentors on the team, Allan Peiper. A professional racer in the 1980s and early 1990s, Peiper had a hardscrabble rise, leaving Australia and an alcoholic, abusive father as a teenager and moving to Belgium. As a *directeur sportif,* he matched great knowledge, passion and empathy with straight-talking.

His presence in this Tour de France showdown was even more surprising than that of Pogačar: months earlier, he had been debilitated by prostate cancer, partially losing his eyesight and barely able to walk. In remission, vision restored and feeling stronger, Peiper resolved not to cut any corners, having seen few talents like the Slovenian prodigy in his lifetime.

On 17 June 2020, two days after Belgium reopened its borders following the relaxing of numerous Covid-19 lockdown restrictions, Peiper got in his car and headed 450 km south from his home in Geraardsbergen to the French town of Lure. Down the road from the home of mercurial French challenger Thibaut Pinot, it would host the start of the momentous time trial on the Tour's penultimate day.

A time trial possesses a purity and simplicity, with every GC contender setting off at two-minute intervals, going up against the clock. Weather conditions may change over several hours of racing, but there are fewer variables, certainly not ones like 145 riders on the road, fighting for every centimetre, attacking or slipstreaming, braking or divebombing. Success demands unwavering focus, precise pacing and cutting-edge aerodynamics.

And so, this was Peiper's equivalent of examining the route under a microscope in a laboratory. He drove the course in the rain, rode it with his own bike the next morning and then, for good measure, drove it again in the afternoon before finalising his notes. He realised a bike change would be essential, going from a wind-cheating time-trial bicycle to a lighter, regular road bike at the point when La Planche des Belles Filles robbed a rider of most of his speed – and the bike would need unusual gears for the climb's changing gradients.

They opted for a 14–29 rear cassette, normally used in junior racing. Most cassettes have two-tooth jumps, but the one obtained from Campagnolo was closer ratio, with one-tooth differences in the middle from 18 to 25, precise and ideal for the slower speeds Pogačar would be going at uphill. The set-up would be another key to success.

A month later, on 16 and 17 July, Pogačar and Mikkel Bjerg, his Danish teammate, rode the same Haute-Saône country roads three times, testing tyres, wheels, gears and equipment. The Slovenian followed the suggestion of former under-23 world champion Bjerg to start with a lone 58-tooth front chainring, making his bike even lighter and more aerodynamic. In a bid to ascertain the optimal spot to change bikes without losing speed, Bjerg spent one training ride going back and forth, testing the bike change six times, seeing where momentum was naturally scrubbed off by the harsh gradient. They found the point of inflection, as the road rose to 9 per cent, soon after turning right off the D16, by the road sign welcoming visitors to La Planche des Belles Filles.

With Pogačar, they drilled the bike change again and again. 'We probably reconned that 13 times,' Wakefield reflects, discussing the roles of the mechanic and *directeur sportif* in the team car behind. 'What was quicker? Does one person get out of the car, do two? How does the mechanic get out? What do we do with the other bike, where does Tadej put the bike – on the car, on the floor? It was super detailed.' Team mechanic Vasile Morari hurt himself one time when he failed to push off Pogačar with a fully straight arm.

They also carried out a full dress rehearsal with the intended skinsuit, wheels, tyres, tyre pressure and time-trial helmet for the race, having Pogačar chase Bjerg. Little wonder Pogačar said afterwards that he knew every corner, every pothole and where to accelerate.

The final touches came on the eve of the decisive stage itself. Pogačar asked Wakefield to put together a TT file from July's recon, showing his time on the course and estimating his speed for the opening several hundred metres, given that he had been unable to do them at race pace in Lure on open roads.

He wanted to know where he could go even faster. There was a calculated gamble they could take: racing the final climb with no power meter. Every gram saved would be milliseconds shaved off his time. Wakefield went to team upper management to tell them that they would instead put a sticker on the handlebars for their partner, power meter brand Stages.

With the Tour triumph still possible, they were worried: it would also mean riding on feel uphill, without an instrument providing real-time data to help gauge his effort. 'I remember saying "I haven't fucked up yet and I'm not going to now. Trust me for what we've done." That was my sales pitch,' Wakefield says.

That evening – as he recounted to *Tuttosport* later the same weekend – Pogačar's agent Alex Carera messaged him: 'never give up until Paris'. The reply was one word: 'never'.

All the homework done meant that there were no questions in Pogačar's head or lingering decisions to be made on race day. He could focus on the task at hand with peace of mind, sleeping in until 10:00 before going for a light spin. In contrast, his rival Primož Roglič rode the course that morning, expending precious mental and physical energy.

'It gave him an advantage. I understood that straight away,' Roglič lamented later to *L'Équipe*. 'Going there that morning was a mistake. I was too enthusiastic, I pushed too hard on my bike, I was going too fast. I should have done something much more relaxed.' He was also wearing a new time trial helmet, which he had not previously worn in a race.

In a rural, accommodation-light area, UAE Team Emirates had snagged a room for Pogačar at the Hostellerie des Sources, 4 km from the start town of Lure. He had rice, omelette and a yoghurt for lunch, watched the 24 Hours of Le Mans and the first few time-trial competitors on the TV and had a short nap.

On the team bus down the road, an hour before the time trial which would decide the sport's blue-riband race, he was singing out loud and dancing to give himself even more energy. Pressure, what pressure?

His teammate David de la Cruz got back to the bus after his race effort, setting the day's second fastest time. 'The TT was super hard. I tried to give him some advice of how I saw the race, but he didn't need it,' the Spaniard recalls. 'He was doing the warm-up really relaxed, even just asking how the TT was for me, but not to get any info. He was showing he was really confident that he will have a good day.'

After warming up with casual sunglasses and Beats headphones on, his Slovenian national champion skinsuit rolled down to his waist, Pogačar went over to Roglič and bumped fists. It was a sign of both their mutual respect and an acknowledgement of the duel about to unfold.

Many thought the race was already all over. At the top of La Planche des Belles Filles, several media were conducting interviews with Uroš Gramc, the experienced sports journalist for the Slovenian daily newspaper *Večer*, about Roglič, preparing their copy ahead of his anticipated victory.

Grand Tours are a slow burn, but by the final weekend, form, the general classification and psychological dominion are well-established, the results tending to confirm what is already known. The winner usually has a secure winning margin. (Indeed, that's how it would be for all of Pogačar's other Grand Tour wins.) Occasionally though, like on 19 September 2020, the race crackles with all the uncertainty and electricity of an Agatha Christie whodunnit and rationale is upturned.

Pogačar rolled down the start ramp at 17:12 local time, two minutes before his older adversary. Quickly into his hunched aerodynamic position, the visor on his Met helmet hiding his eyes, laser-focused on the road ahead, he took 13 seconds over Roglič in the flat 14 km to the first time check. His shoulders rocked a little more than his rival, but he was going marginally quicker.

In contrast, the race leader looked nervous and even started a split second slower than his adversary, spinning his pedals round as the final beep sounded on the start ramp in Lure when he should have accelerated away.

Those in the know felt that Pogačar was going out of his comfort zone to pressurise Roglič, to disrupt his focus and race plan. Even Pogačar's teammates, watching on the team bus, wondered whether his fast start would fade. 'But it was not the case. It was like he was gaining, gaining, gaining time. Everyone in the bus was absolutely in shock,' De la Cruz says.

Pogačar also had the added carrot of Miguel Ángel López, the man in third place, to chase. He zipped past with 18 km to go, catching the Astana leader who had set off two minutes ahead of him. (Adding to the day's upheaval, the Colombian had an abysmal performance, losing over six minutes to Pogačar and falling off the podium to sixth overall.)

Pogačar gained 36 seconds on Roglič in the rolling 30 km to the foot of the climb. The gradual loss of time was surprising, but not yet disastrous for Roglič. It was to be expected that the long-time yellow jersey would peg back time on La Planche des Belles Filles, having held something back.

However, this made the bike change even more pivotal, the precious seconds won or lost mattering even more. Tour organisers Amaury Sports Organisation (ASO) had put metal barriers with advertising hoardings for several hundred metres, aligning with Pogačar's change point at the 30.4-km mark, with 5.7 km left to race. As Pogačar slowed, the UAE Team Emirates team car door was already open, and mechanic Vasile Morari sprinted out. As planned and tested, the Slovenian placed his bike against the right front wing of the car, got on his new steed and was pushed off by the running mechanic. Gone in seven seconds. He had a slug of his water bottle and chucked it away, like a knight throwing down the gauntlet.

Roglič changed bikes a full 500 m later on the route, to the point that his *directeur sportif* had to put his hand out of the team car window to make space among the fans. It looked rushed and he struggled to clip into his pedals for a couple of seconds, adding to his decreasing advantage. With 5 km to go, Pogačar had slashed Roglič's virtual Tour de France lead from 57 seconds to 20 seconds. With 4.5 km to go, it was down to 10 seconds.

Pogačar was just getting going. As the gradient steepened and relented round the serpentine bends of La Planche des Belles Filles, Pogačar felt lifted, liberated, lightened. Somehow, he was able to maintain a brutal pace. His body language spoke of his will to win: springing out of the saddle to glean more speed, adrenaline coursing through his veins, turning the pedals around in a light and fluid manner despite the strain. After almost three weeks of racing, the Tour de France would be decided, mano a mano, on the last mountain.

In contrast, Roglič's cadence was high and choppy. His rhythm had been wrecked. Uncharacteristically, he gripped the handlebar drops and rose out of the saddle, trying to go faster. But he was still losing time.

The TV graphics from France Télévisions had been showing Roglič's lead ebbing away slowly on the flat, the seconds like grains of sand slowly falling. Now, it felt like the hourglass had emptied in one fell swoop.

Moments after the race leader went under the 4 km to go banner on the road, its graphic showing Roglič's lead changed from green to red. Pogačar was now leading the Tour de France on the road – and he did not know it yet.

On the climb, he could hardly hear his race radio through the screams of the crowd. One message came into his earpiece, telling him, 'You have a four-second lead.' He thought it related to the stage win; Allan Peiper meant the whole race.

The GPS timing shown on television was erratic, adding to the tension and confusion. At one point, it showed Roglič leading the race by eight seconds before changing to zero. Minutes later, it went haywire, switching between a deficit of 16 seconds for Roglič to one of just 4 seconds. Pogačar's parents initially thought the clock was mistaken, as did many of his peers watching on. *How was this possible?*

The Planche des Belles Filles saves its worst pitches until last. Cheered on by a three-deep crowd – strict Covid restrictions on spectators seemed to have gone out of the window on this baking September day – the champion elect hauled himself out of the saddle for the final, terrible ramp of 20 per cent.

Because of the steepness, riders pop up in the final metres on top of the climb as if appearing from a vacuum. Pogačar's fresh face, lined with the effort, was the colour of his white skinsuit as he threw his bike at the line like a seasoned sprinter.

Roglič had overtaken a tortoise-like Miguel Ángel López and even got a push from a fan, but nothing could propel him fast enough to stop the rot. As he approached the final 250 metres, his deficit to Pogačar ticked over 57 seconds. Now, his Tour defeat was official. His face wore a haunted, hollow expression, mirrored by that of his watching teammates at the finish. He had lost his form in more ways than one: his groundbreaking Lazer helmet was skew-whiff on his head, his elbows were out as he pedalled to the line. If you were being uncharitable, you'd say he looked more like an amateur cyclist on a sportive than the leader of the Tour de France.

Those 6 km of La Planche des Belles Filles made the difference. Pogačar did the climb in 16 minutes, 10 seconds, Roglič in 17 minutes, 30 seconds – slower by 1 minute, 20 seconds and only 11th fastest on the day. Only four riders were within a minute of Pogačar's time for the climb. In short, he crushed it. In winning the stage and moving into the race lead, Pogačar had also ensured victory in the King of the Mountains and young rider classifications.

Comparisons to Greg LeMond's eight-second victory over Laurent Fignon in 1989 came thick and fast. Next to the closest winning margin in race history, this was a landslide: 57 seconds down before the stage, Pogačar emerged from it 59 seconds up. Many people, especially in Slovenia, will remember where they were when he won the Tour and Roglič lost it. This was sport at its most unexpected, gripping and cruel.

Seconds after Roglič crossed the finish line, still catching his breath, Pogačar put his bare hands over his face in disbelief. 'You win the Tour!' someone next to him shouted, as soigneur Michele del Gallo, press officer Luke Maguire and team doctor Adriano Rotunno engulfed him in an embrace.

Sitting in the following team car behind Tadej, Allan Peiper had broken down and wept when they realised the result; his grizzled Australian mentor later called it the best moment of his life. Matxin was also in tears. Behind him, in the car's back seat, Pogačar's Slovenian mentor Andrej Hauptman, who had seen Tadej as an 11-year-old, wished he could cry, but he was numbed by shock.

No Pogačar win before or since has been met with the same raw astonishment and adrenaline rush by the champion himself, his wider team or the larger cycling world. Years later, his victories were expected and usually comfortably in the bag after long-distance attacks or following weeks of domination; his own voice usually a controlled monotone in immediate post-race interviews. This time, Pogačar's timbre wavered with emotion and he kept shaking his head with incomprehension: 'I don't know. I think I'm dreaming. I really don't know what to say. Unbelievable. My head will explode.'

Pogačar had spent half his life dreaming of simply racing the Tour de France; now, at 21, he was about to win it on his debut, its youngest champion since 1904, in a thrilling finale. He was in a state of conflict as well as shock. Roglič was a compatriot, not an opponent, the elder he looked up to – and had now beaten. The doyen and the young upstart shared a sweaty, brief hug, interrupting Pogačar's post-race TV interview. Deep down, that gesture meant the world to the young man. 'I'll never forget that moment ... it was as if he was allowing me to savour it, as if he were telling me, it wasn't my fault,' he told *L'Équipe* in 2021.

As fate would have it, the team buses of UAE Team Emirates and Jumbo–Visma were parked next to each other down the hill at the race start in Lure. After 3300 km of racing, ahead of the largely processional Paris stage where attacks are traditionally not made on the race leader, this outcome had the emotional heft and frayed nerves of a World Cup Final being decided in a penalty shoot-out, even if a time trial is anything but as capricious.

'We were going crazy, it was a carnival,' John Wakefield says of the reaction at UAE Team Emirates. Staff members were weeping and hugging; the usually reserved team principal Mauro Gianetti was bellowing and punching the air. 'I turned around to go back to the car to speak to my wife, and Visma… it was as if people had been murdered. I'll never forget, it was such a contrast, which you fully understand. It could have gone both ways,' Wakefield says.

Heads in hands, pure agony. There was one more insult added to their and Roglič's injury that day: driven to the press centre 20 km down the hill in Ronchamp, Roglič found himself in second place again, arriving just after the BMW carrying Tadej Pogačar. He had to wait for the new yellow jersey to finish his lengthy press conference, given to over 200 members of the media.

Many of them were still getting to grips with how to say the champion elect's surname correctly (Poh-gah-char), let alone the transformed race dynamic. This was a hell of an introduction to the wider world. 'I'm just a kid from Slovenia with two sisters, one brother and I don't know what to say. I like to have fun. I like to enjoy life and the little things. This press conference is too big for me,' Pogačar said, microphone in hand.

He was full of sympathy for his vanquished compatriot. 'Roglič was the best rider of the Tour with a really good team,' he insisted. 'They did a really fantastic job. They raced super good. I have so much respect for him, he's a good friend of mine. I feel for him. I feel his loss, because he had to lose the yellow jersey on the last day. It's really difficult. I know how he feels, but that's racing. We all try to win,' he said.

It should have been one of his happiest moments before shouldering the weight of expectation, of having to be the hunted, not the hunter. Instead, Pogačar held back celebrating the Tour triumph the way he would have liked, something he admitted later regretting.

Though they had the yellow Colnago bike frame delivered to the team at four o'clock in the morning ahead of the Tour's Paris finale, neither he nor the team was ready for this outcome, emotionally or functionally. 'We had nothing, we didn't even have a yellow sock. We were so unprepared to win,' Wakefield recalls, laughing. He says that on the way to the finish in Paris the next day, some mechanics and soigneurs were given money to buy something yellow for the staff members to wear in Paris as part of the celebration.

There wasn't time to book a fancy restaurant for a party, especially given the Covid restrictions after the final stage around the French capital. 'In the end, we finished in a pizzeria – something quite cool, but really informal,' David de la Cruz says. 'But it was special because it was really, really, really unexpected. It came by surprise, and things that come by surprise are probably the nicest things in life.'

Allan Peiper later likened their feat to a heist. Beating Jumbo–Visma and Roglič in that manner was akin to getting a crack squad to plan and break into an impregnable bank, then pinching the bags of money off them at the last moment.

Of course, there were no goodies and baddies, just two likeable Slovenian champions, for whom being in contention was an against-the-odds success.

As Roglič approached the final corner of La Planche des Belles Filles, Bradley Wiggins, a Eurosport pundit and winner of the Tour de France in 2012, said something oddly prescient about Pogačar into his commentator's microphone: 'This guy could go on to be the greatest of all time and better the likes of Merckx . . . in 10, 15 years' time, we will realise why that happened [today]. I think this is the start of something very special for this man.'

▶ Fast learner: at the start of his days racing in the junior category as a 16-year-old, Pogačar struggled to keep up with stronger and older boys, but he got up to speed rapidly.

2

KING OF THE HILL

1998–2013, childhood

As dusk fell, the yellow jersey stood alone on the podium in the shadow of the Arc de Triomphe. The Slovenian flag, with its white, blue and red horizontal tricolour and coat of arms featuring Mount Triglav, was billowing behind him.

Moments earlier, Primož Roglič had been next to him on a lower rostrum step. A fair few cycling fans around the world must have been wondering how the main protagonists of cycling's most prestigious race had both come from a European country of just two million people. This was a rare moment in the global spotlight for Slovenia.

'You have to remind people we exist. We always assume that nobody knows where we are, nobody knows *who* we are. In contact with a foreigner, we kind of have a duty to educate them,' English teacher Nina Jerončič tells me over coffee in the staff room at Komenda Moste school, Pogačar's alma mater.

If Slovenians didn't laugh at some of the misconceptions about them, they might cry. Shortly before Pogačar won the 2020 Tour, one leading French daily newspaper erroneously referred to him as Slovakian. Then there is one of the most popular auto-generated questions on Google: 'Is Slovenia in Russia?'

The answer: no, not even close. The road signs on the outskirts of this central European country's capital, Ljubljana, give directions for Italy to its west, Hungary to the east and southerly Croatia, all within two hours' drive. Austria, which shares a northerly border, is even nearer. Among the dozen smallest countries in Europe, Slovenia can be easily forgotten about given its larger, older neighbours.

Those next door have often coveted its land: positioned between the Balkans and the Adriatic Sea, Slovenia has been the strategically valuable middle ground of clashing kingdoms and converging worlds over the centuries. For much of their history, Slovenians have found themselves under the rule of others – the Romans, the Franks, the Habsburgs, Napoleonic France, the Austro-Hungarians, to name a few – having their borders shifted and foreign values foisted on them.

In recent history, the two world wars brought further occupation and division for Slovenes. During the Second World War, this little country was split between Italy, Germany and Hungary, and afterwards it became one of six republics in socialist Yugoslavia.

For a minnow among giants, it has been a struggle to simply exist. 'I think we definitely have some kind of a complex because we're so small and we've been invaded so many times during the past,' Jerončič says. 'We're quite proud of the fact we're independent, very proud of the country.'

Independence came at last after a 10-day war in 1991, the country enduring a fraction of the bloodshed, lives lost, territorial disputes or bitter ethnic tensions seen between other republics, as conflict spread to Bosnia and Herzegovina, Kosovo and Croatia. 'So far history has not presented us with any gifts. We have had to achieve everything with hard work. And this is the reason we have been able to maintain our existence,' Slovenia's first president Milan

Kučan said in a famous address following Slovenian independence in June 1991.

Unsurprisingly, the idea of Slovenians as tenacious, patient and industrious flows through its country people like the Sava River through the nation. In an Instagram Live interview months after his first Tour de France win, Pogačar reverted to national character when asked how Slovenia could produce such good cyclists: 'I think it has to do with our nature: we were born with stubbornness and the will to fight.'

In a little more than 30 years, Slovenia has quickly assimilated into modern Europe, the first among the former Yugoslav states to gain full membership of the EU and NATO, a rare post-socialist democratic success story. But misunderstandings still crop up.

'If you say to a Slovenian that he or she is from an Eastern European country, that would be like "Are you asking for a fight?" It's not something we like to hear. But I think we're kind of like the discipline of the Austro-Hungarian Empire – order, work, everything a certain way – with the soul of the Balkan people, mixed together. Work hard, party harder,' Jerončič says, laughing.

Then the next day, exercise even harder. Slovenia is Europe's second most active nation, ranked on residents exercising or taking part in sport on a regular basis. While football is number one for popularity, skiing and ski jumping have a special place in the hearts of the winter sports-loving public. 'I remember my dad talking to some foreign tourists about one very successful Slovenian ski jumper and how incredulous he was because they had never heard of him,' Jerončič says.

Mountains are on almost every horizon, obstacles to be hiked, cycled up or skied down. Towns like north-westerly Kranjska Gora become a summer hub of people walking or pedalling around in Lycra, ready to tackle the testing, scenic climb of Vršič.

· · · ·

Tadej Pogačar and his family hail from the heart of the country and the outskirts of Komenda, a town 20 km to the north of Ljubljana. Pogačar's father, Mirko, was raised on a farm to the west of the town, working hard on the land from the age of 14. He went on to become head of production in the Donar chair factory, looking after the manufacturing line while continuing to help out on his brother's farm in the afternoons. His horizons expanded far beyond the fields outside, watching Federico Fellini and Sergio Leone films and reading the likes of Steinbeck, Dostoevsky and Kafka.

Pogačar's mother, Marjeta Štebe, lived just outside Komenda, to its east, in a little village called Gora pri Komendi, *gora* meaning 'mountain' in Slovenian. (Given that Mirko lived on the other side of town in Klanec pri Komendi, *klanec* translating as 'hill', it seems that Tadej was made to take flight up steep gradients in his life.)

The Pogačars settled in Klanec, a 355-person hamlet close to Komenda. In reality, the two are virtually one and the same: the vast majority of local amenities are in Komenda, and the Pogačar home is a five-minute walk from the main street which runs through town.

This was an idyllic place to grow up, overlooked by wooded hills and nearby ski resorts of Velika Planina and Krvavec. The loftier Kamnik-Savinja Alps beyond – including the peaks of Brana, Grintovec, Planjava, Skuta and Ojstrica – rise like horns on a dragon's back on the horizon.

Just beyond the Pogačars' back garden, with a little stream tinkling next to it, the single-lane country roads around the town are framed by fields, farmsteads and *kozolec* – wide, free-standing wooden haystacks used for storing and drying cut grass to feed livestock.

Komenda has everything a small town needs: a post office, library, doctor's and pharmacy, all on the same main street. As I walk around, one January morning, the air is fresh and cold, the cloud hanging low and blanketing the nearby mountains. Children in woolly winter hats pass the local Spar supermarket, coming home from school for lunchtime. I spy a lot of basketball hoops in the neatly manicured gardens – fodder for kids dreaming of being the next Luca Dončić – and neatly stacked, covered wood piles.

The town's only roundabout, a tree growing from its centre, has become a shrine to Pogačar and a gathering place to celebrate his victories. Its outer ring is painted yellow and pink, in recognition of the Grand Tours he has won. A few hundred metres further down the road, by the Komenda town sign, a fan's placard sums up how they feel about him. On a cut-out rainbow jersey are the words *svetovni prvak je naš junak* – the world champion is our hero.

Komenda's most famous son was Mirko and Marjeta's third-born, arriving on 21 September 1998, two years after Tilen and seven after Barbara. As a baby, he was walking by 11 months and displayed impressive early motor skills, able to shoot and score in a football goal before his second birthday.

Tadej the toddler was a bundle of energy with an innate sense of mischief. Before his first birthday, he somehow climbed the steep, slippery side of the garden slide before getting scared and gliding back down. When his mother put him up on the kitchen counter one day, he touched one of the boiling hot stoves out of curiosity and burned his hand. The result: a blistered palm. 'It was my fault, I put him on the level that he could reach it. But when his hand healed, he verified [again] if it was still hot or not. The second time, it wasn't, luckily. He had a little luck in his life – a lot of luck,' Marjeta told me in 2021.

Marjeta also had trouble getting him to wear his seat belt. She would brake gently while doing less than 15 km/h in the car to try to make him see the danger.

His older brother, Tilen, was a little more docile and sensible. The two always played together, Tadej boisterous but never malicious, following and looking up to Tilen. Barbara, their older sister, was like a teacher at times, instructing them how to write and leading the games – volleyball, basketball, rollerblading, football or badminton.

There was healthy competition from his family members. Everyone wanted to win the various card games – tarok was Tadej's favourite – or chess matches. Usually the youngest sibling playing, and at a cognitive disadvantage, Tadej got used to losing.

'We always told Tadej that there will not only be successes in life, there will also be defeats and that they come to you for a reason,'

Marjeta said to Slovenian radio show *Sol in Luč*. 'In our family, he learned even from a young age when we played board games to tolerate defeats and now we can see that Tadej tolerates failures quite well. We also always said that everything is good for something and that you have to learn something from it. You never know for what reason something happens to you. But you can always "take" something from a situation.'

The good nature and positivity on show years later was already present in Pogačar as a kid. 'Tadej is very kind. Joyful, cheerful, patient,' Mirko told me in 2021. His mother would sometimes sit with him over breakfast and enjoy his sense of calm washing over her.

'When he was a child, whenever he felt that something went wrong in the family, he tried to cheer us up and he played the clown. Every time; he needed there to be no tension in the family. He tried to break the tension, and he stayed like that,' Marjeta said to me for *Rouleur*. That might involve dances or songs; sometimes, he would change the words of a song to his own. The aim was not just an amusing silliness, but to be a kind of mediator.

Tadej's parents sought to pass on to their children many of the 'old' values they had learned growing up in the former Yugoslavia in the 1970s. 'We tried to teach them to be honest, hard-working and kind to other people,' Marjeta said to *Rouleur*. 'We wanted our children to participate in a sport activity in order to be a part of a group, where they find their place. And because, in our philosophy, we thought that if a child is a member of one group, if he feels good in this group, he won't have many problems growing up as a teenager.

'Also when they started something, a sport or whatever, they sometimes wanted to quit during the year and we didn't let them,' Marjeta adds. 'We wanted them to finish the season, to finish the work they started. I think it was the right philosophy.'

They also tried not to give their children things as soon as they wanted them. 'If they wanted a toy, we couldn't afford everything because we were building the house and we didn't have much money at this time,' she told me in 2023 for a *GCN* documentary. 'We couldn't buy everything they wanted and we recognised after two or three weeks that the toy they wanted before wasn't interesting any more. We knew soon it would switch and there would be a new object of desire for them.'

Pogačar believes his character has come from his family and the way they raised him. 'I'm lucky to have a good family,' he told *Cyclingnews* in 2021. 'I owe a big thanks to my parents, my brother and my sisters. They made me who I am.'

His parents' core values, simple in the best sense of the word, have changed little with Tadej's astronomical success. Being bought a swanky mansion in Slovenia's equivalent of Beverly Hills or regular dinners in Michelin-starred restaurants is not for them. They still live in the same family house in Klanec.

The Pogačars were no sporting stars passing on their athletic abilities, but they were avid walkers, and often made their children come along for four-hour outings in the surrounding hills. As they grew older, the Pogačar kids might occasionally moan at being dragged out yet again for a Sunday walk, but it did them the world of good.

Outdoors became the young Tadej's playground. He would climb trees and come back muddy, tired and happy. In this *Boy's Own* childhood, Pogačar was also a member of the Boy Scouts. His first bike was a battered BMX hand-me-down from his cousin as a four-year-old, good for getting air on makeshift jumps he made with his brother.

The young Tadej also took part in a couple of ski and ski jumping competitions – par for the course for any Slovenian child living close to the mountains – and he flew as far as 20 m. At the Občinski Veleslalom at Soriška Planina ski resort in March 2009, a 10-year-old Tadej placed second in his category. He also competed in several orienteering races.

Over the years, his parents have received many questions from the media looking for tangible signs of precocity or a voracious competitive attitude. Their son's race-winning ability is certainly predicated on a remarkable physiological capacity, itself reliant on both nature as well as nurture. You cannot be a cycling world-beater if the genes don't fit, but the family has no obvious sporting heavyweight passing on dynamite DNA.

Marjeta and Mirko's fathers were only casual sportsmen, playing local football in Yugoslavia. Mirko's father also trained in gymnastics, while Marjeta's grandparents were farmers. Perhaps a latent ability was channelled principally into agricultural labour.

Occasionally, they visited Mirko's father and brother on their farm. The whole family would muck in, preparing feed for cows, planting potatoes or harvesting tons of them by hand. The Pogačar children saw that they needed to put in hard work to get the desired outcome.

Their parents were giving them responsibility, rather than handing them things on a plate. At home, household jobs were assigned to the children, such as cleaning the bathroom, washing the dishes or mowing the lawn. Sometimes, Mirko wished they had a farm where there would be more jobs to do. Whether at work or at play, the Pogačar children were rarely idle.

'If we help children with the smallest obstacles from the beginning, how will they be able to overcome the more difficult and bigger ones when we are gone? In life, we have to fight again and again, and sport definitely helps us with that,' Mirko wrote in *Delo*.

· · · ·

Cycling came into Tadej's life through a family friend and fellow Komenda citizen. While studying at Ljubljana's Faculty of Sport in 2002, Miha Koncilija coached volleyball weekly in the new sports hall in Komenda, adjoined to the secondary school. For around 10 years, he played midweek games in a group that included Marjeta. He can remember the little Tadej watching from the sidelines.

Koncilija had started racing in 1993 at Kolesarsko Društvo Rog (KD Rog), one of the oldest cycling clubs in Slovenia, stemming from the Rog bicycle company, a renowned brand in Yugoslavia. A Slovenian national junior road race champion, he shelved racing at the age of 20, wanting to commit himself to study and envisaging himself as a teacher in the gym.

He rejoined KD Rog as a coach, initially reluctantly. According to Koncilija, 80 per cent of a trained sport coach's salary is paid by the government, making it viable and affordable for communities to hire them. KD Rog had age categories going all the way up from under-12 to a modest professional team, sponsored by the mineral water brand Radenska, with a pink and blue jersey. For most of his career, Koncilija oversaw the club's under-17 youth category.

Intake at the club was low, and his goal was to get more kids on bikes, giving them a larger talent pool. Before his arrival, the search was casual, a school here and there every year. Koncilija made the pursuit more focused, going to 20 to 30 schools annually, rising to around 40 later, surveying around 1000 students. Every country could use someone driven, dynamic and passionate like Miha Koncilija.

He would come to the school gyms – virtually every school in Slovenia has one – with a flashy Scott CR1 carbon road bike and a Tacx home trainer. 'You need to impress them,' he explains. Each test lasted two minutes with a cycling computer sensor on the back wheel measuring distance.

Sometimes, Koncilija had only an hour to test the ability of 30 participants. If he could see someone who didn't have the talent, he would stop them before the full time was up. He was looking for determination as much as quality. Sometimes, he would call on those who were third and fourth in terms of distance, seeing if they would be interested in going to a club training session. 'It was much more [a case of] someone who was smaller and fighting on the bike than someone who can get more metres in two minutes,' he says.

One day in 2007, he set up his rig in the sports hall adjoined to Komenda Moste school. Tilen Pogačar stepped up, performed strongly and Koncilija subsequently got on the phone to Marjeta. 'I called her: "Look, we need some new members in cycling, maybe Tilen could try." And that's how it started.'

Koncilija was persistent and proactive, sometimes calling the parents of promising children several times to convince them to give it a go. Slovenian talents Žiga Jerman, Žiga Ručigaj and Luka Pibernik were also discovered by his tests. 'This was the only way we could get the kids. I don't know whether Tadej and Tilen would have taken up this sport without this system in play,' Koncilija says.

'I remember when I drove Tilen home from training and I said to his parents: "How about Tadej? Maybe he can start this." It was "No, no, Tadej is playing soccer, he will not be cycling." You know how it is: I think most younger brothers try to do what the older brother is doing, right?'

It was only a matter of time. Within half a year, Tadej did start – in January 2008, at the age of nine and a half. His first bike ride was inauspicious, falling off when he tried to unclip his pedals (a painful rite of passage for any recreational cyclist).

The equipment – shoes, helmet, bicycle, even sunglasses – was all given to him by the club. Just as well too: with Marjeta working part-time and caring for Tadej's baby sister Vita while there was building work at their house, money was tight.

Tadej and Tilen's first bike was a trusty, handed-down green Billato. One of the smallest boys in his age group, Tadej had to wait a few months to be tall enough to ride it.

The kids would meet for training three times a week, sometimes playing football and basketball – on Monday, a midweek session and Saturday, with one in the gym at the primary school in Šmartno.

As the weather improved in early spring, they would restart cycling sessions outdoors, going to the Tacen police training 'polygon' ground for skills drills, next to their Vikrče HQ on Ljubljana's northern outskirts.

'Immediately, it was really fun for me. I was enjoying [it], I had new friends. It was a nice challenge. And then every year that passed by, I was enjoying it more. I was thinking, "This is really cool, I want to do this forever,"' Pogačar later said.

In Slovenia, the youngest available racing category is C for those aged 12 and under, putting Pogačar at a great deficit when he began racing in 2008 at the age of nine, up against his brother Tilen and boys who were up to three years older. In his first race, doing laps of a 3-km circuit in Trstenik on 12 April, he finished in 23rd and last place, with little knowledge of how to approach a race or the tactical intricacies. His best result in that first season was a modest 15th place. Tiny Tadej and his pipe-cleaner arms had a physiological mountain to climb.

Those early years were a prime, unintentional example of the underdog effect. Every race against older, stronger and more developed racers helped him to learn better strategic and technical abilities, positioning himself in their wake to save energy as well as building mental fortitude.

It was a paradoxical advantage of sorts, given that the early maturers at the front of the pack may not have been taxed physically or tested mentally in the same manner. On the other hand, the little tadpoles that hide lower on the results sheets are not always spotted by coaches and encouraged to progress as proportionately as the winners.

While the likes of Belgium, the UK, Italy and France all start official competition with under-8 categories, Koncilija is against the idea of introducing younger racing in Slovenia. 'I think our riders in Slovenia are so good because competition starts so late. I think it's very important. Plus when you start competition, it just becomes, "Who wins, who was second?" It's not so fun.

'So at first, they have technical skills and they love cycling. After that, the racing must start.'

Koncilija didn't see winning as young Tadej's burning goal. 'Maybe he was [competitive], but he didn't show it. I think it was much more important for him to have a good time with his group of boys. But of course, he wanted to beat them, like every normal person.'

He did not have to wait long for a win. Pogačar's first major victory came at the age of 10 on 29 August 2009 in a C category race up Krvavec. The boys rode up only the first 4 or 5 km of the climb.

'This was the only race I remember for such a young category on Krvavec. Because it's too hard for them, in my opinion. Thinking about it, we can say also that he was something special because they were three years older than him,' Koncilija says.

Krvavec is as close as it comes to Pogačar's local climb, 15 km from the front door of his home. It is a meditative ascent, climbing steeply from the valley floor in Grad past a sheer rock wall.

Pogačar rode up countless times, past the yellow and red snow poles, testing himself on the climb's average gradient of 8 per cent and taking in the scenery. A third of the way, just below Ambrož pod Krvavcem, the tarmac wriggles left and right past green pastures, wood piles and a smattering of chocolate-box chalet buildings. Only a few hill top churches and settlements are visible above a blanket of low-lying mist in the valley below. The view there, let alone the one from the summit, is more than enough to fire a youngster's imagination and make him think: *cycling can take you to some otherworldly places.*

Winning on Krvavec as a 10-year-old was also the moment Pogačar realised he could be a good climber in the mountains. 'After my first year on the bike, I wanted to become a top cyclist,' he told *Siol* in 2019.

However, his older brother was the one showing more talent at the time. When they were riding together, Tilen would perennially pip him in their childhood sprints up hills or for waypoints on the road. 'He always found a way to beat me,' Tadej reflected later to *The Times*. Keeping up, let alone getting the better of him, was another driving force.

There is a tangible 'little sibling effect' in sport, whereby younger brothers and sisters tend to outperform their elders. On average, elite athletes (who had reached senior international competition) have 1.04 older siblings, while those who are non-elite (who attained junior national or senior domestic level) only have 0.6 older siblings, according to an analysis of Canadian and Australian athletes across over 30 different sports. Younger brothers also outperform their older brothers in Major League Baseball. The Pogačars might only have been racing each other for the Komenda town sign or playing games in the garden, but they were motivating each other to go out riding in the first place.

The Pogačar brothers' activity was not limited to normal bicycles. Their parents acquired unicycles for them after being impressed by a local acquaintance riding one around at a local event and showing kids how to do it. Tilen and a 10-year-old Tadej became famous around Komenda as the acrobatic, unicycling brothers.

They would take it in turns on their unicycles to deliver milk in a metal urn to their grandparents over a kilometre away in Gora pri Komendi. Unfortunately, both unicycles were later lost or stolen (Marjeta Pogačar is not sure which), ending their adventures.

Despite his aptitude on one and two wheels, Tilen quit cycling at the age of 14. He came back to it six months later, having not done any training, and could still keep up with the best, according to Koncilija. But he dropped it again, two years later.

'He was very good, also very talented. But maybe he was not so – it's hard to find the right word – focused and motivated,' Koncilija says. 'When he was younger, one hour of training was no problem, but after that, when you need to go to three hours and more, I think this was the problem. But in my opinion, he could also be a professional rider.'

Tadej was just getting going with chasing that dream. A chance encounter with the 2011 Tour de France had a galvanising effect. Heading west in the family Hyundai for a summer holiday in France, his parents eschewed the pricier Fréjus tunnel route, opting to take the slightly longer way via Sestriere. They found the road closed after the pass ahead of the arrival of the sport's biggest race. A fan of the Schleck brothers and Alberto Contador, Pogačar could cheer them on and encourage Slovenia's three remaining competitors, Kristijan Koren, Borut Božič and national champion Grega Bole too.

Cycling was soon on his mind all the time. One day, when a school teacher asked him what he was thinking about because he was looking out the window, not listening, he answered, 'The route I will take for training this afternoon.' 'And another time, he didn't know how to answer a question,' Mirko told me in 2021. 'And he said to the teacher he wouldn't need this knowledge because he would become a professional cyclist.'

Pogačar attended Komenda Moste school between 2004 and 2013, a 15-minute walk from his home in Klanec along the town's main thoroughfare. 'They still teach them values here. It's not like Ljubljana, the city. People are polite here in Komenda, they help each other,' says teacher Mateja Kavčič as we walk through a photo exhibition dedicated to Pogačar opposite the school.

It has changed little since his time there, with the same pale yellow lockers, red and blue banquettes and cream walls. However, there are visible flourishes for its most famous alumnus. On a noticeboard by the doors is a display dedicated to Pogačar, with a centrepiece mosaic of a yellow-jersey-clad cyclist. A framed, autographed white jersey from the 2020 Tour de France hangs on its right side; to the left side are various A4 pieces of paper detailing his best results, his coach and his early races, with photos of Pogačar and his Olympic bronze medal.

When school was in session during the 2020 Tour de France, the various stage profiles and Pogačar's daily results were pinned to boards outside the technology room to keep the student body updated. (After he won, many wore yellow to celebrate.)

Walking into the school gymnasium, the dull thud of bouncing basketballs mingles with the squeak of trainers on the synthetic, rust-coloured floor. In the adjacent teachers' office to the side, above the gathered coffee mugs and computer screens, there is a Tadej Pogačar-branded calendar, emblazoned with his motto *Never quit trying and never give up*.

For Slovenian children, there is a lot of trying, one reason why Slovenia punches above its weight as a sporting nation. Until seventh grade (the ages of 12 and 13), students have three PE classes a week. Sport is financed transparently from public funds, seen as a public good. Basketball, skiing, football, athletics: there was barely a mainstream sport Pogačar didn't try.

'I think we have a good school system to introduce different sports to children,' Pogačar said in a 2020 Instagram Live interview. 'I think almost every kid does one sport when they're young. In the end, you get a lot of different kids doing a lot of different sports so you can find good ones and then talent in this way.'

Miro Šlebir taught him PE in the fifth, seventh and eighth grades, when Pogačar was aged 11 to 14. 'He was good at football, [playing] in the team, and longer-distance running,' Šlebir says. Pogačar apparently featured in the 1000 m, but he was no standout.

'He was a bit special, introverted, he didn't speak to people. He was a little bit in his own world, maybe also because he was already starting cycling, so he had his own thing. He wasn't a person who would disrupt other students. Well, not like it was an obvious introversion, but you could see he was a bit more shy. A bit reserved.'

Šlebir can remember seeing Pogačar riding his bike around the school before *valeta* – a prom ceremony for 14-year-olds to celebrate the end of primary school. This was a surprise, because he was unaware that the boy had been cycling or even how good he was.

Back then, if you'd told Šlebir that Pogačar would win several Tours de France, two world titles and many other top races, what would he have said? '*Nikoli*,' he replies – never. 'It really was a well-kept secret.'

Unbeknown to most of his classmates, Pogačar would hit the road after school to train, chasing the feeling of going faster every time and working to improve himself.

'When Tadej was 13 or 14 years old, he was very focused on cycling. He was training very hard in this time and he wasn't a difficult teenager,' Marjeta told *GCN* in 2023. 'So he didn't have time to do things like the others, going out in the evening or the weekend. He didn't celebrate his birthdays, not even those of his classmates.

'He passed school very well, but it was not the most important thing for him. Cycling was. Already at the age of 13 or 14, he said "I will be a professional cyclist. I will go to the Tour de France,"' she says. 'I always said to him it's very difficult to realise this wish. Because not every cyclist can become a professional cyclist, so you have to work hard and perhaps you can do it.'

His horizons were expanding. Komenda was only an hour's drive from the border with Italy, a cycling heartland with many more races, tougher courses and more competitive fields – and regulations that welcomed outsiders. In a decision dating back to the early 1990s, hot on the heels of independence, Slovenian cyclists were allowed to race as Italians in the most easterly regions of Friuli-Venezia Giulia and Veneto. If they had a racing licence and insurance, that was enough.

Pogačar started to compete abroad more frequently, filling his weekend days. A fifth place at the Trofeo Vida in Italy in May 2012, one of his early races outside of Slovenia, as a 13-year-old, showed he could mix it with the speediest neighbours too.

Nevertheless, it took his parents years to realise his potential. 'We didn't see how good he was when he was young,' Marjeta says. 'All his trainers, Miha Koncilija and the others, said he was very talented. I asked, "How can you say this? I can't see it." Because Tadej didn't win races when he was young because he was very small.'

Pogačar once reckoned that the most his father and mother had done for him to be such a successful cyclist was that they had no idea about cycling. His parents had to learn about this alien sport fast to keep up. First, there was nutrition; his beloved pancakes with cottage cheese and bread dumplings were phased out for more pasta.

Their support included ferrying him to races and buying a few necessary items. As he grew older, the prize money he won contributed to new or second-hand kit.

Over time, coach Koncilija noticed his mental aptitude. 'Every mistake that he maybe made, he didn't do it again,' Koncilija told *The Times* in 2023. 'Everything he did in races and in training, he just memorised it and he didn't ask a lot of me. I think he has a lot of [skill in] … self-teaching problems.'

However, there were crashes that he could not evade, learning the rough, fickle side of the sport. Koncilija remembers being afraid in one youth race in Austria as Pogačar screamed on the floor after a fall, making the coach fear that he had been hit in the back by another rider. Most racers would have quit at this point. But when Koncilija suggested he get in the team car, Pogačar insisted he would continue. They untangled the bikes and Pogačar cycled back to the bunch, over two minutes up the road. Koncilija did not fully realise it then, but Pogačar had the ability to switch off everything else and fight with everything he had.

With racing and training on the open road, cycling carries inevitable risks. Koncilija considers that peril to be one of the main reasons that some parents do not bring their children to KD Rog.

However, there was no question of stopping Tadej or Tilen. 'I know that if you do something with a great pleasure, I couldn't remove this sport from my children. Because Tadej would die, perhaps, without cycling,' Marjeta told me in 2023 for *GCN*, smiling. 'He was really into it,' she adds, her hand clenching into a fist.

Still, it did not help to calm any natural parental worries when the two brothers would sit at the kitchen table boasting about how fast they had gone downhill during training. 'What can I say? I know it's dangerous, but I love adrenaline,' Pogačar told *Siol*, years later.

The Pogačars' model of parenting was a paradigm shift from the well-publicised Western concept of 'helicopter parents', hovering over their offspring or pushing them on aggressively from the sidelines. Instead, aside from necessary support, they put their full trust in the coaches, giving them agency; these were the people who knew what they were doing, starting with Miha Koncilija. The parents took the same approach with Barbara, who pursued orienteering; Tilen, basketball; and Vita, dancing.

'The more you let your child be active, the more he [or she] will learn his own limits. Then there is less chance of him having accidents later on. If you hold his hand the whole time and suddenly let him go, he will fall,' Marjeta told *Delo* in 2023.

For her and Mirko, results did not particularly matter, as long as their children were happy doing activities and engaged in a nurturing community. They were set on raising well-rounded, respectful, outdoorsy children and ended up with a winner of multiple Tours de France – four and counting.

▶ Running up that hill: the young Pogačar got very familiar with the wooded climbs to the north of Ljubljana during his unorthodox winter training sessions with KD Rog.

3

—

SMELLS LIKE TEEN SPIRIT

2014–2016, junior cycling years

In Slovenia, it feels like there is a hill on every horizon. Šmarna Gora is the green giant which dominates the capital city's skyline. Its two wooded crests, like camel's humps, are visible far above Ljubljana's enchanting, pastel-coloured Habsburg-era houses.

'You who go to the holy Šmarna Gora, blessed are you!' Slovenia's greatest poet France Prešeren wrote in the 19th century, after mixing with pilgrims on the way to the dinky baroque church dedicated to Saint Mary, 669 m above sea level. The sunrise and sunset from its summit have enchanted generations of walkers, with views over patchwork fields and across to the Julian Alps, the Karawanks and the Kamnik-Savinja Alps.

However, mention Šmarna Gora to a generation of KD Rog cyclists and its name will elicit masochistic memories of burning legs rather than exaltation. Of crunching along the leaf-covered paths and between the tall oak trees on club training sessions with a single goal in mind.

'Šmarna Gora was some kind of test, deciding which bike and how good the bike is [that] somebody gets,' Miha Koncilija says. 'Because we don't have so many bikes, we had a scoring [system]: every time we went to Šmarna Gora, first, second and third up it gets points.' The more points, the better the bike you got.

There were numerous routes up, the most direct being 1800 m long, which the world's best mountain runners cover in 10 minutes. It was not a race every time they went up during winter, but it is hard to hold back competitive kids. 'They were probably the hardest training sessions of the season,' Blaž Debevec, one of Pogačar's friends and former KD Rog teammates, says. 'Those were not the times where it was winter training in zone 2. All the time, it was just full gas, every training on Šmarna Gora.'

That a young Tadej Pogačar was one of the fastest was no surprise. As an 11-year-old in 2010, he finished second in his age category in the celebrated, annual Rekord race to the top of the hill, winning a backpack in the process. By being one of the quickest years later, as an under-17 youth rider trained by Koncilija, Pogačar made sure of getting a bright yellow Scott CR1 bike. The chirpy little talent also gained a new nickname from those spirited sorties up Šmarna Gora and its twin peak, Grmada – *criček*, The Cricket.

These lung-busting sessions epitomised the unorthodox winter training programme for Pogačar and his teenage clubmates. With the temperature dallying around zero Celsius for several months, Slovenia in winter is no country for regular road biking.

October to March saw an eclectic training programme for the budding cyclists. The weekly schedule included football and basketball at the school gym in Šmartno and there were two after-school sessions on Šmarna Gora.

There was also a dedicated annual training camp for cross-country skiing at Pokljuka or the ski jumping mecca of Planica, with its world-famous jump. These offered opportunities to bond and get to know cycling clubmates even better, such as Blaž Debevec. He joined KD Rog as an under-14; the 2014 team photo on the steps of Ljubljana Town Hall shows both him and Tadej front and centre in the first row, among the smallest kids, smiling into the camera in their black-and-pink cycling kit.

'We knew that he was a good rider, but there were better riders in our team, like Žiga Jerman and some others,' Debevec says. 'Maybe the other riders had a little bit more self-esteem, a bit more of an ego. Tadej was the nice guy who was working hard. That's my first memory of him – and that he was very strong on the climbs, probably the most important thing.

'Maybe some guys, their character was a bit stronger. Maybe they were a bit cocky to the guys who were not that good in training. Actually, it was part of the motivation for me: if this guy told me, "You suck, you're such a bad climber", I thought, "I will train on the climbs a bit more and get better."'

Pogačar did not receive that treatment. Even in a club with only 15 other boys in the same age group, there were levels and he belonged in the top one, often travelling to Italy to race at the weekend. It was a couple of years before Debevec had progressed enough to join them.

Going to compete over the border could be like rolling into a town for a gun-toting Wild West showdown. 'You had the feeling it was a big thing,' Debevec says. 'A proper cycling event, not a town criterium in Slovenia. We had the highest expectations and bigger motivation there. The races were much faster, much more aggressive, much harder courses with more climbing.'

It was a stark contrast to the 30-rider fields at home with the same familiar faces fighting for victory. 'It was far more aggressive … if you know the guy, you're not planning to push him in the ditch. But in Italy, it's not like that, it's just a fight,' Debevec says. 'Luckily, we had one rider in the team who was our protector for younger riders: Žiga Jerman – the same guy with the ego I was talking about. He was like a bully but at the same time our protector, and he's also a very good rider and person. When some other riders tried to fight with us, he just came out of nowhere and put them in their place.'

Given how regularly the visitors scooped the top prizes, there was plenty of cause for unpopularity with the locals. In the Medaglia Oro Val Lapsina one-day race in March 2014, Sava Kranj club member Jaka Primožič outsprinted KD Rog riders Pogačar and Jerman, just ahead of their teammate Matej Merčun, making it four Slovenians in the top 5. Weeks later, Merčun won the Circuito del Bosco, taking it in turns with Pogačar to attack a poor Italian rival until he wilted. Crossing the line in second place, pointing into the air with one finger while Mercun celebrates with two arms over his head in front, Pogačar looked as happy as if he himself had won. Miha Koncilija still considers that 'Class of 1998' to be the strongest in Slovenian cycling history.

The bigger and tougher the race, the better Pogačar seemed to go. Against a mammoth 356 starters at the 2014 Coppa d'Oro, including some of Italy's best youth riders, Pogačar finished sixth after his late attack was caught with 2 km to go. 'I didn't regret it,' Pogačar recalled years later to *L'Équipe*. 'In fact, I've kept the same mindset I had when I played with my brother when I was little: I always try to win, but first and foremost, to have fun. I like to fight against my competitors but I accept defeat, it doesn't make me sad. In truth, winning or losing doesn't change anything for me.'

A post-race photo from the podium captures a trophy-clutching, pubescent Pogačar. Just a week away from his 16th birthday, with a forehead pockmarked with angry spots, he poses in the Slovenian champion's jersey. Awaiting a growth spurt and up against more developed riders who were 10–15 kg heavier, he was constantly forced to go on the offensive.

His friend Žiga Jerman was more physically mature, his sprint was faster, and he was suited to the punchy races, which rarely exceeded two hours in Slovenia. 'From under-13 to under-17, Žiga won, let's say, 30 races [a year] and Tadej 10 or maybe less,' Koncilija says. 'But then if you look further, my opinion was if Tadej stayed in cycling, he would be a better cyclist.'

During the winter of 2014, Pogačar moved up into the junior (under-19) racing category, coming under the oversight of Andrej Hauptman at KD Rog. Hauptman was one of Slovenia's greatest cyclists: with his bronze medal in the 2001 World Championships road race, the sprinter claimed the country's most significant elite international road racing result before Roglič, Pogačar and Matej Mohorič transformed Slovenia into an unlikely cycling superpower.

After racing for several Italian teams, including Lampre and Fassa Bortolo, Hauptman left pro cycling prematurely at the age of 31. Suffering with ulcerative colitis and intestinal problems, he was in and out of hospital for a year. He then returned to his childhood club KD Rog, helping out there as a coach, transmitting his love for the sport to the next generations.

Despite those difficult moments, Hauptman is quick to smile, with his black-rimmed glasses and Desperate Dan stubbled jawline. He is known as 'Hempi' to many in the Slovenian cycling community, a nickname owing to his junior days racing in Italy and his name's resemblance to the American cyclist and Giro d'Italia winner Andy Hampsten.

Hauptman first came across Pogačar by chance, several years before coaching him. He turned up late to a race near the club's Vikrče HQ and saw a little kid seemingly lagging behind, battling a bike that was too big for him. He protested to the officials that the minnow should be pulled from the race – only to be informed that this unlikely leader had just lapped the field. As Mark Twain wrote, it's not the size of the dog in the fight, it's the size of the fight in the dog. Little did Hauptman know that he would become a pivotal influence, his 'cycling father' in the champion's own words.

'Sometimes I said to friends, "Remember this guy, he will go far." But who expects it? Nobody, really,' Hauptman says, drinking coffee in his living room as his Australian shepherd dog Mars sleeps at our feet.

'Compared to his teammates, he was always a bit behind, he was smaller, without muscles and he was already competitive. When I started to work [with him], he came to every winter training. When the season started, from the first race to the last, he always went full gas. Even if the race was flat, he was there, with his determination. Maybe he was smaller, but in his way of thinking, he was already years in front of his teammates. I always had the feeling he would become a good professional.'

Getting to that level is an even tougher uphill battle than running to the top of Šmarna Gora. According to the estimate of Chelsea Warr, former director of performance for Team GB, about 10 per cent of all people have the capacity to be among the best in sport. Pure physical talent gets a promising athlete only so far; at a certain level, everyone possesses the necessary ability. Reaching the very top of elite adult sport is a marginal game, requiring a combination of physiological, mental, tactical and technical elements, which grow and contract in importance at various steps along the journey. It takes a village to help raise any sportsperson, and that included Pogačar's parents, his peers, Koncilija and Hauptman.

Responsible for the junior category's training sessions at KD Rog, Hauptman did not want to rush their development. He mixed up the distances and decided when they did sprints or speedwork or went all out on climbs. 'We do it more through playing games, not just strict intervals,' he tells me.

Hauptman would instruct riders to go full gas for a certain hill, meet at the top, ride more gently to the next one – and then go all out for the next summit. At the time, Blaž Debevec did not realise he was doing serious training masquerading as fun. 'Riders training now like we did would probably change the coach immediately, but in that time, I think it was the best stuff we could do. Also, for Tadej, it looks like it was good for [his] development,' Debevec says.

'Nowadays, I think it's even a bit too much, too structured. They're still developing. You have to keep it interesting for these young people so they don't get over their head when the serious stuff comes … maybe it's sometimes good to take it easy and play on the bike.'

Debevec can still remember one of Koncilija's recurring messages: to enjoy the suffering – and when other riders are suffering more than you. Now a cycling coach himself, working alongside Koncilija, he attributes part of his friend Pogačar's rise to his wise guides.

'I think he had the right coaches at the right time. This is one of the most important things in his young career. A lot of riders from Italy were much better than him at that time, but they're not riding any more because they were probably burned out.

'It's probably not just their fault but the fault of their coaches. If you get a good rider and you try to heighten your reputation as a coach, you try to get good results right now to make a world champion, not five years [later] when he will be a pro. We know that Tadej could also have been a world or European champion when he was a junior, but I think "Hempi" knew he could achieve much more than that.'

Miha Koncilija also believes that Pogačar could have been a junior world champion, but he was doing '20 or more per cent less' training than the best in the world at the time. Asked how much Pogačar was doing at the age of 16 and 17, Hauptman estimated approximately 600 hours of training annually, including football, basketball, Šmarna Gora runs, hikes and skiing in the winter. That equates to around 12 hours per week on average. No great shakes compared to modern-day juniors, but taking the steady route would pay dividends in the long run.

Hauptman was also big on holistic winter training. In regular sessions at the school gym in Šmartno, he and his wife Teja had the cyclists doing burpees, HIIT training, stability and core work. He challenged them to stretch and do 20 push-ups.

'They said, "Bleurgh, this is not cycling. It's better [we play] just soccer,"' Hauptman recalls. 'First, you need to be an athlete, then a cyclist. Now, 90 per cent of professional cycling teams do the same.'

Hauptman was well aware of what his new charges could do on the bike: Pogačar almost beat him in KD Rog's annual coaches versus riders contest on their March seaside training camp in Strunjan.

'Sixty kilometres full gas [to Umag],' Hauptman says. 'Tadej was still a cadet [age 15 to 16], I was in the breakaway with him. He was so small, he went so fast. I suffered behind him, I said, *What the fuck is this? Better that I wait for the others.*'

In March 2015, after his varied winter schedule, supplemented by some weekend road rides from Ljubljana to the coast and back, Pogačar's first international junior race, the GP Città di Loano, rolled around.

Hauptman had a motivational tactic: if any team member finished in the top 3, he would buy every rider a Garmin cycling computer from his own pocket. After a long drive to the town 100 km from the

French border, they checked out the final lap and its decisive climb of 5 km. After dinner, standing in the hotel elevator, Pogačar asked him how far it was from the top of the hill to the finish.

The young cyclist was working out when to attack, showing his self-confidence. Hauptman was impressed, and the next afternoon he waited on the climb and could see six riders coming by, including a flash of pink and black. This was Pogačar, who attacked before the crest and was caught with 300 m to go. Close, but no Garmin. 'OK, I'll never bet with him again,' Hauptman says, recalling his thoughts.

The junior category is a better chance for 16- and 17-year-old cyclists to gauge their ability in more pan-European events, to see if their dreams match up to harsh reality, even if this is a category where an age difference can still have a significant effect. In Loano, race winner Michel Piccot was a full 18 months older than Pogačar.

There are even a few events that correspond with the sport's most prestigious, historic races. After an April 2014 youth race in Tišina, Pogačar had gathered round a friend's phone on a bench with his teammates and watched Dutch star Niki Terpstra ride to a lone win over the cobblestones of Paris–Roubaix. A year later, now eligible for the junior race, he wanted to do it himself.

Pogačar asked Hauptman to speak to Andrej Cimprič, the Slovenian national junior coach, because he wanted to compete in the French event, with its 16 sectors of rough *pavé*. 'Paris–Roubaix? 50 kilos?' Hauptman says, remembering the request, referring to the lightweight Pogačar with doubt. He risked being a lamb to the slaughter, bashed around by bigger rivals or the fearsome rough sectors. In the end, he finished 30th and the best Slovenian in the 111 km race. 'He never crashed. First time on those cobbles,' Hauptman says admiringly. The next year, he finished 13th.

As KD Rog's junior racers approached adulthood, Hauptman became a wise friend as much as an authority figure, full of humour and positivity. After training, the riders would sometimes go back to his home and watch the spring Classics while his wife Teja made cakes for them.

Weekends in spring and during the school summer holidays developed a familiar rhythm. The riders would meet at KD Rog's HQ in Vikrče, load up their white Peugeot Boxer minibus and hit the road.

If competing in Italy, the team would often leave at the crack of dawn on a Sunday morning, get to their destination for mid-morning, have a provided lunch of pasta, prosciutto and mozzarella and then race. They usually left late because Pogačar was on the podium, collecting the breakaway competition or the climbers' classification prizes for winning hill sprints. That led to some sleepy moments in class the next morning; the boys normally got back to their homes at midnight or later.

In their living room a decade on, the Hauptmans look back and laugh over photos from the past, which spark more stories. At the GP Loria Pogačar wound up winning a box of pasta as big as his torso for fourth place. At the GP Gramoni Cav Michele, the race was paused due to drawing pins being put on the route, by which point Pogačar was already on the attack, by himself. After the road was swept and the event restarted, he finished fourth.

KD Rog was supported by the mineral water maker Radenska, but still had only a small budget. Needing to stretch it across several categories and age groups, the club handed down kit, mirroring Hauptman's own beginnings in the club in the mid '80s and a more socialist approach. 'I found everything for free. Now, they [children] need to pay. I always raced with Northwave, so they supported me and gave me a lot,' Hauptman says. As a junior, Pogačar often raced in bright orange Northwave shoes, with white socks from the same brand. 'The best six riders maybe got Fondriest bikes; for another three, it was used bikes from the Continental [professional] team. We made it [work], somehow.' It was frequently just Andrej and Teja at races; bringing more staff might mean paying them with money they did not have.

Tadej Pogačar learned to be similarly adaptable. At the Trofeo Guido Dorigo race around Solighetto, deep in Prosecco country, in May 2015, he came to Hauptman 20 minutes before the start, saying his gear shifters were not working. As usual, they had come in the minibus without a spare bike or a mechanic and their best efforts could not fix the problem.

Fretting, Hauptman went over to the MCipollini Assali Stefen Alé team a few steps away, run by his former teammate Nicola Minali, and asked if he had a bike to lend. Pogačar needed a small size frame, but Minali only had a large one with Campagnolo gears to spare, when Pogačar was used to riding with Shimano.

Well, it was better than nothing. They whacked the saddle and the handlebars down so that it would fit him. The young Tadej crashed during the race, but chased back to the bunch. On a hilly route that went over the stiff Ca' del Poggio climb three times, Pogačar shouted to his roadside coach that the new bike wasn't shifting. Keep going or stop, Hauptman said, recalling his instructions with a shrug.

On the final lap, he was shocked to hear a familiar race number over race radio: Pogačar was on the attack. 'With that L-size bike, first-year junior, and they caught him with three or four hundred metres to go,' he said. 'Already there, you see that he is something special.'

His slender build was made to attack climbs and helped him to become Slovenian national youth road race champion on a hilly course at Gabrje in 2014. However, yet to have a growth spurt, he rarely featured in the top 10 of the leading European junior events that year. Nevertheless, Hauptman says he did not see Pogačar upset post-race.

'Because his generation was so strong that if he didn't win, probably Jerman or someone else did, so they were happy. They were really friends, they spent time together, even outside of training. I think this was also very important for that generation: at first, it was fun, then there was training and cycling.

'He was so behind in his maturation, but this was good, I think, because he needed to be tactically clever to be competitive,' Hauptman adds. 'Even when he was young, he was really in front of others, always at the right place, at the right moment.' Pogačar was helped by competitors watching fast-finishing teammate Jerman, which gave him more strategic freedom to go in breakaways and stay away.

'Mentally, he was always something special because he was so self-confident,' Hauptman adds. 'Sometimes you see that after a few months or at the end of the season, a lot of riders don't have motivation for training, or at races. But he was always prepared to race.

'He was not really powerful but the longer the race was – maybe he suffered on the first climb, but by the last one, he was more competitive,' Hauptman says. 'Then the last year junior [2016], he grew up a lot and put on maybe six or eight kilos. I said, "*Now* we will see how you climb."'

. . . .

Bike racing is both a cut-throat, individual pursuit and the ultimate team exercise. Only one rider can win the race, but no champion crosses the line first without the sweat and sacrifice of a whole back-up team. Hauptman compares each member's contribution to putting a tile into a mosaic picture.

United teamwork and camaraderie are integral elements of leadership, and Pogačar understood that from an early age. At the Grand Prix of Vir Island, an early-season stage race off the Croatian mainland in April 2016, the Radenska juniors turned up with the strongest team. On the opening day, teammates Debevec and Pogačar escaped up the road together.

'In the last kilometre, we knew we could come to the finish. I was very happy – Tadej was the captain, for sure he will win and I will be second, a great result for me,' Debevec says. 'Then he said, "No, Blaž, this one is yours." He let me win there, the first victory in my career. It really meant a lot to me.'

Not that being in the lead for two hours with Pogačar was easy. With one part of the course uphill, the stronger rider did far longer pulls than Debevec, who helped on the way down. He was glad to see the finish line and end the suffering.

'That was probably my favourite moment with him,' Debevec says. 'And he did the same the next day with one other rider, I think he was second twice. That's when I saw he's more than just a rider and a captain, he's a really nice person. He's not just thinking about himself and his results, he cares a lot about his team.'

As he grew stronger in 2016, Debevec was able to lend a hand to Pogačar, racing at times with the best KD Rog juniors. 'When I did good, he always said, "You did a great job." And if I didn't do what I was supposed to do, he also told me: "Why didn't you do that, try this to be better next time?" But always in a polite way, not with anger, in a normal way, talking as someone who wants to get you better.

'If I think back to those times, I don't remember one situation where he would be cocky or try to push other people down,' Debevec adds. 'He was a regular guy, really the most regular guy you can imagine.'

Debevec got to know Pogačar better during their junior years training together, putting in five-hour rides in the mountains. Along the way, they usually chatted over the normal teenage fare: films, music, video games. 'I remember when Pokémon Go for Android phones came out [in 2016],' he says. 'After training, we were just riding at 5 km/h and catching Pokémon on the bike. It wasn't the safest stuff, I know.'

By this point, 'The Cricket' had acquired another nickname: *tamau*. 'It means the little one [in Slovenian],' Debevec explains. 'Even now, when we are talking about him, it's "Did you see what 'Tamau' did yesterday?"' Pogačar even used it for his Twitter handle, @TamauPogi, when he signed up to the social media platform in 2016.

There was another small Slovenian with a big engine who would sometimes pip him or Jerman in their races at home and abroad: Jaka Primožič, a bright-eyed, blonde-haired climber from rival club Sava Kranj.

There were numerous youth and junior racing battles in Italian races between him, Pogačar and the Italian riders Samuele Battistella and Filippo Zana, who also went on to become established WorldTour professional cyclists.

'It was pretty rough,' says Primožič. 'We were enemies in Slovenian races and Italy, but when we went away in the Slovenian national team we were best friends.'

They had plenty of time to get to know each other. Given the tight budget of the Slovenian Cycling Federation, their transport to and from every international race was usually a white Renault minibus. 'I have so many stories from this minibus,' Primožič says. 'If you asked

Tadej about this, he would just laugh. We were *living* there. We didn't have money for plane tickets, we drove to Belgium for 18 hours with our junior national coach Andrej Cimprič. He's a legend, he's the guy who cares the most about cycling in the world.

'When we were [training] in St Moritz at altitude with Tadej, Žiga Jerman and everyone else, he drove over the mountain to Livigno to check how the French and Italians were training, spying. And he went to buy meat because it's much cheaper in Italy than in Switzerland,' Primožič says, struggling to contain his laughter. 'It's bonkers. But only he is able to do everything. We went on a training camp with Andrej Cimprič alone: he was mechanic, masseur, cook, everything. He knew everything about cycling.'

On the lengthy drives around Europe, there were soft mattresses on the minibus floor, so that two riders could sleep under the seats, two could sleep across the pair of rows at the back, with a couple seated in the front row and one in the passenger seat. Unsurprisingly, the minibus retained a distinct odour because of the umpteen hours riders spent sweating inside during its years of faithful service.

In 2016, their second and final season as junior racers, Primožič had even better results than Pogačar internationally, winning the Oberösterreich Rundfahrt in Austria and finishing third in the Junior Peace Race, while Pogačar won a stage there from a breakaway. As the season wore on, the Slovenian pair were rarely out of the top 10, among the best in Europe.

'In 2016, Tadej's progress was crazy. From the start to the end of the season, he was just going up and up and up,' Primožič says. 'I can say that I was more serious than Tadej was. I would also say Žiga Jerman was too. Tadej just did the things that other people said to him. He was not strict about food, exercises and training. He was a super-talent then, we all knew.'

One of his final races as a junior, the flat 120 km of the Gran Premio Valli del Natisone just inside the Italian border, underlined that. He attacked early and was joined by two fellow Slovenians before they were caught by the bunch. He joined another four-man escape briefly, then crossed solo to the race's six leaders after missing the initial move.

'Who is leading the chase of the escape? It's Tadej Pogačar again. Tireless, always on the attack,' the Italian commentator of the race's highlights on YouTube channel Oradelciclismo said. 'He's taken more wind today than a sailing regatta.' He still had the punch and timing to beat his breakaway rivals in the sprint for victory, his legs spinning out in the saddle on the restricted junior 52×14 gear ratio like windmill blades in a gale. On a day that favoured faster sprinters, he had turned it his way.

Something was burning inside Pogačar, pushing him on. His training rides became longer and he started doing motor-pacing sessions behind cars. The pursuit of a place on the WorldTour, road cycling's top tier of teams and races, was starting in earnest, because international junior events are where leading agents dig around for hidden gems. Every inferior result, deflated tyre or race-ruining crash feels a lot more consequential, and Pogačar was not impervious to self-reproach. 'Whenever he was not doing well in a race, he would first carefully lean the bike against the van at the finish line and then start a volley of curses. The bike was never at fault, always and only him,' Miha Koncilija told *Delo* in 2022.

However, Jaka Primožič was struck by Pogačar's sanguine nature. 'He is still the same now. When everyone is judging him – ah, he's shit, he didn't win, or he's 12th – actually, he just doesn't care. He knows this race is for preparation and the next one will be better. I was always surprised by his mentality because I was always *Ah fuck, I did a bad race*, I had bad thoughts.

'Him, never: he came to a race and he had a good time. He has the perfect mentality for a cyclist, we knew that then,' Primožič says. 'But now, you can actually see it. Because if you think one evening before the queen stage of the Tour de France that he's nervous and not sleeping during the night? No, it's not a problem for him because he just doesn't think like that.'

▶ Champions are born and made. Pogačar possesses a supreme physiology, with characteristics that favour the extremes of human endurance performance, even if they are only maximised with a winning mindset, unstinting workrate and the right training.

4

—

RARE ABILITIES

The Physiology of Cycling

Sport is a sobering reminder that all human beings are not created equal. Beyond the bike racer's pained grimaces and sheen of perspiration, individual performance boils down to the physiological nuts and bolts under the bonnet: a higher number of red blood cells delivering more oxygen to the muscles, the mitochondrial density that facilitates efficiency, and increased power and the genetic make-up.

Matter decides much more than mind does. Champions can be moulded, but they must be born with genetic and epigenetic variations that provide a winning potential, to be maximised through the right guidance, training and lifestyle.

From the age of 17, Tadej Pogačar had the opportunity to understand his own physiological capabilities in detail. He and Jaka Primožič were among 10 Slovenian cyclists from their year group chosen by their national coach for annual testing at the University of Ljubljana Faculty of Sport, a concrete block on the city's eastern side.

Dr Radoje Milić, the head of the physiology department, and his fellow specialist Samo Rauter were the ones putting them through their paces in 2015, and the pair are still there now, testing tomorrow's world-beaters. Part of a programme funded by the Slovenian Cycling Federation (KZS), Milić has over 30 years of data from up-and-coming Slovenian athletes, and is able to objectively compare their results over time.

Their laboratory is dominated by a treadmill designed for the testing of cross-country skiers, taking up a quarter of the room. The cluster of signed, framed sports jerseys hanging on the walls is testament to the gratitude of their charges: Pogačar's UAE Team Emirates yellow jersey accompanies a Giro d'Italia *maglia rosa* from Primož Roglič and many ski suits and photographs. Milić's desk in the room's far corner is next to a retired-looking white Monark Peak Bike ergometer 894 machine missing its pedals. It might be old, but it is the gold-standard machine for the cycling tests they carry out.

According to Milić, Slovenia has a catchment of around 200 youngsters that are talented in sport. 'One percentage of the 20,000 newborn [annually],' he says. 'If you live in China, it's quite a different number [nine million]. In our situation, it's too hard.'

That limited quantity adds to the unlikeliness of Slovenia's modern cycling success. 'I think it's a miracle in the sense of the outcome,' Milić says. 'A miracle because other teams also prepare themselves and have good riders, different tactics.'

When it comes to finding these needles in the haystack, Milić is a firm believer in the concept of countryside over city. He thinks Pogačar's geographical circumstances were also advantageous. '*Klanec* means "hill". So the theory is when you're trying to do something in the world, you're suffering more. Do you remember one top performance cyclist from the centre of Ljubljana? Only sprinters,' he says.

'So, countryside is winning. When he wants to move from one part of the village to another, it's not flat.' Perhaps: Pogačar's home village might be called Klanec, but there is only a gentle incline, even if lengthier mountains are only a short bike ride away.

Coming to the facility three times a year, Pogačar and his peers did two different tests on each occasion. The Conconi Test gauges aerobic capacity by testing maximal oxygen uptake, while the Wingate Test, 30 seconds long and all out, shows anaerobic maximum power and anaerobic capacity. Modified by their staff, the Conconi 'ramp' test started at 100 watts, going up in 20-watt increments per minute, or for young women or those who weigh less than 60 kg, starting at 60 watts and heightening in 15-watt increments, while the sport scientists collect blood lactate samples from their earlobes. It is an indirect test to measure anaerobic threshold, which can be used to work out one's VO_2 max – a measurement of an individual's aerobic system. The higher the number for the volume of oxygen (ml) that's consumed per kilo of body weight per minute, or ml/kg/min, the more sustained power that can be produced.

Due to data privacy, the professors cannot disclose the teenage Pogačar's test numbers; Milić puts his VO_2 max in the average standard deviation range of 72.5, plus or minus five, for the 18-year-olds tested. His results gave an early hint of his versatility. 'We can easily say that Pogačar was good in both tests . . . the majority of them are not,' Rauter says.

The physiology experts were struck by Pogačar's placid demeanour as much as his data. 'One time, he came here and had been bitten by a bee,' Rauter says. It was clear the incident affected the quality of the test. 'And he did the test, with that [swollen] face, and we said to him that maybe it's good he comes tomorrow, or the day after tomorrow.

'He did the first test, came in two days' time and did another test. He did it without problems – because we have some of the athletes who have a lot of questions when something goes wrong.'

Each coach was sent their charge's data. While also unwilling to disclose Pogačar's teenage VO_2 max, Miha Koncilija says that it was 'high but nothing special. From that generation, four riders were better.'

In contrast, a few years earlier, Milić tested Primož Roglič, in his early twenties and making the transition from ski jumping, a sport with markedly different physiological requirements, such as greater explosive power and core stability, to cycling. 'He scored 81.4 when he tested the first time … 7.14 watts per kilo, that was his first test as a recreational cyclist. We told him that he definitely is not for recreation. He was for a Grand Tour front group, that's it,' Milić says. He later quipped to Roglič's first pro team manager Bogdan Fink that if he didn't sign him, he would create his own team and draw up a contract for this rare specimen.

Still in the developmental phase, Pogačar's VO_2 max was a work in progress, rising towards its peak. His fully fledged, adult VO_2 max was reported as 89.4 ml/kg/min in 2021, though the source is unclear. He is part of a very select physiological elite: one modern study has shown Tour de France riders ranging between a VO_2 max of 79 and 86; historically, Tour de France winners tend to have a VO_2 max over 80.

A high VO_2 max number rightly catches the eye as a key measurement of output for an endurance athlete, but it is not the be-all and end-all. Just as relevant is the percentage of the VO_2 max that is maintainable in a race scenario. The watts per kilo a rider can put out in a metabolic effort and its repeatability is just as important as the watts per litres of oxygen – in other words, how efficiently he produces his power.

A primary factor in that is mitochondrial density, and Pogačar's is magical. His coaches in the WorldTour later realised that he possessed an exceptional recovery capacity on a muscular and mitochondrial level. Blood analysis showed he was ready to race or train hard again after a few days when others were still knackered. Such capacities are part-trainable, part-genetic. He was a physiological rough diamond in need of polishing.

However, it was too early for these men of science to see anything extraordinary in the adolescent Pogačar's data. 'You cannot say that Pogačar will be a Tour de France winner at the age of 16. I am a big liar if I say to you that I knew that,' Rauter says. 'The generation before the Pogačar one, by the data, are all really good.' Millennial compatriots Grega Bole, Simon Špilak and former under-23 world champion Janez Brajkovič had results of a quality which matched or exceeded his before turning professional.

Pogačar was still far from the finished article. There was room to improve his VO_2 max and physiological efficiency. 'He did the same test as me, but I had – I don't know – 6 per cent fat and he had 17. It's crazy,' Primožič says. 'He had a lot in reserve.' This links back to the ml/kg/min part of the VO_2 max equation: losing weight leads to an increase.

'He has the perfect body for a cyclist, the perfect structure. My hand is as big as two of his hands. And a really skinny upper body, but his legs are twice as big as mine. And he has a fat butt,' Primožič says, in a complimentary tone. The gluteus maximus is the body's biggest muscle, helping to improve pedalling efficiency. That might be why Pogačar stands up out of the saddle on the attack, which is the best way of activating the muscle.

Junior races rarely brought out the best in Pogačar, often lacking long climbs that could take more powerful rivals over their lactate threshold and into trouble. The 2016 World Championships road race in Qatar exemplified that, as well as the all-round quality of Pogačar's year group. Slovenia was the only nation with three riders in the top 10, thanks to Žiga Horvat in fifth place, Žiga Jerman in sixth and Primožič in ninth. On the flat route, Pogačar was in an early, short-lived breakaway, later missing the decisive split.

However, weeks earlier, his rivals were reminded of Pogačar's raw talent when the road pitched uphill. The Giro della Lunigiana is a leading junior stage race and its selection of sharp, medium-length hills inland from Italy's Ligurian coast were rare beasts in the under-19 category.

The race's decisive stage, or *tappone* as they say in those parts, came on day two, finishing north of La Spezia after a climb of 5 km to the village of Fosdinovo. Escaping with Kazakh rider Vadim Pronskiy and Samuele Battistella, the 17-year-old Pogačar sprinted to third place, hitting an average heart rate of 211 bpm for 90 seconds on his Garmin Edge 500 computer, according to Strava, and maxing out at 214, even higher than his publicly stated maximum.

He saved his best for last, winning the last stage's uphill finish to confirm his overall victory, pounding his chest in the emerald-green leader's jersey as he crossed the line. 'I remember the race really well because we slept in a campsite, which was awful,' says Primožič. 'That's where I saw that Tadej is much more than we expected [him] to be and he's mature.

'He was just flying there,' he adds, 'he was so comfortable racing exactly like he should … There, I really saw that he was much better than me.

'Especially the last stage: there's a nice photo where the whole team is pulling, helping Tadej. We were really brothers in arms,' he says. On the podium afterwards, Pogačar sprayed their coach Andrej Cimprič with a bottle of Astoria fizz and took a hearty swig.

His most prestigious result came weeks later at September's European Championships road race in Brittany, finishing third behind French duo Nicolas Malle and Emilien Jannière. As he moved up to elite races with adults in 2017, there was no doubting his potential.

In one of his first interviews with international media, Pogačar spoke to French website *Velo-Club* for their Champions of Tomorrow franchise in late 2016. 'I like long climbs and difficult finishes, and I also like time trials, though I'm not very good at this discipline. I think I need to work at this,' he said, telling readers what kind of cyclist he was. Asked what his dream was, the answer was simple: to become professional and win the big races.

He mentioned too that he had been a fan of the Schleck brothers and Lance Armstrong as a youngster. This was only four years on from the American's dramatic fall from grace, stripped of his seven Tour de France titles after being found guilty of doping in a USADA investigation. It was another stain on a sport that had seen damaging doping affairs surrounding various champions in previous decades.

Neither Tadej nor those close to him could be ignorant of this harmful history.

Over dinner with Andrej Hauptman, his mother Marjeta asked for him to stop cycling. 'We talked about it a lot. I knew that if he went any further, they would want to dope him. That's when it starts,' she told *L'Équipe* in 2021.

It was a conversation Pogačar said he did not find out about until later. 'Mothers whose children ride bikes are afraid of two things: accidents and doping,' Hauptman told the French newspaper. 'It's true that there have been several cases in Slovenia. I had to personally commit to protect him from that.'

► Level up: performing on the under-23 circuit, in a tough calendar of races against the most talented and cut-throat competitors in his generation, could put Pogačar in the crosshairs of top WorldTour teams.

5

BREAKAWAY

2017–2018

Moving up every rung of the cycling ladder is a laborious task for a bike racer aiming for the top. Going from junior to the under-23 ranks and then into WorldTour races is an exercise of repeatedly proving yourself in bigger, more intense environments, year after year. The proverbial dial does not go all the way back to zero – the best take along ability and a certain reputation – but the transition is far from easy.

The races get longer and faster, against more international fields with deeper quality. Many older rivals have similar ability and plenty of power too, so making the winning difference often relies on putting out the numbers at the crunch point in races, when already in a state of fatigue. Tactics matter more and brute strength does not cover up positional sins as effectively any more; a lax approach to training shows up more clearly too.

Then there are bigger bunches and intimidating adult rivals, also chasing their WorldTour dreams or simply trying to make a living.

After his graduation on to Rog-Ljubljana, the adult professional team part of the KD Rog set-up, the lessons continued for the 18-year-old Tadej Pogačar, on and off the bike.

Making the step up was even tougher with school in the way. In between competing in pro races, he was also embarking on his last, most important year at Mechanical Engineering High School in central Ljubljana. His parents told him he had to finish his studies, then he could carry on racing.

At his technical school, the majority of the subjects were about mechanical engineering. That also comprised practical work in the workshops, totalling around eight hours a week, and included welding, programming on CNC machines and pneumatics.

Karin Klun was his homeroom class teacher for four years there. 'I'm surprised at how confidently and comfortably he appears in the media,' Klun wrote in an e-mail before our conversation over Zoom. 'His responses to journalists are increasingly self-assured and even humorous, which is quite a contrast to the reserved and somewhat shy student I once knew.'

Klun remembers a calm, well-mannered teenager who did not cause trouble. 'He was just an average guy in class, he never stood out. I think his parents raised him well. He developed into a nice person.'

Once the bell rang to signify the end of the school day, the rest of the afternoon was for cycling, though Klun says he never skipped classes due to training. The only significant absence the teacher can recall was when Pogačar went to the United States for the World Championships in September 2015.

Klun heard about his cycling talent only because a colleague's son was a fellow cyclist. 'I'm sure that no one [at the school] knew about Tadej. They never told us about his successes and I didn't know that he wanted to be a future professional cyclist.' However, he would sit next to fellow racing cyclist Jaka Oven in the classroom's back row.

In his final years, Pogačar was studying Slovenian, English and maths alongside mechanical engineering. He would be marked between one and five, needing two for a satisfactory pass. For his important springtime graduation assignment, he was helped by Rog-Ljubljana teammate Žiga Ručigaj, whose engineer father advised him while he built a battery-powered wheelbarrow.

Even as his older sister Barbara became an accomplished engineer and brother Tilen went on to work in logistics, the prospect of employment away from cycling was receding for Tadej. 'I can't imagine doing anything else. I would suffer in the office, here I am free,' Pogačar once told his grandmother Anica when she asked if he could do something else that wouldn't require him to work so hard, she recounted to *Aleteia* in 2021.

With his increasing school workload, he had missed the Rás race in Ireland in May 2017 and suffered through another race in the Czech Republic, off his best form. However, Pogačar wanted a strong showing at the mid-June Tour of Slovenia. His home race was the biggest event of the season for Rog-Ljubljana, registered as a UCI Continental team, the sport's third and lowest tier, designated for pro-amateur teams. This was a chance to test himself against WorldTour top dogs for the first time. The problem was that it also coincided with Slovenia's compulsory *matura* exams which mark the end of secondary education.

This clash was an annual headache for the race's youngest homegrown competitors: years earlier, a teenage Matej Mohorič sat a chemistry exam wearing his cycling jersey in the stage start town before rushing off to race.

Pogačar took three written and one oral exams in the days before the race start in Koper. He also rescheduled the presentation of his final project in mechanical engineering so that he could compete.

When the race hit Rogla, the 14-km finishing climb of stage 3 in the hills west of Maribor, there seemed to be little apparent impact on his form, whether from missed training or study stress.

With 10 km to go, Pogačar was still hanging on to the eight-man lead group. He looked ragged on the bike, his elbows flexing and upper body rocking as he struggled to keep up with the repeated accelerations of Rafał Majka, the reigning Tour de France King of the Mountains champion riding for Bora–Hansgrohe.

While the Pole attacked and won the sprint for victory ahead, Pogačar finished fifth. Moments after crossing the finish line, the smiling, exhausted teenager high-fived spectators reaching their hands out. Fighting Majka on Rogla made his father Mirko fully realise his son's quality as a cyclist. The result also secured Pogačar a place on the final podium in Novo Mesto, wearing the white jersey of best young rider.

'This is one of the first podiums in my career. I hope there will be many more and it will continue like this. That one day I might even win the Tour of Slovenia and something else of a higher rank,' Pogačar told *Siol*.

Only at this moment did Karin Klun realise what a sporting gem had been under her nose. But no rest for the gifted: he went from sharing the bunch with sprinting great Mark Cavendish to sitting his *matura* oral exams 48 hours later. 'Of course, I would like them [my teachers] to look kindly on me, but that's not going to happen,' Pogačar said, adding with no little understatement: 'It's very tiring mentally when you have to prepare for school and compete at the same time.'

Despite the juggling act, Pogačar passed his exams and high school. With education out of the way, he could finally focus fully on cycling and was able to put in more hours of training.

Pogačar's Tour of Slovenia fifth place was the highlight of his debut year in the elite ranks. He had already shown his climbing ability at one of his first races, the Istrian Spring Trophy, a March stage race on the Croatian Adriatic coast. Stage 2 finished in the charming, medieval hilltop town of Motovun on a lung-busting hill 2-km long and dotted with misshapen cobblestones. The finish in Josef Ressel Square was unconventional: metres after racing under a narrow 17th-century gateway in the town walls, breathless riders went under the finish line gantry flanked by restaurant tables and tourists tucking into their lunch.

At 186 km in total, the stage had been the longest race of Pogačar's life. But after almost five hours in the saddle, he seemed to be up to the challenge. One hundred and fifty metres from the finish line, on the attack in front, Pogačar's foot came out of the pedal and he briefly lost all his speed. He was overtaken by a couple of other riders. Seconds later, with the finish line beckoning, it happened again.

Speaking to *Prijavim*, he professed to being a 'little disappointed, but still very satisfied' as he held on to fourth overall. The 18-year-old was the only rider under the age of 25 to finish in the top 10, making the transition look easy.

'Everyone else was fighting to finish races and ride in the bunch, and he was top 10 everywhere,' Jaka Primožič says. 'From the start, he never struggled with the bunch or anything. He was just racing normally, like he was in juniors. At that time, it was a *big* step. It's different to now when you're a junior and come to elite: you're racing with development teams, you have all the best gear, all the best everything.'

Pogačar's performance caught the eye of Joxean Fernández Matxin, a leading talent scout working for Quick-Step Floors. The Spaniard talked to both Pogačar and Andrej Hauptman at the finish, seeing whether the squad would be allowed to test the young rider in Belgium before the under-23 Tour of Flanders. It never took place, simply because Pogačar's race schedule changed, according to Hauptman.

Matxin kept an eye on him, though, also noticing him finish second to South African rider Stefan de Bod at the following year's GP Palio del Recioto, a leading Italian amateur race. 'His legs were of a non-cyclist, of a normal guy starting cycling one month ago. There was no muscle, no tone, nothing,' Matxin told me in 2021, recalling their first encounters. 'This is important for me, remembering the amazing margin of development of this guy. He is a winner, he has the character of a winner, he had the level, but nothing of the professional, no super body.'

Yet Quick-Step would miss out, as a deal with another WorldTour team was in the works. During the summer of 2016, Hauptman had called Fabrizio Bontempi, his former *directeur sportif* as a rider at Vini Caldirola, and suggested: 'Take this one, I never trained someone like this.'

Bontempi was team manager with Italian squad Lampre-Merida and had been given an unofficial remit to seek out emerging talents by its general manager, the Italian cycling great Giuseppe Saronni. The squad was about to become UAE Abu Dhabi as backers from the Middle East came in to save the team from extinction ahead of 2017.

Thanks to long-standing relationships with Hauptman and compatriot Milan Eržen, a succession of accomplished Slovenians had already signed for the team in the previous decade, including Simon Špilak, Grega Bole, Jan Polanc and Luka Pibernik. Pogačar and many of his KD Rog teammates even wore Lampre socks for bike rides or gym exercises.

Tipped off by Hauptman, Bontempi had duly been, incognito, to see Pogačar compete at four junior one-day races that summer, including Montichiari-Roncone (where Pogačar was third) and La Piccola Sanremo (seventh). More important than the results, the Slovenian was a protagonist in all of them. 'He was born with the spirit of a big attacker,' Bontempi says. 'He was a lot smarter than many other stage racers and knew how to handle his bike.'

Sufficiently impressed, he went back to Saronni to report on his findings. However, Pogačar was not an easy sell. When Bontempi brought him up again at the team headquarters weeks later, the two-time Giro winner replied: 'Fabrizio, are you still proposing these Slovenian kids to me?'

At the time, Lampre also had Matej Mohorič, Marko Kump and Jan Polanc on their books. 'They didn't cost too much, but we were an Italian team, we couldn't take too many Slovenians. Now, teams are international,' Bontempi explains.

He persevered and in January 2017, Saronni drew up a pre-contract between his team and Pogačar, stipulating that when he was ready to turn professional, the UAE Abu Dhabi team had the right of first refusal. There was also already a sum involved – €50,000, according to Bontempi. The pathway to the pro ranks was being laid.

Bontempi suggests they signed Pogačar without seeing physiological test data. 'But I have to be honest: nobody could have thought that this kid would become the rider he is in a few years,' Bontempi says. 'He was very strong, yes, but to think he would win the Tour de France and the other races right away … in the races, he did not dominate. I've got a load of results sheets: in one youth race in Kranj, as a first-year, he finished 14th.'

During the winter of 2017, the Rog-Ljubljana team became Ljubljana Gusto Xaurum. Taiwanese bike manufacturer Gusto came on board alongside Slovenian cryptocurrency company Xaurum.

Slovenian team manager Tomaž Poljanec joined as general manager, accompanying their existing *directeur sportif*, Marko Polanc. With the additional sponsors, the overall budget increased; Poljanec estimates it was upped to €250,000 – still modest, but allowing more spaces for international riders and a broader European racing calendar.

The team size doubled to 16 riders, but Poljanec was still well aware of their underdog status as an outfit made up predominantly of undercooked foreigners and riders under the age of 21.

'Usually when you come from the juniors and are on the start of the first elite/under-23 races, you always watch these older guys like this,' former Yugoslav junior champion Poljanec says, miming putting his elbows out. 'Now things are changing, but before, the hierarchy in the peloton was really strict. The guys from the big teams always look on the young guys like "Go away junior, fuck off." This change came because of Pogačar. He was not afraid of anybody.'

At the 2018 season opener, the GP Laguna Poreč, Pogačar had to endure conditions of minus one Celsius, freezing rain and snow. He could barely eat an energy bar as his hands were frozen, but he was in the winning breakaway with Jaka Primožič and finished fifth. Pogačar went to the team van afterwards and asked them to turn on the heating. It was already blasting, but he was so chilly that it still felt like he was outside. This would go down as one of his worst days on the bike. Little wonder some of the first Slovenian words his newly arrived Australian teammate Ben Hill learned were *mrzlo da popizdiš* – so fucking cold.

He and his compatriot Tim Guy joined a team that also included three Taiwanese riders and a Japanese rider. Aged 27, Hill was chasing his dream of turning professional in Europe, playing the role of sprinter alongside Žiga Jerman.

'I remember rolling out every day for training and one of my teammates being like "It's just like another screensaver." Beautiful, picturesque mountains in the background every day,' Hill says.

He did not get the early impression that Pogačar was the special one. 'Žiga Jerman had just won the under-23 Ghent-Wevelgem, he was kind of "the man". Žiga Ručigaj was a [European youth] Olympic champion,' Hill says. 'I felt like the hype was more around those two. And even [Izidor] Penko was a good upcoming time triallist, talked about the same way Tadej was.'

Hill and Guy were struck by the 'hardcore' attitude of the team. Some training sessions could be like races. If a rider dropped back, unable to keep up with the fierce pace, nobody stopped and waited. On one ride with the club's junior group, a coach attacked up a hill, leading to more accelerations from other riders, dividing the pack by the crest. One kid then crashed on the wet, twisting descent, chasing hard. They did not stop to regroup. 'He knows his way home,' the coach bellowed as they continued roaring downhill.

If Ljubljana Gusto Xaurum had a bad performance at a race, their no-nonsense *directeur sportif* Marko Polanc ('democracy doesn't belong in sports … I've never been a democracy,' he once said to *Siol*) frequently had them doing hard team training sessions the following week, with motor-paced efforts or long days sticking to certain effort zones.

'But whenever Marko wasn't there and it was free rein, we'd just race up every hill – for speed signs, for Strava segments and doing lead-outs,' Hill says. 'Pogačar and Ručigaj would always be Strava-hunting, going for stuff. Tadej was really easy to gee up for any mini race or Strava attempt, he loved it.'

The team would sometimes turn the steep wall at the foot of Krvavec into a training race, with Ručigaj and Pogačar often going toe to toe. However, in the longer mountain training rides, sometimes doing five hours into Austria, Pogačar had few equals.

'He destroyed everyone because he just seemed to not fatigue as much,' Hill says. 'I thought it was "Ruči" fatiguing quickly at the time, that he's only good for one effort … I didn't realise maybe Pogačar was actually way better than everyone else for that.'

The penny fully dropped for Hill at the 2018 Tour of Croatia, where the Ljubljana Gusto Xaurum team were one of the smallest squads up against six WorldTour teams. During the toughest stage to Poklon, containing three ascents and more than 3000 m of elevation, Pogačar did a new 20-minute power PB on the climb to the finish.

'Pogačar said he did 410 watts or something. And I was like "*That's when you do your 20-minute PB?*"' Hill says, his voice going up an octave. 'If I do a 20-minute test, I'm tapering into it, doing it fresh and going as hard as I can. Stage 5 of a UCI *hors-catégorie* race, he's like "I'll try now." … That was mind-blowing in terms of his fatigue resistance.' Pogačar finished fifth that day, ending the race just outside the top 10 overall.

That is the real litmus test of a top pro cyclist too: giving your best at the optimal moment, days into a race when already in a state of heightened tiredness. As the level of racing rises from junior to under-23 and elite level, when every single promising rider can carry out the required watts per kilo to challenge, it gets harder and harder to do the same at the crucial moment in the race – and to be positioned in the right place to do it. More mental and physical energy is being burned.

'In training, sometimes I was dropping him at 400 watts,' Žiga Ručigaj says. 'But in races, the whole group was going 400 watts, one guy was attacking and Tadej was just going with him, full gas, the whole climb. I didn't know how, but I was suffering. Where is this guy putting energy in his legs? Sometimes I was really shocked.' He believes it was due to Pogačar's exceptional ability to clear lactate, which is produced in greater numbers by high-intensity exercise, helping him to make accelerations again much more quickly, whereas Ručigaj's own levels tended to fluctuate more, necessitating greater recovery time.

Pondering the difference between the pair, Ručigaj says: 'He was really focused, he knew how to really suffer … mentally, you cannot break him down.'

Three years older than Pogačar, Ručigaj was based in the large town of Kamnik, 7 km down the road from Komenda. The duo got to know each other better as Ručigaj gave him regular lifts to and from training in Šmartno or races in his grey Smart car – just big enough for two bikes, two people.

They would talk gaming, fast cars and WorldTour racing; Pogačar encouraged him to watch more pro cycling and they both took part in the popular Pro Cycling Stats fantasy cycling management game, where players can pick pro riders who earn points depending on their performances. 'He also beat me there,' Ručigaj says, laughing.

After training, they would play long online games of League of Legends, the popular multiplayer battle arena, sometimes going deep into the evening. 'He was really good. When I start to think back now, he was like in cycling: he never gave up,' Ručigaj says. 'Every game, he did not want to surrender – I was always that guy who did, which pissed him off sometimes – and wanted to play to the end. He played it a lot, maybe he could also turn pro in League of Legends esports.'

On the bike, Ručigaj tended to shine more in training than racing, freezing when he felt the expectation from the team to produce a result. He remembers one under-23 Italian race when the team's trainer suggested the leader as Pogačar, who countered that Ručigaj should be their frontman.

'I was really nervous. In the middle of it, I said to Tadej, "No, no, we'll race for you, I can't [be leader] any more"', he says. 'He always said to me, *Never give up and never stop fighting*, that's how this slogan came out,' he says, referring to a motto which became Pogačar's personal one during his early years as a pro cyclist.

Pogačar was determined to make it to the upper echelon of the sport. 'Sometimes talking on training rides, he was telling me he would just be happy going to the WorldTour,' Ručigaj adds. 'His dream was just to be at the Tour de France. In the end, the first time he tried it, he won it.'

Despite not being the largest rider by a long shot (1.77 m / 5 ft 9.5 inches), Pogačar could hold his own in the bunch's fights for position. 'Sometimes he was yelling at one guy a head taller than him, sometimes you need to tell him to chill [out]. Going full gas to the last climb, he wanted to be in the first row to start it in the first 10 positions,' Ručigaj says.

The Ljubljana Gusto Xaurum general manager Tomaž Poljanec sees similarities between the characters of Pogačar and fellow Grand Tour champion Jai Hindley, who raced under him for the Attaque Gusto team in 2016 before turning pro and going on to win the

Giro d'Italia. 'They're both very kind and grateful for every small thing. This is something that always frustrates me. I think it's getting worse from generation to generation. It's just "What will I get?" Not what they will give you back,' Poljanec says. 'Now, nothing is good enough any more.

'If our mechanic used five-year-old cranks and not the best Shimano chainring, it was like: "Sorry, Tadej, but this is what I have", he went: "Ah, it's OK, good, no problem, thank you"'.

Ben Hill wonders whether the team's tech equipment might have held Pogačar back at times. 'I don't think the Gusto bikes were very good. Especially the early iterations we were on. Pogačar's winning on it, they can't be too bad … but maybe he just wins on anything,' Hill says.

'They were pretty heavy rim-brake bikes. It was an old-school design, so it wasn't aero at all, painted with this thick gold paint. They were bomb-proof: we crashed a lot and never broke any.'

Countering that viewpoint, his compatriot Tim Guy suggests that the team went to every degree to ensure that Pogačar's bike, at least, was as close to the UCI limit of 6.8 kg as possible, costing them extra money at times.

Either way, it was some distance from the richer set-up of WorldTour squads – and Pogačar's pathway was unusual, given that he feasibly could have signed for a vaunted WorldTour development team.

Pogačar did not grumble, able to appreciate what he had at Ljubljana Gusto Xaurum: regular leadership opportunities in a familiar, tight-knit environment which would likely have been harder to come by elsewhere. His salary – Poljanec says that Pogačar was on no more than €1000 a month – was as modest as his attitude, but big money could come later.

. . . .

Ushering in a summer he would never forget, Pogačar took his first win of 2018 in spectacular fashion at June's under-23 Peace Race. Part of the Nations Cup, the foremost UCI season-long series for that age group, he won with an audacious, last-day attack over two climbs and 35 km, through the pouring rain into the Czech town of Jesenik, jumping from sixth to first on GC in the process. The rival Swiss and Great Britain teams chased hard, but made few inroads into his advantage. Even a couple of years later, after winning his first Tour de France, Pogačar talked about that day as his best memory of racing on the offensive.

The subsequent Tour of Slovenia was a big success for Pogačar and his team. Ben Hill took enough intermediate bonus seconds from breakaways on the opening two stages to slip into the green jersey of race leader.

'I'm leading the tour and there are fellas still not giving me the wheel,' Hill says of the lack of respect afforded to him. 'Whereas Pogačar didn't care, he was sat back in 50th by himself, moving up when he needs to move up. As soon as it started going uphill, he just rode around everyone.' Pogačar finished fourth, helped by a strong time trial, though Primož Roglič was the comfortable race winner.

The young team captain's happy-go-lucky side also shone through. 'I was tucked up in bed one night and Pogačar bust in at 10:30, handing out pizza sticks,' Hill says. 'He was like "This town is a great pizza stick stop, you *have* to have these pizza sticks." I was like "Mate, we've got a race tomorrow, what are you doing?" He was so relaxed about it ... life seemed to come pretty easy to him. Win races, have fun, no problems.'

Despite his consistent top 10 finishes through the year, Pogačar never slacked off working for teammates. 'I remember stage 1 of Friuli [the 2018 Giro della Regione Friuli-Venezia Giulia], there were 20 of us or so coming into the finish and he was chasing down every move for me for the last 20 km because he was like "Ben, you're a sprinter, you can win this." He was all-in helping me, leading me out, even though he was the one that was going to win the tour, it had a big hilltop stage. He was really happy to ride for someone else if they had a chance.' Pogačar dropped him off at the front for the finish; unfortunately, Hill's back wheel slipped out of his frame and he crashed.

After Pogačar duly won the race overall days later, they dropped equipment off at the team's headquarters and then went into Ljubljana, to the local pizzeria. 'I think they were drinking Long Island iced teas that night,' Hill says, laughing. 'He did [too]. I'm not sure if it was a common occurrence for him, it was a kind of end-of-season party.'

Pogačar did not miss out on teenage kicks completely for sport. He went to a few parties and after training, he and his friends would occasionally stop off at Bar Julija in Domžale for a beer or two. But largely, he stuck to his goal of becoming a WorldTour cyclist without distractions. 'I sometimes thought that cycling was making me miss out on all the fun,' Pogačar told *Siol* in 2019. 'But in the end, it's worth putting so much effort into what you love to do. Cycling has given me a very special life. Without a bike and fellow cyclists, I would probably be bored.'

While the Slovenian riders and foreigners on Ljubljana Gusto Xaurum were inevitably a little divided, Hill and his compatriot Tim Guy found Pogačar to be one of the most welcoming riders. 'Off the bike, you didn't get the idea of this unbelievably dogged, selfish, directed person,' Guy says. 'That's not the vibe he gave. I remember doing some interviews with him [for the team], and you're just laughing around.' When the team went go-karting for Guy's 29th birthday, Pogačar was one of the best, showing his ability at taking risks and following the racing line.

Guy regards Pogačar's finished superstar form as partly down to KD Rog's successful 'gamification' of development and training, rather than making him conform to a strict structure. 'Because you can try to force someone into [being] a robot, and you probably don't want him as a robot. You *want* him doing stupid moves with 80 km to go. You could easily beat that out of someone … you could see that personality and it seems like that stayed.'

. . . .

An unexpected force was pushing Pogačar on through the summer of 2018 like a tailwind: love. During a shared training camp in Livigno in late July, he and fellow cyclist Urška Žigart became boyfriend and girlfriend. For nine days, they did many training rides together in the

Italian Alps location. It is little wonder that Livigno and its majestic mountains became a 'special place' for him.

The pair had first met in 2017, at a training camp for Rog-Ljubljana and BTC Ljubljana, the professional women's squad and KD Rog's sister team, in Poreč. Having to rush off to Ljubljana, *directeur sportif* Marko Polanc had asked the men to go training with the women.

They paired off to do 30-second sprint accelerations. As a climber, not feeling particularly good at these, Žigart asked for a male counterpart with similar attributes, and Pogačar volunteered. After doing the first one on his wheel, with her heart rate spiking at 196 bpm, it was clear he was not nearly as bad as he had indicated.

Pogačar's friends noticed him light up as the two played table football on the same team together later. He had met his match. Two years older than him, thin with long blonde hair, blue eyes and a smile as ready as his, Žigart had done seven years of music school and was able to play the piano and sing like an angel. She also went to law school, harbouring ambitions of being a state prosecutor before putting her studies on hold to pursue her sporting dream.

Formerly a runner and volleyball player, she had turned to cycling after installing an exercise bicycle in the corner of her house to pedal while doing homework or watching films, spending several hours a day on it. The learning curve was steeper than Planica's main ski jump: within a year of starting cycling in 2017, she was doing WorldTour races.

Tadej and Urška kept in touch, talking and hanging out, though living 100 km apart in Slovenia without immediate access to a car meant they couldn't see each other so easily.

Together, they brought out the best of each other. 'At first, he was quite shy. It took a while. He was a bit like he is in the media now, serious. But with me, he makes jokes, Tadej is more self-confident, he is relaxed. He is funny, he is a joker,' she told *Le Parisien* in 2022.

Both seemed energised by their blossoming relationship. Žigart rode to the best results of her embryonic career after their Livigno camp, finishing inside the top 30 at La Course par le Tour de France. Meanwhile, Pogačar embarked on his first Tour de l'Avenir, the focal point of his season.

'The Tour of the Future', run by Tour de France organisers ASO, was one of the longest races on the under-23 calendar and the go-to test for budding stage racers. Since its inaugural edition in 1961, 10 of its champions have also won Grand Tours, including Felice Gimondi, Joop Zoetemelk, Greg LeMond and Miguel Induráin.

After another interminable minibus drive with his Slovenian national teammates, Pogačar lined up for the start in the little Breton town of Grand-Champ. It could have been worse: Nejc Grilc had driven the TTT bikes overnight without stopping, leaving Slovenia at 8 in the evening. 'I couldn't go to sleep because I had €50,000 of bikes on the roof,' he remembers.

Now a sports journalist with *Delo,* Grilc was there doing PR for the national federation and helping team manager Martin Hvastija. He remembers the 19-year-old Pogačar as being 'a bit shy. He did not stand out in any way. He never was a diva, I think he still is not a diva. He didn't have anything special: he's not loud, he's not the person who is the centre of attention.'

'That group of guys, they were great friends, really having fun. I didn't sense a pressure among them.' Grilc remembers them listening to loud Slovenian music constantly, in particular playing the parody song 'Midva Sva Iz Tacna' ('We Are from Tacen') by Blaž and Mali Mišo in the car, over and over and over. Its lyrics 'en, va, tri' – one, two, three – became a particular catchphrase between the riders. (No doubt it helped that Tacen was well-known to many of them, down the road from the KD Rog HQ.)

Pogačar started as an outsider for victory. The first difference-maker was the stage 4 team time trial. The Slovenia team was easy to underestimate, especially given that the nation had not even qualified for the race the year before. However, Jaka Primožič had pedigree and Izidor Penko had finished second in the European Championships under-23 time trial. Performing better than Pogačar expected, Slovenia rode strongly to eighth place. Rivals Colombia, the team of pre-race favourite Iván Sosa, had a disaster, finishing 22nd of the 26 teams.

Pogačar was already competing on a Colnago time trial bike, the brand used by UAE Team Emirates, and two days later, his two-year contract with the team was unveiled in a team press release. Given what was about to unfold at the Tour de l'Avenir, the announcement was perfect timing, akin to hanging a 'hands off, he's ours' sign around his neck.

Pogačar was in his element when the race entered the Alps for a series of short, sharp, pass-packed stages. On stage 7 to Méribel, Sosa won, outsprinting American challenger Brandon McNulty and Pogačar from their escape. However, the Slovenian TTT performance meant Pogačar was ahead of them in the GC. He donned the hallowed yellow jersey, but his team support was dwindling. That day, Žiga Jerman abandoned the race; the next, it was curtains for a sick Penko.

Pogačar knew he was likely to come under fire from rivals. He asked his team manager, Martin Hvastija, what he could do, and *attack is the best defence* came the answer. 'The classic advice, but he has to do it: it's easy to say, but not that easy to realise it,' Hvastija says.

Not for most. But on the ninth and penultimate stage, the *maillot jaune* broke away with Luxembourger Michel Ries with 20 km to go and gained a cushion of over a minute on the rest.

After finishing that day in Val d'Isère, Pogačar and Primožič sat in their wood-cabin-like hotel room. Their remaining teammates, Nik Čemažar and Žiga Horvat, joined them, munching on snacks and *crostini*. Horvat sat on the wooden-plank shelf in the closet. 'It broke and he fell on the floor,' Primožič says. 'It was such a stupid thing, but because we were so tired, it was so funny. We were laughing for half an hour.'

One decisive day in the mountains remained. The last stage was set to leave Val d'Isère, go over the mighty Col de l'Iseran at 2754 m and the 13.1-km Col du Chaussy after a long descent and then finish halfway up the Col du Glandon. Team manager Hvastija was nervous: Pogačar would be isolated and especially vulnerable to attacks, with heavy *rouleurs* Čemažar and Horvat likely to be distanced on the first ascent and Primožič weakened by mononucleosis.

At 10 in the evening, they got some unexpected meteorological help. It started snowing – in late August. Grilc and Hvastija drove up to the Iseran, filming the couple of centimetres of snow and icy conditions on their phones. At a team meeting, they showed their evidence and suggested the race couldn't possibly ride over it. It was too dangerous, someone would get killed.

The next morning, the race jury postponed the start and decided to skip the first 35 km because of the snow, travelling by car to Bessans. 'It was a bit of luck. The Danish guys were particularly angry with that decision,' Hvastija remembers.

Horvat and Čemažar rode on the front of the bunch, keeping the race together in the valley. Still, the nail-biting moments were far from over as Pogačar came up to Primožič before the Col du Chaussy, needing to take a comfort break. As one of his support riders, he was tasked with stopping and pacing him back on. Primožič's stress levels skyrocketed, waiting for a minute with him to do his business. It was a bad time to stop, with the race about to ignite on the steep climb.

He set off all out, with the race leader tucked safely in his slipstream. 'We catch the back of the group at the start of the climb and then I went 10 minutes, [gave] everything I had and we got to the front. I left him there and pulled over to the side,' Primožič says. 'I would say he won the race himself. The first two hours, we could help him when the tempo was not that high,' he adds later.

On the descent of the Chaussy, disaster almost struck. Pogačar's rear wheel locked up and he missed a left-hand bend, riding straight into a meadow. He stayed on his bike and manoeuvred back on to the road over the grass. The heart-stopping moment didn't prevent Slovenia's first Tour de l'Avenir win. In fact, Pogačar extended his winning margin, to 1 minute 28 seconds over Thymen Arensman of the Netherlands.

The toll of the Tour de l'Avenir on Team Slovenia's young hotshots did not quite end in France. Primožič says that they later received a bill for €900 for a new hotel room shelf and the labour. 'What we earned on the Tour de l'Avenir, we had to give it back. The national team took it directly from our prize money, which we then split,' Primožič says, smiling.

Nobody could now be left under any illusions about Pogačar's potential. He had saved some of his best performances in the under-23 category until his last summer. 'To have a talent like this who could possibly become a great rider for Grand Tours was really a big deal for us,' Nejc Grilc says. 'It just cemented this idea that he could be the next best thing.'

Pogačar would graduate to the WorldTour in the crosshairs of other teams, having won cycling's version of the under-23 Tour de France.

'All the teams – Sky – started calling him. But he had already signed for us,' UAE Team Emirates manager Fabrizio Bontempi says. Teams taking an interest ranged from WorldTour heavyweights such as Quick-Step, Bahrain Merida and Trek–Segafredo to smaller, second-tier Pro Continental squads like Delko Marseille and Nippo-Vini Fantini.

Bontempi says that while Sky and Quick-Step both showed interest, no team wanted to pay the large premium in his contract to free up Pogačar. 'If they pay it, will he be a great rider? Nobody thought, *I'll pay this, take him and then we'll see*. It was an unknown,' Bontempi says.

Every cycling team wants to consolidate their position and be first to sign the next precocious young superstar, but judging a rider's margin of development is an inexact science. Vaunted talents come and go like passing clouds every season in pro cycling. However, with the benefit of hindsight, this was a sliding doors moment unlike any other. Team Sky – and their rivals – missed out on the rider able to single-handedly transform a sport and a team's fortunes. Instead of going to one of the front runners, he went to the 12th-ranked team in the WorldTour standings.

Nobody saw what was coming. Years later, as Pogačar blazed a consistent, imperious trail in Grand Tours and Monument one-day races and the stranglehold of Ineos Grenadiers, who took over the sponsorship from Sky, ended, their management would probably privately rue missing out on a monstrous champion. Had he joined them, everything could have been very different for them – and Pogačar.

Such is professional cycling's transfer system that Ljubljana Gusto Xaurum and KD Rog both received nothing financially from his move to UAE Team Emirates. However, for Pogačar, the value of his cycling education there was priceless. From his first moments riding gingerly on Slovenian country roads to his final race with the adult team in Japan a decade later, the Slovenian club had helped him grow into a rare talent with an enviable work ethic.

'They [Tilen and Tadej] found friends in the club that they still hang out with today and they found values that they still live by,' his father, Mirko, wrote in a letter of thanks, published in *Delo* in 2021, after joining the KD Rog board of directors. 'Let [children] know that with hard work and willpower, they can shake stars from the sky.'

The trust built up in his teenage years was holy. Pogačar himself would not forget the lessons inculcated or the fellow travellers on this early part of his journey.

▶ 'I'm always nervous before the new season because I always want to improve. What if I stop getting better? If I get stuck in some place? That's my fear.'

6

—

TIMING IS EVERYTHING

2019

Fernando Gaviria, UAE Team Emirates' star sprinter, stands at the far end of the nine-man row, wearing a dark blue Elvis Presley suit, smiling into the camera. Each of the teammates alongside him is clad in a different item of garish fancy dress. Former Paris–Nice winner Sergio Henao is in a floppy hat with an inflatable horse in front of him, making him look like a cowboy. Jasper Philipsen has perhaps drawn the short straw, in a lurid red and black dress, showing his formidable sprinter's calves. Linking arms with the Belgian at the end of the line is a beaming Tadej Pogačar, dressed in a baggy, electric-blue tuxedo with over-long sleeves, looking every inch a 1980s prom king.

What resembles a bunch of university students on a bar crawl is simply a moment captured from the light-hearted initiation ceremony for the new riders joining UAE Team Emirates in late December 2018 from their winter training camp hotel in the Spanish town of La Pineda.

Other riders chipped in a few euros each and sourced the costumes as part of a time-honoured tradition across the peloton. More than just jocular team bonding which ended up on social media, the photograph encapsulates the new-look UAE Team Emirates and its fresh impetus.

Of the nine new riders – a third of the team's entire rider complement – pictured, all except Henao were 24 years old or younger. The Oliveira twins from Portugal, Rui and Ivo, would become good friends and trusted helpers for Pogačar, as would Colombian rider Juan Sebastián Molano. Philipsen evolved into the world's fastest sprinter. A winner of two Tour stages the previous year, Gaviria would go on to add another at the Giro in 2019. And then there's Pogačar himself.

Timing is everything, and he had joined the squad at an opportune moment. Perennially mid-table finishers in the WorldTour, UAE Team Emirates were looking to soar up it, rebuilding with intent and international talent. This was a time of transition for the team following two seasons of consolidation.

There was very nearly no UAE Team Emirates at all. Their involvement in the sport came in a haphazard, rushed manner, morphing out of the established Lampre-Merida team.

Backed by a company specialising in pre-coated steel production, the Italian squad had existed in cycling's top tier since 1999, spearheaded by champions like Alessandro Ballan, Damiano Cunego and Gilberto Simoni in their blue and fuchsia kit. They had lined up a Chinese consortium to take their licence in the sport's top tier at the end of 2016, but the deal never happened.

A former professional cyclist who won Liège–Bastogne–Liège and the Amstel Gold Race in 1995 during his long career, Mauro Gianetti was the consulting project co-ordinator who had been part of brokering the abortive deal.

The bald, gaunt Swiss swept into action again, galvanising his contact, UAE property mogul Matar Suhail Al Yabhouni Al Dhaheri, the president of Kopaonik Property Investment.

Perched on the end of the Arabian Peninsula, the predominantly deserted UAE possesses the world's sixth largest oil reserves. Investment in sport has become a key part of the drive to diversify its highly fossil fuel-dependent economy, and the country has put in billions in recent decades. A Formula 1 Grand Prix circuit was built in Abu Dhabi at a cost of over $1 billion, while Abu Dhabi United Group, led by the UAE's deputy prime minister Sheikh Mansour, bought Premier League club Manchester City in 2008. Backing a professional cycling team was pocket change in comparison.

The original intention had been to launch a UAE-based squad with Matar in 2018, but time was now of the essence, with Lampre's existence and over 60 jobs hanging in the balance. Plans were laid out at the Formula 1 Grand Prix in Abu Dhabi in November 2016 to take over their UCI licence; Giuseppe Saronni, general manager, indicated that everything was defined in just 10 days, a remarkably short space of time.

The team became UAE Abu Dhabi Team, and then a few months later, UAE Team Emirates, as the world-renowned airline took over. Emirates' backing was unveiled in a swanky launch, with riders flanked by air hostesses. The new kit, with its red, green, white and black colours, echoed the go-getting Middle Eastern nation's flag.

In a heartbeat, the team went from being a more parochial unit advertising an Italian company specialising in metal coating to a moving billboard promoting a nation and one of its flagship brands. The avowed aim was 'to be a representative for the UAE, for a culture to promote a healthy lifestyle [and] to promote the use of bicycles in the UAE,' Gianetti said to Eurosport.

Critics have argued their association is a form of sportswashing, given the country's debated human rights record and suppression of free speech, peaceful protest and dissent. Not something that will cross most cycling fans' minds when they see Pogačar finish in first place or mess around in charismatic social media videos, with the country's abbreviated letters emblazoned across his jersey chest.

UAE Team Emirates were here to take over, not just take part. Within months of the change, Saronni talked of their ambitions to be among the world's best three teams and win Grand Tours.

Bold words: Lampre had been a staple of the WorldTour lower rank and had not won a Grand Tour since 2011, when Michele Scarponi was retroactively given the Giro d'Italia title. Lampre's budget, estimated to be €10 million, was one of the smallest in the WorldTour, almost four times lower than that of big-timers Team Sky.

Despite added investment – Fabrizio Bontempi suggests that the team's budget doubled immediately – there was a lot of work to be done.

'The first years, the staff and almost all the sports managers were maintained. And they increased the budget, new people came in from different countries … they made a big investment to get the best riders and said from the first year they wanted to have the number 1 athlete in the world and be the number 1 team,' Bontempi says. 'It was already said from the first year [2017] … that for two years, there was no problem. But the third year [2019], they wanted to see results.'

In the winter of 2017, the squad had made eye-catching signings: Fabio Aru, the former winner of the Vuelta a España; Alexander Kristoff, sprinter and winner of the Tour of Flanders; Rui Costa, the 2013 world champion; and Dan Martin, the two-time Monument champion.

Even so, the team was far behind the sport's leaders. Martin's autobiography, *Chased by Pandas*, paints a picture of a backwards, old-school atmosphere during his time there in 2018 and 2019. His bike fit, in a state-of-the-art laboratory at the team's HQ, was on a saddle that looked 50 years old, with cranks two sizes too big for him.

'Rather than working on marginal gains, the staff felt they should stick with their old habits,' Martin wrote. 'I suggested getting input from researchers, sports scientists, biomechanics and materials engineers. Equipment, tyres, textiles, nutrition: everything needed to be reviewed. But every time I proposed something the staff got upset … we were 20 years behind our rivals.'

Looking into his struggles with performance after a so-so 2018 spring campaign, Martin claimed that the team's technical assistants had used only 10 per cent of the manufacturer-recommended amount in their energy drinks – 4 g of carbohydrate instead of 40 – so as not to make it too sweet. Little wonder they were running out of energy.

Martin and Kristoff won Tour de France stages that summer, but it takes time to transform a sports team's culture, way of working and fortunes. Ahead of the 2019 season, there was a back-room overhaul. Giuseppe Saronni stepped down as general manager and Mauro Gianetti became team principal and CEO, bringing in a concurrent change of mentality to help build the world's number one squad.

'Some football teams buy big players, but this is not the goal, it is to create a team,' Gianetti told Sport360 in 2017. Leading scout Joxean Fernández Matxin joined from Quick-Step at the end of that year and became his right-hand man. He lent his gimlet eye for talent, attracting the new wave of precocious youngsters from around the world.

Together, they oversaw sweeping changes to the team's performance staff. The Spaniard also hired Mitchelton-Scott *directeur sportif* Neil Stephens and followed the Australian's recommendation to sign his compatriot Allan Peiper, a canny, thorough and disciplined team manager who lived and breathed the Belgian races.

Colorado-based sports scientist and exercise physiologist Iñigo San Millán, who had previously worked with Gianetti and Matxin in the early years of the Saunier Duval team in 2004, became the new head of trainers.

He brought in South African Jeroen Swart as medical director, asking him to assemble a medical team. His overall brief was to create an outfit that was more structured, evidence-based and cutting-edge. Numerous other South Africans arrived, including Jason Suter and Adriano Rotunno, part of an agreement with the University of Cape Town. On the performance side, South Africa's John Wakefield, Adrie van Diemen and former Lampre rider Rubens Bertogliati joined the squad.

'In past teams, not just Lampre but many others, the way it worked was the team manager had everything on his shoulders: contracts with sponsors, riders, staff, furniture, vehicles,' Bertogliati says.

In came a more shared, modern way of working, with less responsibility solely on the general manager or CEO. Italian Andrea Agostini was responsible for operations and logistics, becoming the third prong of their organisational trident with Gianetti and Matxin, while San Millán oversaw performance. 'There was a person dedicated to every area. OK, they also had the budget to do it,' Bertogliati says. 'But it moved from one centralised person to sharing the power – and Mauro was good at that and having trust in people below him. Then he was also more free to go on the market and pick up good riders.'

While the squad maintained its relaxed, convivial Italianate atmosphere, English became the team's official language, having previously been Italian.

There was no time to waste in their drive for improvement. During their training camp in December 2018, Stephens and Peiper set up training on a Spanish racetrack, working on time trial, 500-m speed efforts, team time trials, starts and lead outs. 'Really specific, really military sort of workouts that these guys weren't really used to,' Stephens says. 'I suppose it started that sort of dynamic [of success] … That was the start of the experiment there.'

Out on the road in Spain, doing tests in the hills, Stephens had already noticed Pogačar in the wake of one of the team's best riders, Diego Ulissi: 'There was this young guy, getting frustrated because he wasn't able to follow. I said [to myself], shit, he's only a neo-pro and he's already good. You could see him chomping at the bit, really ready to go.'

The youngest rider on the team had worries about how he would fare in the big leagues. 'I'm always nervous before the new season because I always want to improve,' he told *Rouleur* writer Nick Christian in late 2018. 'I'm always nervous because what if I stop getting better? If I get stuck in some place? That's my fear.'

However, he was already keen to carve out his own path and style of racing. Asked if team leader Fabio Aru was someone he was looking up to, he replied: 'He's the guy to look up to, but I don't want to be like him. I can learn a lot from these riders, but I want to be something different. Not to be like him or anybody else, but to be me. I want to be the best of me.'

Pogačar's debut came at the Tour Down Under in January 2019, a gentle introduction to the sport's top tier in warm weather while the team stayed in the five-star Hilton Adelaide. It helped that he had his friend and fellow KD Rog alumnus Jan Polanc on the same team.

The Slovenian duo were riding in support of team captain Ulissi. However, a flashpoint arose on the finish of stage 3, a fast downhill sweep into Uraidla. They sprinted full bore, passing him metres before the finish. 'He got a bit heated,' Stephens says of the Italian. 'He said, "What's the story? I got no help from these guys," and this and that.'

Wanting to implement a culture of calm, constructive debriefs rather than knee-jerk reactions, Stephens sat the trio down together at the hotel later to discuss what happened. 'The guys didn't do anything wrong … They wanted to help out, but they just fucked it up … there was Ulissi the champion, Tadej who really wanted to be up there with the champion, but he was there doing his work.

'The significance of that conversation: because of it, Ulissi had a lot of respect for him. Ulissi and him always got on really well after that.' Later that season, Pogačar helped Ulissi to win the Tour of Slovenia, sacrificing his own chances at his home race.

Fellow debutant Jasper Philipsen went on to win a Tour Down Under stage and the UAE Team Emirates line-up won the race's teams classification, clutching boomerangs on the final podium. Pogačar finished 13th in his support role; remarkably, this was to be the only time he finished outside of the top 6 in a stage race up to and including the end of the 2025 season, a run totalling 27 events. 'I said to Mike Turtur, the race organiser, this kid will win the Tour de France one day. And I don't say those sorts of things very often,' Stephens says.

However, Pogačar's first race as a WorldTour pro had been beset by travel nightmares. According to Stephens, snow grounded his flight from Ljubljana to Milan. He flew to Frankfurt instead and found a late-night bus that got him to Bergamo, getting one of the last seats, and was then ferried to Milan Malpensa airport by a team car to make the outgoing flight. 'We arrived in Australia and Tadej, and one other rider maybe, had no suitcase [turn up]. Another challenge. Anyway, he just dealt with it,' Stephens says.

Three weeks later, hours before setting off for the long journey home following the Cadel Evans Great Ocean Road Race, Pogačar called his *directeur sportif* Allan Peiper at the crack of dawn with bad news: he had lost his passport – on Australia Day, a national holiday on which most public services were closed.

'OK, he was nervous. But most guys would have been panicking and Tadej didn't panic,' Allan Peiper told me in 2021 for *Rouleur*. 'He stayed happy, friendly and compliant because he had to do a load of things, go to the police, go to the bank, organise some things … it struck me how relaxed under pressure he was and I think that's one of his strongest traits. And that was the first impression I had [of him].'

He spent another night in Australia, contacting the consulate and embassy to get the necessary documents to fly back.

His next race came at the Volta ao Algarve in February. Pogačar was not supposed to be competing but was drafted into the line-up late after a teammate was not ready. On day one, opportunity knocked. A crash divided the bunch and he, Philipsen and teammate Simone Consonni were in the front group. Team leader Fabio Aru was caught behind, losing over a minute.

The next day, finishing on the Alto da Fóia, Pogačar attacked for victory, outsprinting Wout Poels, a former winner of Liège–Bastogne–Liège. He then extended his lead in the 24-km time trial, despite not having a time-trial bike at home and having raced it only twice previously.

I was also there in Portugal, covering the early-season event for *Rouleur*. I had gone there to write a feature on the five-day race, not to interview Pogačar. But with him surprisingly in front, he had become one of the stories of the race. The team's press officer was only too happy to help facilitate a one-on-one interview. On the morning of the penultimate stage, Tadej and I strolled over to a shaded courtyard in Albufeira for a five-minute chat, my first encounter with Pogačar in person. Future ones would not be quite so casual.

'It's incredible, I was not expecting this,' a beaming Pogačar told me. 'I think it was the time trial, I was really not expecting to extend the lead, I was actually expecting to lose the jersey. But that's how it happened and I'm really happy.'

He talked of there being a big difference, between this experience and that of leading the Tour de l'Avenir – not that race leadership weighed on his mind. 'I'm sleeping OK, I think I can handle pressure really good, so no problems,' he said, adding, 'This week, I am learning a lot.'

After going into himself and his Slovenian background, he talked about his interests: going out with friends, living a normal life and watching films. 'My favourite is maybe *Harry Potter* or *The Matrix*,' Pogačar said.

Just so I know, for the future, how do I say your name? 'Tah-day poh-gah-char,' he said patiently. He would answer the same question a fair few more times, though that did not stop it being mangled by many commentators.

'Hopefully see you on the podium tomorrow evening,' I said by way of farewell – which is what happened. Pogačar held on, rebuffing several attacks on the finish up the climb of Malhão, for a surprise overall victory. It confirmed the sense that the 20-year-old was a rising star.

Days before Strade Bianche, Andrej and Teja Hauptman brought him to the factory of Colnago, the Italian bicycle manufacturer for UAE Team Emirates, where he would meet founder Ernesto Colnago and tour their museum. Hauptman seemed to sense that the young man's career was about to go stratospheric. Akin to a father dropping off his son at university before saying goodbye, the moment was charged with meaning.

'I was just telling him, "Remember, you do this because you really love cycling. You train and then you don't have pressure, then you're just playing and enjoying like it's a game,"' Hauptman recalls. 'It's difficult to play when you become the best one and have a big salary. The game changes. It's a big pressure.

'I said, "Remember, as long as you manage to remain simple and play, you will be successful."'

When his team leader Rui Costa suffered a puncture at Strade Bianche with 50 km to go, Pogačar gave up his wheel. After waiting minutes for a replacement, he did the rest of the race alone, catching and passing fellow backmarkers, a show of his tenacity and teamwork. Afterwards, he told Hauptman that he had enjoyed the race and fighting for position. 'One day, I will win Strade Bianche,' he said.

That spring, Pogačar – or 'Pogi' as some teammates had started calling him – seemed to raise his level at every race. Competing at the Itzulia Basque Country, a gruelling week-long WorldTour stage race through the green, rainy hills of northern Spain, he finished sixth. His role was to support leader Dan Martin, riding by his side in case he was required to hand over his bike, given they rode the same size frame.

He had already gained Martin's respect on their first encounter, at a UAE Team Emirates training camp in January 2018 in Sicily while still riding for Rog-Ljubljana. 'This little fat kid showed up from Slovenia and, to be honest, I saw a lot of myself in him – his whole enjoyment of racing,' Martin told *The Cycling Podcast* in 2022. 'We were playing around, attacking each other a little bit, and he was literally the only guy to go over the top and attack me. And that's where I saw something different. This kid had the cheek to attack me, try to drop me, and even then I had to struggle to get back on to his wheel.'

Many other UAE Team Emirates teammates and staffers had similar eureka moments during Pogačar's first months. 'Tadej is an exceptional rider. But I saw many other riders that had almost the same values or even better values. But the good thing about Tadej is that he can do it when he wants,' says Rubens Bertogliati, the former UAE Team Emirates trainer and assistant *directeur sportif*. '"OK, today, let's do 6.5 watts per kilo." This is the difference between him and the others.

'The fact that Tadej could do it on demand was really special. He came ready to the race, but also ready in his head: he knew in that moment he needed to do his best.'

Every young rider goes into the WorldTour wanting to win, but there has to be a confluence between talent and opportunity. In a top cycling team, there is a hierarchy and younger riders often come to understand their position from the first camps: carry bottles, learn the ropes, adapt to the physical load of top-tier racing. Some are even told to chill out and not train so much.

The prevailing dogma had it that new pros were not necessarily supposed to perform at the highest level, and besides, were rarely given the chance by team managers. Sometimes, that came more from logic than crystal-clear instruction – if a *directeur sportif* tells a neo-pro to work and take the wind for 150 km, he will not of course be able to contend for victory afterwards.

This conventional approach meant less pressure, developing gradually out of the spotlight, but far fewer results or unfettered opportunities to show what they can do. And in a team sport where there are inevitably a lot more workers than winners, many prospects find their permanent place as valued *domestiques*.

The Swiss rider Tom Bohli had experienced this attitude during his first years as a professional with BMC Racing Team. Like Pogačar, he was also in his first year with UAE Team Emirates in 2019, having joined from the American-registered squad.

Bohli says there were fewer limitations at UAE Team Emirates, with talents able to use their winning momentum from the under-23 ranks. 'Nobody is restricting you, they're supporting you, you're able to race freely,' Bohli says.

'The journey a young rider has to go through has changed completely [nowadays], and also the approach from the team has become much more professional and evidence-driven ... there are no more "training" races any more to prepare for bigger races. That doesn't exist any more. Every race is considered extremely important.

'Hierarchy doesn't only mean the older you are, the higher up you are. Hierarchy is clearly always the stronger you are, the higher you are,' he adds. 'In my opinion, he [Pogačar] really helped strongly to flatten this hierarchy. Because also the way he helps you, how he interacts with his teammates, the way he interacts with normal people on the street. This is very nice.

'To be honest, I didn't perceive him as a neo-pro. He was always mature, he knew exactly how to race. Sometimes, neo-pros don't know how certain structures work, how to do things. With him, I never had this,' he says.

Bohli noticed Pogačar's stress-free style of leadership. 'He's not telling you "I need you there." He's keeping it calm because he has a way of talking with his riders where nobody gets nervous, but everybody knows what they're doing. It's very simple. And on the other hand, you have leaders who put a lot of stress on the riders [around them] because they are insecure themselves. So when you have a leader who is secure like him, he's not putting insecurities on the riders. That's super-important.'

In the spring of 2021, months after Bohli left the team for French squad Cofidis, Pogačar sought him out and gave him autographed jerseys from the previous year's victorious Tour de France campaign, thanking him for the nice times racing together – despite the fact Bohli was not on that specific team and that they had rarely raced together at UAE Team Emirates.

'This is something very beautiful when you think about it, that he considers you not only a teammate, but also a friend. When I saw him in the bunch after I left the team, he would start talking to me … that's something contributing to a flatter and more fair hierarchy. A more appropriate ambience where all riders feel welcomed in a race, such as the helpers … it's who he is, and not just somebody who wants to get the extra 5 per cent out of his riders,' Bohli says.

'But obviously when you have a team structure that supports such positive behaviour like that, that enhances the performance of the team. This is one of the key reasons, in my opinion, why UAE Team Emirates became so very strong, because they have cohesion inside the team that is beyond other teams.'

In May 2019, Pogačar took another important step forward in the hierarchy by winning the Tour of California. On the decisive stage, finishing on Mount Baldy at 1959 m, he took full advantage when rival Sergio Higuita overshot the final corner, carving down the inside and sprinting to victory. He was the youngest ever WorldTour stage race victor – just months before his 21st birthday which, given American law, meant that he could not drink the sparkling wine on top of the podium.

Mid-race, his UAE Team Emirates teammate Kristijan Đurasek was provisionally suspended and later given a four-year ban for violating anti-doping rules between 2016 and 2019 (by the use of prohibited methods/substances), uncovered as part of Operation Aderlass, a joint German-Austrian investigation into blood doping. Đurasek was not prosecuted. Slovenians Borut Božič and Kristijan Koren were also implicated and sanctioned with a period of ineligibility of two years in October 2019 by the UCI – Božič for anti-doping violations committed in 2012, Koren for anti-doping violations committed in 2011 and 2012.

Speaking to *Siol* in 2022, Koren agreed with the assessment that he was a 'victim of the system' because he was unable to defend his innocence at the Court of Arbitration for Sport (CAS), as the costs of litigation there are extremely high.

This led to some of Pogačar's first dealings with media questions relating to doping. 'I know about this thing as much as you do. I'm unhappy. We actually just push away the bad thoughts. It's not really good, but it didn't really affect us,' he said in a post-stage press conference.

At the end of his long journey home, Pogačar met a group of 30 of his closest supporters at arrivals at Ljubljana Airport, including his family and Miha Koncilija. The first thing he did upon walking through the automatic sliding doors from the baggage area was to hug his onrushing little sister Vita and plant the giant cuddly bear he had received in her arms. His fans chanted 'Pogi! Pogi!', whirring wooden football rattles and shaking national flags. The wholesome scene was a rapid-fire change from the international to the hyper-local: he shook hands vigorously with Komenda's mayor, Stanislav Poglajen, took a bouquet of roses from him and greeted more wellwishers individually before giving an impromptu speech. All the while, tired but curious compatriots walked past after their holidays and business trips, trying to work out the identity of the young man receiving such a homecoming.

'I certainly didn't expect anything like this in my first season,' Pogačar told *Siol*. 'I didn't expect such a leap when I moved from the older juniors to the under-23 ranks. It's the same now. I surprised myself this year.'

Slovenian riders were stunning the cycling world. This was the start of an unprecedented period of international success for the country. Matej Mohorič had won seven races the previous season, including a Giro d'Italia stage. His compatriot Primož Roglič had been a model of consistency for Jumbo–Visma, winning the UAE Tour, Tirreno–

Adriatico and Tour de Romandie consecutively. He then wore the leader's jersey at the Giro d'Italia on the way to third place overall, moving into number one spot in the UCI World Ranking.

Coming straight from the race finish in Verona, Roglič was the toast of the capital city for a much bigger welcoming ceremony in Mestni Trg, one of Ljubljana's main squares. Hundreds of fans gathered in front of the stage, waving national flags and banners with his face. Pogačar and Jan Polanc, who had worn the race leader's jersey for a day in Italy, joined him: three smiling faces of Slovenian cycling success abroad.

The trio also met President Borut Pahor at an informal reception at the presidential palace. It must have been a strange juxtaposition for Pogačar: clinching a WorldTour victory and meeting the nation's leader while still living at home in his childhood bedroom in Komenda.

He and Roglič were no strangers, chatting over the years at World Championships when part of the Slovenian national squad. Even while sitting at the top of cycling's tree, Roglič perhaps sensed the threat that the young man posed. Asked in the subsequent press conference in Ljubljana about when he would be going for three-week races, Pogačar suggested his debut might be at the Vuelta a España. Seated next to him, Roglič patted him on the thigh and said, to laughter: '*Raje počakaj, da mi nehamo.*' *You'd better wait until we stop.*

'He was joking about it, but I think he knew he was quite a big contender already,' says *Večer* journalist Uroš Gramc, who was in attendance. 'What surprised me was that Roglič was already speaking of him as if he was a really top cyclist. Like he was a bit afraid of him.'

Plans for Pogačar's Grand Tour debut at August's Vuelta had been fast-tracked by team management. While the sweltering summer climate took no prisoners, it was a kinder Grand Tour for a debutant, its shorter stages and relaxed atmosphere allowing youngsters to do a three-week race without a blinding media spotlight. The surfeit of summit finishes and the late-season fatigue often lent itself to opportunistic racing and surprising breakthroughs. Here was Pogačar's big chance to go from learner to leader.

▶ Brothers in arms: every champion needs a trusted team around him, attuned to his needs. UAE Team Emirates principal Mauro Gianetti (left) and soigneur Joseba Elguezabal (right) with the fresh-faced champion after another striking showing.

7

CHANGING OF THE GUARD

September 2019

The 2019 Vuelta a España started in the Costa Blanca city of Torrevieja with an evening team time trial, pro cycling's great test of the collective.

Mastering this art demands a Formula 1-style attention to detail. Each team's analysts run their rule over the course, deciding on the best gear ratios, tyre pressures, pacing strategy and order of each rider in their paceline. Stronger ones tend to take longer turns on the front, getting the most out of each individual's strengths. The TTT mixes hurt and harmony, requiring repeat maximal efforts at 55 km/h while flowing smoothly around corners, centimetres behind a teammate's back wheel.

In previous months, riders have drilled practice sessions at training camps, helped by video analysis. Team leaders have tweaked bike positions minutely on the track and in the wind tunnel, employing all their team partners' most effective tech trappings to cheat the wind. Pre-race, the competitors ride the course again and again to commit more demanding parts to memory.

Then there are the uncontrollables which can wreck all the best-laid plans. Minutes before UAE Team Emirates were due to race round a sweeping left turn on the 13.4-km route, a pipe with a garden hose attached broke in a nearby garden and started leaking water, which streamed across the course. Two seconds after riding over the wet road in formation at 60 km/h, slicking their tyres, UAE Team Emirates were all scraped carbon and grated skin. Maybe that sums up modern pro cycling, able to go from the cutting-edge sublime to the ridiculous in a heartbeat, all because of a resident watering their flowers. This would never happen to Max Verstappen.

So much for a gentle introduction to Grand Tours for Pogačar. After regrouping, the cut-up UAE Team Emirates finished 21st of the 22 teams, with a 1 minute 7 second deficit to make up on winners Astana Pro Team. Pre-race favourite Primož Roglič suffered the same fate too, his team crashing minutes later on the same corner.

Fabio Aru's heart must have sunk as he lay on the Torrevieja tarmac for a few beats. This was the latest interruption in a stop-start season for the leader. The Sardinian had been seen as a successor to Italian star Vincenzo Nibali after winning the Vuelta in 2015 and finishing second in the Giro d'Italia. However, since joining UAE in 2018 as a big-money signing earning in excess of €2 million a year, the climber had struggled with injury problems and the team's new methods.

He missed three months of the 2019 season after surgery on a constricted iliac artery. Then, after finishing 14th in that year's Tour de France, he went on to the Vuelta as UAE Team Emirates' frontman, with Fernando Gaviria on hand to target sprints.

Aru had precious little confidence or momentum going into the race. In contrast, Pogačar was at the other end of the scale after his blistering neophyte season.

Despite feeling the TTT crash in his legs, Aru went on the attack the next day, finishing fifth into Calpe, the winter training hub for WorldTour teams. However, it was a last sign of quality from the Italian rather than a return to form. On the mountain stage to the Astrophysical Observatory of Javalambre three days later, Aru finished over 90 seconds behind Pogačar. It begged the question: who was the team leader?

Going into stage 9, a punchy, mountain-packed stage through the microstate of Andorra which finished at Cortals d'Encamp, Pogačar was ninth overall and a minute ahead of Aru. He had special motivation. 'He already said before the start [of the race], Urška will come to visit me here and I would like to win it,' Andrej Hauptman recalls. Pogačar's mentor had joined the team as a *directeur sportif* in May 2019.

Lashed by a deluge as darkness fell in the final 10 km, hail hurting his back, Pogačar was in his element. 'When I saw the weather forecast for today, and I read that it would be rainy, I was actually happy because I knew I had it in me to do something special,' he said afterwards.

Pogačar had followed the attack of Movistar rider Nairo Quintana, bridging across to his teammate Marc Soler. Shaking his head repeatedly and throwing his hand up at having to sacrifice his own chance of victory, Soler was a picture of begrudging teamwork. As the pair were about to make contact with the recalcitrant Spaniard, Pogačar accelerated away – ignoring his team manager Matxin's instructions to hold back and wait for the group of chasers – and became the youngest Grand Tour stage winner since Moreno Argentin in 1981. 'Attitudes and actions like that confirmed to me how much natural class he has as a rider. You can tell him what to do, but he knows it anyway, and better. He's thinking, moving and acting like a winner,' Fernández Matxin told *Procycling* in 2021. Urška was there to embrace Tadej, moments after crossing the finish line.

In three hours of racing, Aru lost 30 minutes and the leadership debate was settled. It was nothing personal, given the pair's mutual respect, just sport. 'I think [Pogačar] was able to wait for when he knew the tactic was going differently than expected,' Rubens Bertogliati says. 'But he was also good at taking his chance – and we come back to the fact he was able to do good [power] values when it was needed.'

Pogačar was just getting started. On stage 13, he added a second stage win, outsprinting race leader Primož Roglič after they escaped on the coiling, concrete ramps of Los Machucos. Both had overcome their inauspicious starts to move into contention, with Pogačar climbing to third overall, 3 minutes 1 second behind his countryman.

With every stage, the 20-year-old was heading deeper into uncharted territory. He had never raced so many days and had no point of comparison for how his body and mind would react to the unprecedented demands and fatigue. Still, any prior discussions within the team about voluntarily pulling the neo-pro out on one of the race's rest days to save his energy were now irrelevant. 'I came to his room [to discuss it] and he said, "No, no, I feel better every day,"' Hauptman says.

On a Grand Tour, recovery and energy conservation are paramount. Quality of sleep matters, but that goes for the mind as well as the increasingly aching body. It pays to be naturally zen – or even wilfully ignorant – to shut out unnecessary, external chatter or social media, to not get irked by the Vuelta's late dinners, to not lie awake mulling over possible race eventualities.

Pre-race, Pogačar talked to his team's YouTube channel about 'going with the flow' and he practised what he preached. He was breezy, telling roommate Marco Marcato he did not mind whether he put on the air conditioning in the cauldron-like Spanish heat. Everything was new and exciting – well, perhaps apart from the dinner routine of eating white rice or pasta for three weeks straight.

'What struck me was his personality never changed,' says John Wakefield, UAE Team Emirates' former trainer and performance-coordinator. 'Regardless of how tired he got or not, when he won and had a bad day, on day 1 or day 21, it was the same. Also, I know it sounds stupid but I would notice the gears he was pushing – he always ran a really big gear. That was really impressive in terms of what he's capable of producing.' Doing so showed his high physical ceiling and impressive fatigue resistance; lighter gears are normally used by others due to efficiency and the Grand Tour's demands.

Pogačar's introductory Grand Tour also helped to cement the team within a team around him, an inner circle that would become increasingly important to him over the years. It was the first time Pogačar worked extensively with soigneur Joseba Elguezabal. A former nightclub bouncer and factory worker, the Basque had been at the Bilbao football academy before switching sports, joining UAE Team Emirates from Spanish team Caja Rural for 2019.

With Eminem or Slovenian rap music usually burbling from speakers at the team hotel hours after the race, Elguezabal gave Pogačar massages, working on his chest, head, diaphragm and legs before dinner. In their daily hour or more of calm away from the cut and thrust of the race, they developed an innate bond and Pogačar asked to be paired with him regularly.

A tattooed bear of a man with a salt-and-pepper beard, Elguezabal also served as a pseudo-bodyguard at the end of the race. After doling out post-race recovery drinks and putting a towel around Pogačar's neck, Elguezabal and the team's press officer Luke Maguire would guide Pogačar around the post-finish crush of exhausted fellow cyclists, reporters and race staff to the team bus, anti-doping control or their press responsibilities.

At first, these were modest: before the race's start, Pogačar had one engagement with a small Colombian radio station while Aru fielded a larger press conference. That was the last occasion requests would be so modest in their number or nature at a big race for Pogačar. Maguire, a genial Irishman working with Pogačar for the first time at the 2019 Vuelta, was chiefly responsible for fielding them and shepherding Pogačar from microphone to microphone.

Meanwhile, his agent Alex Carera was a crucial figure behind the scenes. He helped to solve daily problems and parlay Pogačar's appeal into earnings, later agreeing brand endorsement deals with the likes of Slovenian supermarket Tuš, Telekom Slovenije, Breitling and the Slovenian Tourism Organisation.

Carera chose to only work with 'high-level' brands to help raise Pogačar's image, opting for fewer commitments in his first years as a star. He was mindful of ensuring Pogačar had more of a private life because lasting at the top of the sport was important. Money would be a natural consequence of his hard work.

Carera also negotiated a sizeable increase on Pogačar's contract in the middle of 2019. Reflecting his stellar performances, he went from an estimated €70,000 a year deal to something substantially bigger, extending it to the end of 2023. By mid-2021, his salary would be worth an estimated €5 million a year.

A shrewd judge of talent, Carera had signed the likes of Chris Froome and Vincenzo Nibali at the dawn of their pro careers to A&J All Sports, the management agency he co-owns with older brother Johnny. Pogačar was already showing a mindset to rival those experienced champions.

His Basque soigneur Elguezabal saw a huge margin for progress, believing his young charge still had 5 kg to lose in those early years at UAE Team Emirates, even as his Vuelta performance provided early glimpses of his incredible ability to recover over the course of a three-week race – or deteriorate more slowly than his competition. 'As the stages go by, other riders show signs of fatigue; they arrive dead, catabolic,' Elguezabal told *El Correo*. 'Tadej, on the other hand, is getting better every day.'

That last statement may be physiologically impossible over a race of that duration and intensity, but his performance did confirm what UAE Team Emirates already knew. Iñigo San Millán, head of performance, had built a metabolomic profile of Pogačar, analysing thousands of body parameters from a few drops of blood, going far deeper than rudimentary blood tests. Here was a young man with remarkable mitochondrial function who could recuperate quickly both between stages and in-race efforts.

Pogačar emphasised that on the race's last mountain stage, 24 hours before the finish in Madrid. Having dropped to fifth place on GC, he went on the attack midway up the penultimate climb, the Puerto de Peña Negra, 39 km ahead of the finish at Plataforma de Gredos.

'My director radioed that I was going well, but advised me to stick to the wheels,' Pogačar told *Procycling* weeks later. 'But when I saw that [podium rival] Miguel Ángel López had attacked and made some mistakes, I went for it – all or nothing.

'I felt like I was throwing a dice,' he added of his gung-ho move. 'What have you got to lose if you do your best? It doesn't matter what the result is.'

Movistar rallied to chase hard with two *domestiques*, but hardly made a dent in his 90-second lead on the final climb as Pogačar rode to the stage win and returned to third place overall and into the best young rider's jersey.

Primož Roglič won the Vuelta, the first Grand Tour for him and Jumbo–Visma, but the youngest rider in the race also grabbed the headlines with his insouciant, breakthrough performance. Having two Slovenians standing tall on the podium in Madrid was a coup for the central European country.

Vuelta a España 2019: general classification

1. Primož Roglič (Team Jumbo–Visma) 83 hours 7 minutes 14 seconds
2. Alejandro Valverde (Movistar Team) at 2 minutes 33 seconds
3. Tadej Pogačar (UAE Team Emirates) at 2 minutes 55 seconds

Pogačar harked back to his childhood days following compatriots Janez Brajkovič and Tadej Valjavec in the late 2000s. 'At that time it seemed incredible to us that a Slovenian could make it into the top 10 at the Giro or Tour,' he told *Delo*. 'For me, they were kings. Now Roglič wins almost easily, times are really changing.'

It was out with the old champions, in with the new: Vincenzo Nibali, Philippe Gilbert and Vuelta runner-up Alejandro Valverde were fading forces, all taking their last prestigious wins in 2019. Months earlier, Chris Froome had also suffered a career-altering crash, ensuring he would not add to his total of Grand Tour wins: seven. There was an interregnum between the old guard and the newcomers; it felt like the door was open for fresh, fearless riders.

However, Pogačar was still not the leading young light. Froome's precocious Colombian teammate Egan Bernal was shaking up the sport at the highest level. In July, the Ineos Grenadiers star had won the Tour de France at the age of 22 with a display of fearless attacking in the Alps. Many expected the Colombian climber to dominate cycling for the next decade, but a life-threatening training crash in January 2022 would clip his wings.

Several other young riders were attracting attention. Dutch cyclo-cross star Mathieu van der Poel announced himself as a force at the Amstel Gold Race that spring, driving the late pursuit of a breakaway before sprinting to victory from the front, showing his remarkable strength. 'He's like a man from another planet,' Pogačar observed to *PEZCycling News* in January 2020. Van der Poel's fierce rival Wout van Aert was showing early signs of his otherworldly versatility, winning his first Tour de France stage that summer.

Then there was Remco Evenepoel. Sixteen months younger than Pogačar, he had won the Clásica San Sebastián at the age of 19 in August 2019. Since his emphatic triumphs in a host of leading junior races, he had been attracting intense media attention in his native Belgium, a cycling-mad country that can simultaneously lift up talents with praise and burden them with great expectation. His salad days in the WorldTour, with every minor result obsessively scrutinised by his national press, were a lot more pressure-laden than those of Pogačar. Evenepoel had been trumpeted as the next superstar, allowing the Slovenian to slip under the radar for longer.

Van der Poel, van Aert, Pogačar and Evenepoel were all unafraid of making long-range attacks, showing a devil-may-care style of racing and incandescent ability. Together, they would go on to dominate and shape the first half of the 2020s in pro cycling.

Pogačar's Vuelta performance capped one of the most successful seasons for a first-year pro in modern cycling history. His eight wins made him the most prolific rider on UAE Team Emirates, finishing individually 15th in the World Ranking and helping the squad to finish fourth in the team standings.

Pogačar had been surprising himself all season with his progress.

'I'm only impatient when I'm not doing well,' he told *Delo*. 'When I want the race to be over as soon as possible so I can move on to the next one,' he added. 'I'm the type of cyclist who always goes "into the red", racing all or nothing, just to stay in front. I don't know if I'm distributing my energy well and I don't know where my limits are.'

▶ Pogačar managed to take four race wins before the Covid-19 pandemic put the world on pause and halted the cycling calendar, leading to one of the strangest fortnights of his life after the UAE Tour.

8

EXTRAORDINARY LIGHTNESS OF SPIRIT

2020

At UAE Team Emirates' preseason bonding camp in their home country in October 2019, Pogačar was the one cutting cake, celebrating their successful year and standing front and centre for their team photograph, surrounded by fellow riders. His status was transformed: 12 months earlier, he was a peripheral figure, looking like a kid who had won a competition to be with established stars like Martin and Kristoff. He had not even contractually been able to wear the team's cycling kit.

Andrej Hauptman does not believe that Pogačar thought of himself as a real leader in his first year. There would need to be some cognitive catching up with his reality. Call it the same issue as a breakout band after an explosive debut album.

'The most important [thing] for me was after the season. A lot of riders win a lot of races in their first year, but nobody actually really focused on you,' Hauptman says. 'But now, people know you. You won three stages in the Vuelta, the Volta ao Algarve, the Tour of California. But the second season is really hard. Because [before the] first race, everyone talks a lot about you through the winter.'

Pogačar himself had a little fear about being able to repeat his 2019 performances, aware of how difficult improvement would be. Turned out there was no need for trepidation.

'Well, first race, he won two stages and the GC. I was afraid – he was not afraid,' Hauptman says. The Volta a la Comunitat Valenciana was a sign that Pogačar was just as strong. As he accelerated to his victories, his style was the same, his body mesmerically moving left and right with the effort.

Little had changed for Pogačar, other than the increased number of interviews he was doing and his home address. At the end of 2019, he found a flat to share with Urška in Monaco, the tax haven favoured by many pro cyclists. Teammates Valerio Conti and Davide Formolo also lived in the same apartment block, sharing a view of the moored yachts and supercars beneath on the Quai Jean-Charles Rey.

The upheaval of a house move would soon pale in comparison to the transformation that put the world on pause. In late February 2020, Pogačar finished second at the UAE Tour to Mitchelton-Scott leader Adam Yates and won a stage on Jebel Hafeet, pipping Alexey Lutsenko. That proved to be the race's final act, as the last two stages were cancelled after two Italian participants tested positive for Covid-19.

The pandemic was spreading and would affect pro cycling for the first time. Initially, riders and team staff were not allowed to leave the hotel before being cleared to return home after testing negative. However, Pogačar and UAE Team Emirates stayed in the W Abu Dhabi – Yas Marina hotel in voluntary isolation for 14 days, a different test of patience and endurance to a long bike race.

At least Pogačar had company, rooming with teammate Sven Erik Bystrøm. Food came and went in plastic bags, left at the door and returned to the hallway for collection. The riders would sneak out into the corridor to socialise with their masked teammates. Above the Formula 1 circuit at Yas Marina, they trained on home trainers on their balconies and Tadej spent hours on the phone to Urška. The welcome arrival of a PlayStation meant he could beat Bystrøm a fair bit at FIFA; he likes to play as Manchester City.

Pogačar adapted quickly to the strange circumstances. 'Tadej was super-relaxed,' Bystrøm says. 'I've never seen a guy so relaxed, he was just taking it day by day. Maybe that's one of the reasons he's so good at racing, I've never seen him stressed.' The Norwegian had more reason to fret, given his wife was heavily pregnant, but after their three-week stint in the Middle East, Pogačar returned to Monaco and Bystrøm made it home in time.

A new social normal set in of unprecedented lockdowns, regular nasal swabbing, self-isolation for positive cases and months of preventative face-mask wearing. Under Monaco's regulations, Pogačar could go only to the shops and back.

He and his fellow UAE Team Emirates riders need not have worried about missing quality training or race time. The Tokyo Olympics were put back a year and an unprecedented, truncated WorldTour calendar was drawn up, restarting on 1 August with Strade Bianche. The Tour de France would begin at the end of August, with October starts for the Giro and Vuelta.

Athletes don't especially distinguish between days of the week, only training and racing. This binary outlook made preparation difficult in 2020, given that initially no one knew whether there would even be a competition. Pogačar's routine consisted of waking around nine o'clock, watching Netflix, morning and afternoon indoor trainer workouts in between lunch or a stroll around town and occasional strength training or core work.

Between training indoors or listening to music, he also made his own rap to camera about washing hands for Covid-19. His favourites, Eminem and Drill, don't have anything to worry about.

Pogačar moved back to Slovenia in early April, returning on the same private jet as Primož Roglič and his wife, Lora. At home, he was able to ride his bike on his local roads.

He was still in good shape. In May, his trainer Iñigo San Millán asked Pogačar to take a week off because he was already in top form, but even so he took himself out for some easy rides. 'I don't know what to do with myself for the whole day if I don't ride my bike,' he told *RTV Slovenija*.

In a welcome return to racing, Roglič outsprinted him at the Slovenian road race championships, finishing at Ambrož pod Krvavcem, 5 km from the top of Krvavec, in late June. A week later, Pogačar got the better of him in the time trial by eight seconds, making it one apiece.

It was an appetiser for a clash at the Tour de France. Roglič considered him a rival and raised talk of an alliance of convenience. 'I hope that we can help each other as much as possible. After all, we don't have many such opportunities to cooperate and we have to take advantage of them,' he told *Siol* a few months before the race. Pogačar echoed the theme when asked: 'Definitely. Slovenians must stick together.'

As the start to this backloaded WorldTour season approached, there was still internal discussion within UAE Team Emirates about whether Pogačar should go to the Tour as leader. Allan Peiper lobbied upper management for months. 'I don't think anyone was under the illusion he was going to the Tour de France as a helper for Fabio Aru,' Peiper told me in 2021. 'My mission was to go to the Tour with Tadej as the leader and everyone knowing his role, even before the preparation started, so they knew what they were committing to and why they were going.'

Peiper had been concerned about simply getting through the race himself. In the previous 18 months, he had endured rounds of chemotherapy for cancer. He had lost his reflexes and barely been strong enough to watch the previous year's Tour pass near his front door in Belgium.

Pogačar trusted his wise counsel, and it was a boon to have him in the team car behind. 'Allan is a very important person for me, he taught me a lot, more about life than about cycling,' Pogačar said later in a 2021 Tour de France press conference. 'He had a big influence on me.'

Peiper's commitment to Pogačar was bolstered further after the cyclist finished fourth in the Critérium du Dauphiné build-up race.

His friend Johan Bruyneel, the former *directeur sportif* banned for life from the sport for his role in the US Postal doping affair, told him that Pogačar could win that year's Tour de France.

The team meeting ahead of the race outlined the aim of Pogačar finishing in the top 5 and going for stages as a goal. 'I was not even thinking about winning it because that felt like it's almost impossible,' Pogačar said the year after in a MET Helmets interview. The bookmakers had him down as a 14-1 shot.

The spectre of Covid-19 loomed large over the *grand départ* in Nice. Holding the race was a considerable gamble. Spectator numbers were limited on some stages and each team entered sanitary 'bubbles', aware that they would have to leave the race if two cyclists or staff members showed symptoms.

Sprinter Alexander Kristoff gave UAE Team Emirates the perfect start after a nervy opening day on wet Riviera roads close to Pogačar's adopted home. 'You are the champion!' the youngster screamed at Kristoff moments after they came to a halt. Pogačar had almost crashed in the last 500 m, nearly locking handlebars with a speeding Caleb Ewan while jostling for position.

Adjusting to the Tour de France's racing rhythm was a test for Pogačar. The Tour is faster, nervier and moving around its peloton is even harder than other races. The front rows are the safest, desirable places to be, at less mercy of crashes, able to see obstacles, unimpeded by narrower roads and not exposed to the concertina effect of changing pace. The problem is, all 180 competitors know that and want those prime spots.

If not at the front, a Tour racer is moving backwards, part of the washing machine cycle of Lycra-clad racers, constantly changing between saving and expending mental focus and physical energy.

Key to winning the Tour is not losing it in the first week before the mountains. Easier said than done, as the flat stage 7 to Lavaur showed. Pogačar punctured 50 km from the end and was then caught behind a crash as Ineos were the instigators of a split in the bunch in a cross-tailwind, riding hard on the front. Pogačar, along with his fellow contenders Richie Porte and Mikel Landa, was left chasing 40 riders, powerless as his rivals put time into him. By the finish, he had lost 81 seconds.

Allan Peiper was furious. In the post-race debrief on the UAE Team Emirates bus, he turned the air blue, asking the riders how it was possible to miss the split. They went over what happened, riders talked to each other as well as the management, taking responsibility and turning the page. Pogačar was unbowed.

'The thing that catches my attention the most about Tadej is the capacity he had to deal with the pressure,' his former teammate David de la Cruz says. 'Everyone was really upset at dinner, like "Oh my god, it's a disaster." Because, the goal was to finish top 5 on GC and win the white jersey. And then he came to dinner like "Why are you so sad? We lost one minute and a half (or something like that), but don't worry, tomorrow we're gonna gain time again."

'And when I was there, he never, ever blamed the team for anything, [like] if he was alone because the other riders were not strong enough to be with him in the crucial moment.'

The following stage took the Tour into the Pyrenees, offering an immediate opportunity for Pogačar to claw back time. He wanted to attack on the day's last uphill challenge, the Col de Peyresourde, its summit reached 15 km from the finish of stage 8. Peiper told him not to, believing it was too far from the finish and not decisive enough, expecting that Pogačar would simply be caught by the other contenders after showing how good his form really was, removing an element of surprise for the rest of the race.

Pogačar attacked anyway. Roglič and Nairo Quintana marked his first move, ensuring stalemate among the favourites before he accelerated up the road again, 4 km before the col.

This time, he created a gap. Roglič sat back and let rivals chase or attack, while Pogačar rode like a charging bull through the roadside tunnel of frenetic fans, some pulling Basque *ikurriña* flags from his path at the last moment. By the finish, he had gained 40 seconds. Roglič and his Jumbo–Visma teammates would come to rue their tactics, letting Pogačar back into the fight for the yellow jersey a day after he had lost significant time.

'Well, that day we completely fucked it, didn't we?' George Bennett says. The straight-talking New Zealander was riding as a key mountain helper for Roglič on Jumbo–Visma. In a few kilometres, he went from having several riders controlling the pace to being isolated, as an unexpectedly hard turn from Tom Dumoulin dropped Bennett. Roglič was left open to attack, without teammates to do the work.

At that point, they were more worried about defending champion Egan Bernal and his potential threat. 'Tadej was the cute little Slovenian friend that was kind of under Roglič's wing, and he was looking out for him,' Bennett says. 'As long as Bernal didn't take time, we didn't really care – that was kind of the vibe.' There were to be no more giveaways to his younger compatriot. 'After that day, the team management went [to Roglič]: "You're not friends any more, right?"' Bennett says.

Back into the top 10 on GC, Pogačar was on a roll. Twenty-four hours later, his first Tour de France stage win followed. Sprinting against four rivals into the Pyrenean town of Laruns, he threw his bike at the line, instinctively grabbing his helmet in disbelief and roaring with adrenaline afterwards as it dawned on him what he had done. Roglič pulled on the yellow jersey, making it double delight for Slovenian fans.

Tour de France 2020: stage 9 – Pau to Laruns

1. Tadej Pogačar (UAE Team Emirates) 153 km in 3 hours 55 minutes 17 seconds
2. Primož Roglič (Team Jumbo–Visma)
3. Marc Hirschi (Team Sunweb) both at same time

It was all the more remarkable because Pogačar had come downstairs that morning after a weight check, saying he had put on a kilo and a half, according to David de la Cruz. 'To any other riders, that would *break* them before a mountain stage. [And he goes] "OK, that means more power." For me, that's Tadej: he sees the positive things. Instead of saying: "Fuck, I have a kilo and a half more", it means he has more energy. That was his approach, it was really cool. And he was still eating Nutella for breakfast.

'After one stage, Tadej and I were sitting at the back of the team bus with [recovery] compression boots on,' De la Cruz adds. 'Two seats, one in front of each other. And we were just lying down and talking. I don't know how many chocolate bars Urška gave to him on the Tour – all these different brands. Every day, he was eating chocolate after the race on the way to the hotel. We were sharing it – OK, if he eats it, I will as well.'

Grand Tour contenders are not supposed to gorge on sweets after every stage, but Pogačar mixed endearing innocence with self-confidence. 'I remember he made a joke – but I don't know if it was a joke or he truly believed it. He said, "If I win the Tour this year, next year I won't go [and race it] and I will go to win the Giro." OK … sounds a bit cocky, you know? Because we came here with the aim to be top 5, you are now seventh on GC and it seems difficult to beat Roglič.'

De la Cruz laughs; hindsight is a wonderful thing. 'When you can win the Tour with the mindset he had at that time, that means that you can still do things every year to be better, you have this room for improvement. There are young riders who are super good who don't have that, it's really difficult. For him, it was the other way round.'

He was racing his first Tour with an extraordinary lightness of spirit. Pogačar also had a bet going with Joseba Elguezabal that he would win a mountain stage. On the rest day, he got out the clippers and shaved the Basque soigneur's head as his payment.

Several of his teammates would have happily had such close shaves. De la Cruz was fighting through the pain of a broken sacrum, sustained in a crash on the race's opening day. Two key mountain lieutenants abandoned mid-race: Davide Formolo, having broken his collarbone in a crash, and Fabio Aru. His issues appeared to be mental rather than physical; speaking on RAI TV, Giuseppe Saronni suggested Aru was having 'problems, also psychologically'.

Racing consistently and looking untouchable, Roglič appeared worry-free. He extended his lead on stage 13, dropping Bernal. Pursuing his attack on the Pas du Peyrol climb, Pogačar slotted into second place overall and back into the white jersey of best young rider. Leaving a handful of rivals behind in their burst for the line 48 hours later, Pogačar outsprinted Roglič on the Grand Colombier for his second stage win.

Tour de France 2020: stage 15 – Lyon to Grand Colombier

1. Tadej Pogačar (UAE Team Emirates) 174.5 km in 4 hours 34 minutes 13 seconds
2. Primož Roglič (Team Jumbo–Visma) at same time
3. Richie Porte (Trek–Segafredo) at 5 seconds

In an indication of their master-apprentice closeness, while warming down the previous day, Roglič had told Pogačar about the difficult last climb and what he needed to do. In the race's second half, the duo became so inseparable that they were dubbed 'the Slovenian Hydra' by French newspaper *L'Humanité*.

On the second rest day, the UAE Team Emirates management meeting, driven by Allan Peiper, focused on how to win the Tour de France. The back-room staff had upped their game accordingly. Performance gurus Jeroen Swart and John Wakefield had devised a monitoring document, trying to maximise how they could use their depleted, climber-light line-up. 'The reason we had done it was because our team, in hindsight, was not the strongest team. It wasn't a Tour-winning team,' Wakefield says.

'And we had to use riders really to what their specialty was, we needed to make sure we could use them over the full duration correctly. We could monitor riders: in terms of what they had done on the day, what they need to do tomorrow and in two days' time.' It was like fitting riders into a puzzle, based on their energy expenditure and fatigue. It helped to institute some 'recovery' days (nobody truly recuperates on the Tour) for Pogačar's five teammates, so they could be slotted in again for the next important stage.

Nevertheless, breaking the stranglehold of Roglič and his pace-dictating team seemed to be mission impossible. The race leader gained 17 seconds on Pogačar on the stage 17 finish at the Col de la Loze when the intention had been to try to drop Roglič. 'It was that one bad day that everyone has in the Tour: you just hope it's better than everyone else's bad day,' Wakefield says. Showing his sense of perspective, the first thing the breathless Pogačar asked press officer Luke Maguire after crossing the finish line was how Urška had done that day at the women's Giro d'Italia.

The penultimate stage time trial between Lure and La Planche des Belles Filles was UAE Team Emirates' long, last shot at overcoming the 57-second deficit.

The day before, Pogačar had decided to not ride the course again and get a few hours more shut-eye, given that they had done their homework in July, reconnoitring the course in detail. After all, at the end of a Grand Tour, every effort – or spared scrap of energy – counts.

Driving to the team's hotel on the morning of stage 20, Allan Peiper was too nervous to speak. He had gone through every detail and made the call about the gears and bike change, so it was principally on his shoulders if Pogačar's race was a disaster. However, he had the young contender's total buy-in.

'I've worked with a lot of top riders, but what I really appreciate in Tadej is the fact he gives me full confidence,' Peiper told me in 2021. 'Many times in the Tour de France, we'd discuss the gears for the next day and other riders would say other gears than I'd suggested. Tadej would say to me, "Look, do what you think is right." And that doesn't happen very often. Most riders think they know. There was never a question about the bikes, gears, anything we were going to do at the Tour de France. He just had full confidence in my decision-making and that's gratification in itself – especially when you see it come off.'

The steep climb of La Planche des Belles Filles proved to be 6 km too far for Roglič, giving the Tour its enthralling turnaround. Pogačar reflected later in an interview with MET Helmets that he was the one who was pressure-free: 'When he started losing some time, games started to play in his head, I think. When your head is all over the place, the legs are also kind of lost.'

After crossing the line to finish the race the next day on the Champs-Élysées, Pogačar became the Tour's youngest winner for 116 years –

at 21, he was the same age as Roger Federer winning his first Grand Slam, as Tiger Woods winning his maiden Major, as Usain Bolt taking a brace of Olympic gold medals. Well, only just: the day after the Tour de France finished was his 22nd birthday.

Tour de France 2020: general classification

1. Tadej Pogačar (UAE Team Emirates) 87 hours 20 minutes 5 seconds
2. Primož Roglič (Team Jumbo–Visma) at 59 seconds
3. Richie Porte (Trek–Segafredo) at 3 minutes 30 seconds

As dusk fell in the City of Light, there was a kiss for Urška and an embrace for parents Mirko and Marjeta, who had flown in from Slovenia and brought him dark-chocolate-covered ginger sweets. Slovenia's president Borut Pahor hugged him, as well as wrapping his arms around Roglič and saying a few words into his ear.

It was hard not to feel sympathy for the older man. He had worn the yellow jersey for 11 stages and looked unbeatable. This was a heart-breaking way to lose, paying for tactical conservatism when his Jumbo–Visma team had controlled the race. Amid their dominance, their cardinal error was underestimating, and failing to distance, Pogačar.

Even Pogačar's own happiness was adulterated. 'I had mixed emotions. Beforehand, I wanted Roglič to win the Tour,' he told *L'Équipe* at the end of 2020. 'I was a fan of his since his first results. Between the ages of 15 and 20, I would shout in front of the TV for him to win, and then, I was the one who beat him, who stopped him from achieving his dream.'

There was similar shock and awe back in Slovenia at the unexpected ending to a fairytale Tour. Forty-eight per cent of viewers (900,000 Slovenians over the age of four) followed at least a part of the race, a record viewership.

Pogačar's first coach Miha Koncilija had watched the time trial in the KD Rog team house in Vikrče, with fellow coaches and riders after organising a race. 'We said, "It will be fun – Primož will win, right?" That time was also very emotional and crazy,' he says.

Having had 24 hours to digest the turnaround, Koncilija was one of hundreds of celebrants toasting the champion in Komenda. Outside the sports hall next to Komenda Moste school, there was a widescreen TV showing the final stage, amid screeching horns and a brass band banging drums. One local turned up on a horse draped in a yellow coat. Fireworks lit up the night sky and fans clutched yellow flares as toast after toast took the party on into the night.

The ecstasy was not universal. A woman in her fifties in her garden had noticed journalists observing the Pogačar house and said, according to *AFP*: 'I know why you are here … you came for him, but Roglič should have won. I cried last night when I saw what they did to him … And I'm afraid he might quit his career now.'

Roglič was not just a champion, but a sporting folk hero in his home country. He had only started cycling in 2012 at the age of 23, with Andrej Hauptman sending him a road bike at the end of his ski jumping career. The only thing he took with him was his telemark celebration on the podium, embarking on a remarkable transition, rapidly learning the technical and tactical elements of bike racing. Since turning pro in 2016 with Team LottoNL-Jumbo, he gradually accumulated more and more prestigious wins, inspiring a generation of fans, many of them new to cycling. He had been Slovenia's first Tour de France stage winner, their first Grand Tour winner and their first world number one, despite coming to the sport late. 2020 felt like the culmination: it was seemingly Roglič's year, his Tour.

'He had more time to gain so much popularity,' *Večer* journalist Uroš Gramc says. 'And people who follow Primož are very loyal to him. OK, they cheer for Tadej, Matej Mohorič and all the other guys, but he's their number one pick.

'Slovenian people like tragic heroes,' he adds. 'Someone who should win but then something happens, an accident or whatever. Sometimes, we glorify those kind of heroes more than the real heroes that win, that go by with no problems.'

Pogačar's victory had caused divisions back home. He read critical articles online and received strange messages from a vocal minority who regarded him as the villain of the piece.

'People who don't understand cycling or sports at all kind of made this resentment,' Gramc says. 'They said "Pogačar should have let him win because he is young and has a lot of years in front of him. Roglič is an experienced rider at the end of his career." But that's not how sport works.'

It reminded Gramc of a ski jumping duel that aroused similar passions in Slovenia. Local hero Peter Prevc was beaten to the season-long Ski Jumping World Cup crown in 2015. In the last round of jumps at Planica in the final event of the year, Jurij Tepeš had soared to 244 m, knocking Prevc into second place and inadvertently robbing him of the points he needed to surpass overall winner Severin Freund. 'Tepeš was jumping before Peter Prevc. He didn't know that Prevc would not jump as far as he did,' Gramc says.

'They said nobody would arrange this thing to happen, only us Slovenians: we are stupid, we don't stick together,' says Gramc, recalling the furore. 'OK, we stick together, but if your neighbour buys a new car, sometimes you have to buy a bigger or more expensive car. This is our mentality a little bit.'

Amid the umpteen celebratory posts praising Pogačar and outpouring of national pride, there were conspicuous bitter sections. Across leading Slovenian internet media, the readers' comments could be extreme:

He proved to be the new Tepeš, a traitor to the Slovenian nation.

Roglič is the winner for me because he is a 100 times better character.

Tadej won the Tour, and Primož won our hearts.

He [Pogačar] could have won the stage with a 20 or even 30 second lead and everyone would have been happy, but no … I will never watch the races he rides again.

I don't feel joy. Ice cold killer.

However, there was no apparent animosity between the two rivals. Their mutual respect remained: on the Tour's last day, Roglič suggested that the best man had won. Pogačar indicated that after this Tour, Roglič was an even greater role model for him.

The devastating defeat did not affect Roglič's performance, even in the short-term. A week later, he sprinted to victory at Liège–Bastogne–Liège, beating Pogačar into third. He then took his second Vuelta a España title in November. Such resilience sums up Roglič's appeal: no modern cycling star has the same bouncebackability from adversity, playing into Slovenian self-image.

'Even Primož falling and then picking himself up, time after time, after each hard crash, coming back stronger – it's like an example of a great person, not only a sportsman, kind of a role model for your life,' Gramc says.

Sadly, in spite of having the support of the majority, Pogačar's life-changing triumph had a bittersweet tinge. In winning the Tour, he had somehow lost a little.

'Because of all the negative comments at the time, I didn't celebrate my victory too enthusiastically. It wasn't the homecoming I'd hoped for as a Tour winner,' he told *RIDE Magazine* in 2023. 'I still feel like I have to prove myself over and over again to some people back home.'

▶ Pogačar has picked up an array of trophies during his career, but the Tirreno–Adriatico trident must be one of the most original and eye-catching. In March 2021, he ruled the 'Race of the Two Seas.'

9

MONUMENTAL

2021

'Life definitely changes after you win the Tour de France,' Chris Froome tells me, stretching out the willowy legs that powered him to four victories in the sport's pre-eminent race. 'That pretty much marked the end of my season in 2013. I think I went and did some other races, but I was nowhere. Just because those weeks and months after felt like such a whirlwind and a blur.'

Nothing could prepare Tadej Pogačar for what comes after the success. More than receiving the Sèvres trophy – an elegant, midnight blue, it looks like a fruit bowl – he became a personal brand, a role model, a cycling poster boy, public property. Selfie requests walking down the street stacked up, let alone around any event. Leaving his hotel for a short walk before a race was borderline impossible. Everyone wants a piece of the Tour champion: media, fans, sponsors.

After the initial discombobulation of his first Tour win in 2013, Froome found lessons in sticking to the process. 'I think not being able to continue the season in that way was a stark reminder for me that if you get too carried up in the fanfare, it's easy to lose sight of what actually got you there in the first place,' he says.

'I learned pretty quickly once I got to my winters, I'd shut it down and try to not get pulled too much into the hype of it all. Keep my head down and keep focused on the next goal.

'You can see it in a lot of guys who win the Tour for their first time,' Froome adds. 'It's really interesting to see how the reaction is, how their preparations are for next season. I think it tells you a lot about what to expect for the upcoming one.'

However, Pogačar did not face quite the same quantity of extracurricular distractions. When past champions would have been visiting various sponsors and attending a succession of glitzy post-season galas, hoovering up awards and vol-au-vents, Covid-enforced caution made for a quieter winter – in person, at least. He deserved a trophy for innumerable hours spent on video calls doing interviews and engagements.

One of the hardest parts of sport is not just winning, it's staying at the top and winning again and again. Having scaled his personal sporting Everest and won the Tour, Pogačar now had to keep his hunger and workrate up for another exhausting, all-encompassing summit push, being chased by the rest this time.

'There are just so many sacrifices which come with it,' Froome says. 'It's literally making the bike and your training the be-all and end-all of everything you do, from morning till evening for years on end. You don't have much of a life outside of training, outside of recovering, and that's just how it is, if you want to be that competitor. So I've a lot of respect for what he's doing.

'It's been really interesting looking out for "Pogi". He seems to do a really good job of knuckling down, doing the work and shutting everything out.'

Pogačar felt the mental effects of his victory: when I asked him what changed the most for him since winning the Tour, he said it was in his head. 'Because preparing for every race [to win], it's quite hard,' he told me in an interview for *Rouleur* in March 2021. 'But I think

I managed this and made some improvements last year. I think I'm more confident and even more motivated. I have pretty clear goals and expectations for myself. It's quite important to not stress about everything too much.'

Pogačar appeared to handle the leap from contender to champion with aplomb. After all, he is not an automaton – he does have stress in his life. But whatever anxieties he has, they seem to not affect him as they have others before. While the fears, pressures and responsibilities that come with being Tour champion can easily weigh any racer down, Pogačar seemingly wears them as lightly and loosely as one of his beloved baggy white T-shirts.

'I think I still haven't quite realised what I achieved. In a couple of years, I'll look at this totally different to now,' Pogačar told *Rouleur*. 'I take it slowly, but also I don't waste too much time thinking about what it was and more about what is going to be.'

The aim was for the first Tour de France victory to be a launch pad for greater things and more wins. He had not 'arrived': he was still in his pro infancy, ahead of any realistic, imagined schedule for his career, and UAE Team Emirates was similarly still 'under construction' as a project.

Over the winter of 2020, the squad invested in a mix of experience and talent. Rafał Majka and Matteo Trentin joined, contenders in their own right, reinforcing the squad in the mountains and one-day Classics. Super-talent Marc Hirschi also came on board.

The new recruits also adapted to the team's slightly different way of training to many other WorldTour squads, which was being led by Iñigo San Millán. The focus was predominantly on zone 2 training.

The zones are set by blood lactate thresholds. From testing done by UAE Team Emirates, zone 2 was identified around 2 mmol/litre, the point where lactate increases significantly. This would correlate to a certain power value / watts per kilo for every rider, as each is different.

The result is a pace between one's lower lactate threshold (LT1, the first lactate threshold), where lactate is produced in the muscles and can be cleared and the upper threshold (LT2) – the top-end of lower intensity training, the metabolic state where a rider burns the most fat to power exercise. In lay terms, riders in zone 2 can just about breathe through their noses and talk, while still exerting themselves.

San Millán has said that Pogačar spent roughly 80 per cent of his training time in zone 2, leaving 20 per cent for more power-based, high-intensity efforts or speedwork, usually around races.

The goal of such sessions was to encourage aerobic adaptations and improve the body's ability to use oxygen efficiently. Zone 2 workouts enhance mitochondrial density within the muscles, stimulating the production of new mitochondria—tiny structures that generate ATP, the body's universal unit of energy, through aerobic respiration. Another objective was to increase sustainable power and develop endurance-type muscle.

Depending on the duration of the session and the proximity and nature of a rider's next competitions, there were hard efforts in the middle, but generally fewer HIIT sessions compared to, for instance, sport-leading team Ineos Grenadiers, driven on by their coach, Tim Kerrison. 'When we were in Tenerife with Kerro, the guys would be close to breaking point. We were given efforts that we just couldn't finish. Tim's philosophy was "more is better". So if you did five hours and you could physically do six, then do six,' their rider Luke Rowe recalled in his book, *Road Captain*. 'It was more, more, more.'

San Millán believed that greater focus on zone 2 work would lead to fewer problems caused by overtraining. Built on firm aerobic foundations, it improves their riders' ability to burn more grams of fat per minute.

The approach generally makes sure that the athlete's heart rate stays in the same zone too (assuming training on the flat), so for Pogačar, that meant a lot of time at 150–155 bpm when fresh. There were no more easy miles or sessions coasting to and from the coffee shop.

'It was almost a bit like old-school training. You go out, you're riding a little bit harder than you're used to, and that's it,' Sven Erik Bystrøm says. 'Everybody just had a new, fresh start. Some change was actually good for us ... personally, I had a really good feeling with it. I felt also the whole team just lifted their level after we started this.'

From physiological testing at winter training camp and his blood work platform, Iñigo San Millán realised during Pogačar's first months with the team that the Slovenian was an incredible specimen.

His ability to clear out lactate while sustaining high levels of power was extraordinary. After an attack, it can take a couple of minutes for his lactate levels to return to normal when other riders might need 20. 'People like Tadej, they got the lottery, at birth: his genes,' San Millán told me in 2023 for *Escape Collective*.

In exercise, lactate is used as the body's dominant source of fuel. When a cyclist sprints or climbs, he or she generates a great amount of lactate, demanding the muscles to use more glucose. The more used, the more lactate is produced as a by-product. As it accumulates, hydrogen ions associated with it increase acidosis of the muscle micro-environment, decreasing power output as a result. Pogačar has one of the highest glycolytic capacities that San Millán has seen, able to break down great amounts of glucose in his cells.

Because Pogačar possesses immense mitochondrial function, he can also ride at great intensity without depleting much-needed glycogen – the best can store around 500 g – and predominantly burns fat while doing so, rather than precious carbohydrates. This protects his fast-twitch muscle fibres and also helps to slow his fall into a catabolic state.

San Millán could see his training updates daily on TrainingPeaks, showing his power outputs over a whole day or effort, and observed how well he absorbed the workload and recovered again. When other riders were usually exhausted and in need of an easy day, he was ready to train hard again quicker and could feel the benefits in the final week of a Grand Tour, when recovery becomes crucial.

'Physiologically, he knows his numbers very well,' San Millán adds. 'He's a numbers guy. Although it seems on TV like there's a lot of animal instinct and that he competes for every race, a lot of things are calculated very well. In his numbers, his trainings, his nutrition. And he knows that whenever he has the numbers, he can transfer that and really win this race and that's when he goes for it ... he's really a perfectionist when it comes to training and nutrition. That is key to be[ing] Tadej Pogačar.'

At times, San Millán felt like he was talking to a veteran pro who had been competing for 15 years, given his intelligence, calmness and nous.

'He doesn't freak out like other ones ... [who have] not just the fear of losing, but the fear of winning,' San Millán told me in 2021.

This enviable mix of mind and matter also means, though, that training with the competitive Pogačar is not always easy. 'Every time you go out with him is hard, it's like a race,' Davide Formolo, his teammate between 2020 and 2023, says. 'I've had many different leaders, I shared teams with amazing riders, but nobody like him.

'His [power and heart rate] zone 2 is like zone 4 of everybody [else]. In the beginning, I was trying to train with him almost every day because he's a good person and I like spending time on the bike with him. But then I just caput the engine and realised it's better to go with him just a few times a week.' He laughs. 'Otherwise I'm gonna die!' Formolo used to do a minute's all-out effort with Pogačar every session, but as time went by, he increasingly just let him go up the road to do it by himself.

Pogačar was the first person Formolo found who trained as hard as he did. 'If you look at the training load in general, it's always been my weakness in the past. I was pushing myself too much in training and maybe I wasn't that fresh in the race,' the Italian says. 'But he was just training harder than me, he could absorb all the work he'd done and be super-fast in the race.'

The UAE Team Emirates riders were not just training their bodies and legs, but also their guts. Gone are the days when hunger flats would pole-axe riders in the last hour and affect racing more. Given that the more intense the effort, the more carbs are required, modern professional cyclists eat more and more often than they used to. They aim to take on 120 g of carbohydrate hourly through food and drink during a race, an amount that would have been scoffed at a decade previously.

Carbohydrates are absorbed from the gut into the bloodstream via different transporter proteins, but there is a limit to how much they can handle. Excess carbs can pool in the gut or lead to gastrointestinal issues: in his first years as a pro, Pogačar had endured stomach problems after long races because of his body not being accustomed to this.

Practice during training sessions made perfect, preparing the body for the hardest stages when such an intake is required for optimal performance, using different types of carbohydrates – glucose and fructose – allowing for a higher absorption rate.

Power-to-weight ratio governs cycling success, especially in Grand Tours. In a sport that obsesses over the number on the scales, the UAE Team Emirates approach was pursuing lightness in moderation. Numerous staff noted that Pogačar had several kilos to lose when he joined the team in 2019, which he gradually shed over several seasons to reach a lean racing weight of 65 kg by 2024.

Joining from Team Ineos in 2020, David de la Cruz found the squad's philosophy towards training and nutrition to be 'day and night' in comparison. 'I came from doing six hours on low carb, really aiming to be as light and thin as possible,' he says. 'At UAE, it was the other way around: super-high carb, it was like "OK, it's better to be two kilos heavier but have power and your hormonal system working well so you don't get sick so much."'

With reduced hunger and energy deficit, De la Cruz found there was subsequently less negative impact on his mood. 'When you have so many restrictions, it's a kind of jail. And then you don't have that fun, that joy any more, and that makes it tougher to be a professional cyclist.'

A former runner and supermarket worker who discovered cycling in his late teens, the Spanish climber likens his career to one of 'catching waves', surfing between squads who were at, or approaching, the pinnacle of the sport. He joined cycling's most prolific team, Quick-Step, in 2015, moving on to the pre-eminent stage-racing squad Sky in 2018 before signing for UAE in 2020: 'At the time, it could be a good team but it isn't the UAE we see now. It was a team where I was also catching the wave.'

After the overhaul of performance staff before the 2019 season, with several new coaches, including San Millán arriving, UAE Team Emirates became more data-driven, drilling deep into their riders' physiology and performance. 'In terms of how things changed, I can say we added a more scientific and validated approach to training, with updated methodologies, testing, coaching prescription,' John Wakefield says.

In the team's performance back room, Jeroen Swart and Wakefield had helped to implement a culture of sub-maximal fatigue testing for riders, carrying out a three-minute at-home indoor trainer session before training, ideally every seven to ten days. This was a way of monitoring performance data and subjective wellness across the year, telling the trainers whether an athlete was in peak form, progressing, regressing or fatigued. It took time for some of the team's riders to get up to speed: during the first months of the new system in 2019, Wakefield would have to chase them to do their tests.

There were weekly coach meetings and comprehensive athlete data reports sent to upper management. Indoor and outdoor testing was done, providing a full metabolic profile for a rider, showing figures such as peak power, FatMax and lactate accumulation.

'Everything was improved ... basically, we came closer to what it takes to win the Tour,' Wakefield says. 'Whereas in 2020, to be honest, if you looked at it on paper, we should never have won it. Simple as that. Fifth place, yeah because he [Tadej] follows wheels and we do our thing. But in terms of performance, we were not a Tour-winning team.'

The level was upped across the board. With 58 km of time trial on the route of the 2021 Tour de France, fine-tuning Pogačar's aerodynamic bike position for the discipline would be an important part of his Tour title defence.

The flame-haired Spaniard Aurelio 'Yeyo' Corral worked with him and the squad as a biomechanics and aerodynamics expert between 2019 and 2021.

Corral reckons that if 95 per cent of performance is physical and conditional, biomechanics and aerodynamics makes up the other notional 5 per cent. In other words, they are very important: the difference between 1st and 20th place, to use the example of Pogačar's first WorldTour TTT experience at the 2019 Vuelta a España.

'I made a plan for it, how much time each rider pulls and at how many watts. When Tadej arrived to the pull sector—,' Corral makes a noise like a throttle going. Pogačar went even harder and longer than anticipated. 'Twenty-five seconds ... 30. Change positions, change positions! He killed the [other] guys. It was amazing.'

Corral's remit was maximising their time-trial performance and pursuing as low a CdA number as possible – the coefficient of aerodynamic drag, which correlates to how aerodynamic a rider is, based on the body's drag size, shape and surface texture and how much resistance the wind creates against a cyclist and his bicycle. Minimising the number will mean that less power is needed to ride at the same speed. (A generic rule is that a 0.01 reduction in CdA means that nearly 10 watts less power is required at 40km/h.) Anything under 0.20 back in 2021 put a cyclist among the fastest in the world; at that year's Tour, Corral told *El País* that Pogačar's CdA was 0.19.

Corral also worked with more of the team's riders in the wind tunnel, including the Oliveira brothers, Mikkel Bjerg, Rui Costa and Pogačar.

'During my three years in the UAE team, he was the easiest rider [to work with],' Corral says of Pogačar. 'If a *directeur sportif* says, "We go to recon the Tour de France these days," OK, we go [Tadej says]. "We will do this track testing." OK, we do it. "I want to analyse putting the handlebar higher." OK, do it. He always has an open mind, and there are no questions, no discussions, no stress over small things. Just full gas. A super-funny guy ... Tadej is very simple in all performance areas: around coaching, nutrition, biomechanics, aerodynamics, tactics.'

Training in Tenerife, Pogačar did substantial road work on the flattish part near the top of Mount Teide at 2000 m, focusing on his aerodynamic position, while Corral obtained real-time data. The quest was for the optimal position, one a rider can physically tolerate with minimal aerodynamic drag while expressing maximal power, requiring a mix of data and subjective feeling.

'We did a lot of track tests in Roubaix and at the wind tunnel in Bike Valley [Tessenderlo, Belgium], analysing skinsuits, the helmet, small details,' Corral says.

'We put the [TT] handlebar higher, we increased the stack [height] and changed the angle of the bar,' he adds.

Once an optimal position had been decided, the wind tunnel was used to confirm what their real-world tests and modelling suggested. Just as well, given that a day's eight-hour session costs in the ballpark of €4000 alone. Pogačar would spend at least three hours in there, with Corral testing which position was faster – and by how much. 'For example, if you improve three seconds in 40 km, it doesn't make sense to do anything to the position if you lose the stability and increase the VO$_2$ max [required],' Corral says. 'The energy you expend in a different position is very important; it's about efficiency.'

Aero gains from the wind tunnel need to be sustainable in a race scenario. 'I remember he was completely looking down. "Hey, look forward because the corner is coming!"' he says, recalling his instructions to Pogačar.

Every miniscule amendment to his bicycle or aerodynamic position was designed to reduce aerodynamic drag or save precious watts. The team integrated his SRM power meter into the set-up of his cockpit, making it slightly more streamlined. They also went tubeless in the front tyre for improved aerodynamics, staying with a tubular in the rear.

A lot of the positional work was done at the end-of-the-year October training camp, capitalising on his racing shape and weight, and then revisited in the spring.

Pogačar himself could see the progress being made. 'I personally think that we as a team have made a really big step in this discipline ... I'm not so far behind in the time trial any more,' he told *Siol* in November 2020.

Ahead of the 2021 Itzulia Basque Country, aided by Pogačar's gym and core work, they changed his time trial saddle angle, so his back was more relaxed and he bent his narrow shoulders more sharply, reducing his frontal area and gaining 15 watts. When Pogačar had raced with his radio on his back previously in time trials, moving it to his chest gained 4 watts, Corral says.

The Spaniard believes that Pogačar is the best cyclist he has ever seen. 'Tadej's aerodynamics are really good, his efficiency is really good and his power is amazing. He has all the things you need to be a champion – and the mind,' Corral says.

In 2021, Pogačar became the team leader while still one of its youngest riders. He was a chilled-out presence in the team bus, with no need for big motivational speeches.

'He's not afraid to speak his mind, but he's not a big speaker,' *directeur sportif* Allan Peiper told me in 2021, adding later: 'Tadej is not opinionated. He's never negative, he's never critical, only grateful and thankful. I think those are big traits that really serve him well.'

Sometimes, actions spoke louder than words. His 2020 Tour teammates all received a special Breitling watch from Pogačar, customised with a yellow strap. While a team leader sometimes has a slightly superior bike to the rest, with a special stem here or a fancy bit of equipment there, the egalitarian-minded Pogačar often asked for his teammates to have the same set-up as him. They were all working together, so for him it was all for one, one for all. (If he then had a bike problem and needed to take a teammate's bike mid-race, this approach also offered a functional advantage.)

Working for a captain who usually finished their work off helped to motivate his teammates. In the spring of 2021, Pogačar won the UAE Tour and Tirreno–Adriatico back to back. His consistent excellence also helped to avoid inter-team leadership feuds or doubt over who was strongest as the squad became more star-studded.

'It's not easy to manage so many egos, so many riders that want to also achieve their own goals,' David de la Cruz says. 'For example, with a rider like Tadej, you go to these races knowing it's for him and that's it, because he's a favourite.'

Ensuring a harmony of rider ambitions and expectations came down to careful rider management by team manager Fernández Matxin, the man responsible for deciding each rider's annual race programme. 'Matxin is really good for giving you the feeling that you're really important for the team, that you will have your sporting space,' De la Cruz says. 'Maybe not in the races for Tadej, but your own ones where you will have your chance to shine ... [Matxin has] the capacity to make every rider feel special. Because it can happen when you're in the shadow of such a big star as Tadej, you feel much less of a rider ... it gives that space and confidence to everyone, that feeling that each rider is an important piece of the machine.'

Pogačar was still willing to sacrifice himself for teammates. As he and Primož Roglič watched each other on the fourth stage of the 2021 Itzulia Basque Country, their teammates Brandon McNulty and Jonas Vingegaard slipped up the road, with the young American becoming race leader. Pogačar was riding in support of McNulty on the race's final stage, but the gamble did not pay off: Roglič attacked mid-stage to take the title and McNulty was dropped, losing more than seven minutes. After doing some of the initial chasing work for him, Pogačar finished third as his rivals sat on his wheel, refusing to help his pursuit of the leaders.

Perhaps it was dawning on team management: why take a risk, even on the exceptionally talented McNulty when you have as close to a sure thing riding at his flank?

. . . .

By April 2021, Pogačar curiously had not won a UCI-rated one-day race in four seasons racing as an elite. April's Ardennes Classics, long one-day tests up and down the steep, forested hills of south Belgium, provided a couple of opportunities to change that.

However, UAE Team Emirates were forced to pull out of the midweek Flèche Wallonne, due to positive Covid-19 tests for two team members on the race's eve. 'Tadej was angry because he was well prepared and he wanted to race,' his mother Marjeta told me in 2021 for *Rouleur*. 'In Slovenian, we have a proverb – everything happens for a reason [*vse je za nekaj dobro*]. And I said to him perhaps because he couldn't take part in the Flèche Wallonne, he would win at Liège–Bastogne–Liège. Perhaps if he did the Flèche Wallonne, he wouldn't. It's always that message that I try to give him: it's not worth worrying, perhaps there might be one positive thing in this misfortune you had.'

Mum knew best, although the bad luck did not end for David de la Cruz. After crashing in the race's neutral zone, before its official start, he rode in the wind for 220 km with a broken rib, keeping Pogačar in the front part of the bunch. 'It was painful, but I really like Tadej. When you have a rider like that, you don't mind to have that pain and work for him,' De la Cruz says. 'You can give this extra bit more in an environment where you feel good.'

The oldest of cycling's venerable five one-day Monuments, first held in 1892, Liège–Bastogne–Liège is a wearing-down affair, with barely a single flat kilometre from the 259 en route. The 2021 edition came down to playing a patient, waiting game. On La Redoute, the vicious third-last climb which rises next to the motorway, Ineos Grenadiers took the race on and whittled down the front group, Hirschi and Formolo staying in front with Pogačar.

With a dozen riders remaining in contention, Formolo went all out close to the top of the Côte de la Roche aux Faucons, the race's final hill. Those training sessions hurting with Pogačar evidently paid off, as he split the group. The Canadian challenger Michael Woods accelerated again over the top, Pogačar, David Gaudu, Julian Alaphilippe and Alejandro Valverde escaping with him.

UAE Team Emirates had raced intelligently and made their numbers count. Seconds behind the leaders, Hirschi and Formolo sat in the chasing group as dead weights on the likes of Primož Roglič and Michał Kwiatkowski, ensuring their chasing efforts were in vain.

Away with fast finishers Valverde and Alaphilippe, Pogačar judged his sprint tactics perfectly. He took the Frenchman's wheel at the back of the group and pipped him on the line with his bike throw, helped by a tailwind.

Liège–Bastogne–Liège 2021

1. Tadej Pogačar (UAE Team Emirates) 259.1 km in 6 hours 39 minutes 26 seconds
2. Julian Alaphilippe (Deceuninck–Quick Step)
3. David Gaudu (Groupama–FDJ) both at same time

'That's where he surprised us, when he could beat those fast guys,' Formolo says. 'That's where we found out "Wow, this guy can also sprint." Until there, we were used to see him winning the races dropping everybody from the wheels.'

In a spring capped by his first Monument triumph, Pogačar showed that he could win different races in different ways – and badly wanted to as well. Being 'just' a Tour de France winner or stand-out stage racer was not nearly enough. He was on the way to becoming the complete, versatile package.

▶ Smiles for miles: in the high-pressure environment of the Tour de France, Pogačar's zen mindset helped to keep him and his teammates relaxed.

10

ON ANOTHER LEVEL

2021 Tour de France

As Tadej Pogačar's closest rivals rolled across the finish line in Le Grand-Bornand, it was hard to tell whether raindrops or tears were rolling down their faces, given the beating they had experienced. A week into the race, in its very first high mountains, their hopes of victory had been shredded by a smiling assassin.

The race's new leader had crossed the line a full 3 minutes 20 seconds in front of them – and had already downed a mini can of Fanta, fist-bumped team staffers and started his post-race warm-down while they were completing stage 8 of the 2021 Tour de France. 'What a ride,' Pogačar said, breathlessly, to press officer Luke Maguire.

After 150 km on a day of cold rain and mist, which the French love to call *Dantesque*, back-weighted with three Alpine climbs, he was in heaven. UAE Team Emirates set a high pace in the peloton, behind a breakaway containing no threats for Tour victory.

The penultimate climb, the first-category Col de Romme, with 8.8 km at an average gradient of 8.9 per cent, was a prime opportunity for Pogačar to test the rest. Its steep gradient meant it would be more a case of every man for himself, with less advantage to be had from slipstreaming.

Brandon McNulty and Davide Formolo set a punishing tempo on its early stretches, reducing the group to a dozen and casting yellow jersey wearer Mathieu van der Poel adrift. When Formolo peeled off the front and ended his effort, Pogačar accelerated savagely. Minutes later, he shed his only follower, Ineos Grenadiers leader Richard Carapaz, with another out-of-the-saddle kick as they hit 13 per cent gradients and climbed into the clouds. Given the era's usual, more conservative team tactics of waiting for the last climb before making a meaningful move, this audacious tactic resembled cycling from another era, an impression only augmented by the headlights of the following vehicles, illuminating him through the gloom. 'Attacking is the best form of defence,' Pogačar said afterwards.

Clad in a sodden best young rider's jersey, he did not seem to notice the rain. His body moved laterally with the effort, his eyes, visible through clear sunglass lenses, locked on to the next suffering rider to be swept past from the day's early escape group.

After negotiating the treacherous, wet descent, he kept his effort going on the Col de la Colombière. His speedy progress and wet tufts of hair spiking through his helmet vents (a Pogačar trademark) brought to mind Sonic the Hedgehog. Behind, it was game over for the chasing group. They were disorganised in their pursuit, with Formolo on hand to break up the rhythm.

Topping the final climb only 15 seconds behind the breakaway leader Dylan Teuns, Pogačar took the descent sensibly, with no need for risks. Moments after crossing the line in fourth place, he pounded his fist on his chest. There was no questioning his heart or opportunism.

The 3 minutes 20 seconds advantage he gained over his bedraggled rivals in his spectacular 32-km lone Alpine raid was the highest amount of time he has taken over adversaries in a single Grand Tour stage between 2019 and 2025, inclusive. The Pogačar era had started with a declaration of supremacy; in hindsight, it was an omen of what was to come.

Pogačar and his team came into the 2021 Tour de France expecting a more drawn-out, draining struggle. It had looked like being a Pogačar versus Roglič rematch, continuing the duel from 10 months earlier. The older Slovenian still seemed to be part of the superior squad, surrounded by the black and yellow 'killer bees' of Jumbo–Visma, who had shown their ability to swarm at the front and sting opponents in other prestigious races. A similar come-from-behind strategy to 2020, predicated on a day of grace from Pogačar, Jumbo–Visma's one-dimensional strategy and misplaced confidence would surely not work again for UAE Team Emirates.

'The year before, we were with no expectations and the problem in sport and life is expectations,' David de la Cruz says. 'And if you don't know how to handle them, it gets really difficult to enjoy the moment or perform … most likely, this year was the inflection point. You go from no expectations and now all the looks are on us. I guess it also makes it a bit more difficult for the management.

'In 2021, there was a lot of pressure inside the team to win the Tour because Tadej had won the year before. But it never came from him. For sure, that really helps the environment. Because when you are in a race and you have a leader who is always really stressed for this or that, for small details they cannot control, needing to be in position, then it's a bit annoying. With Tadej, it was not the case.'

Theirs was a cosmopolitan line-up consisting of eight riders from eight different nations, with only Pogačar, Formolo and Vegard Stake Laengen, the hulking protector on flat stages, retained from the 2020 crew. Rafał Majka, Rui Costa, Marc Hirschi and Tour debutant Brandon McNulty bolstered their mountain forces, with fellow first-timer Mikkel Bjerg adding firepower on the flat.

The first five days of the Tour, always full of jangling nerves and hidden pitfalls, were particularly crash-marred. The mega fall on stage 1 was a sign of what was to come, caused by a fan holding a cardboard placard reading *Allez Opi-Omi* leaning out too far and knocking German rider Tony Martin off at 45 km/h. Ten kilometres from the finish in the Breton town of Landerneau, a touch of wheels through a turn led to another high-speed wipeout. Pogačar came through unscathed, while GC hopefuls Miguel Ángel López and Richie Porte were injured and lost time.

The process of attrition continued on the road to Pontivy 48 hours later: Ineos Grenadiers leader Geraint Thomas crashed inside the opening hour, dislocating his shoulder, while Primož Roglič fell 10 km from the finish, losing 81 seconds despite a desperate chase with teammates. Pogačar himself was delayed behind yet another fall with 4 km to go, finishing 26 seconds behind a small group of leaders. 'A teammate fell in front of me. I caught myself and managed to go around everyone lying on the ground in front of me. It was awful, like on the battlefield,' he told reporters afterwards. In the hectic flat stage finales, Pogačar tried to avoid taking excessive risks. He made an 'air bubble' of space around himself, creating a little more room to manoeuvre left if an incident happened on his right, and vice versa.

Allan Peiper was absent from the Tour, going through treatment for prostate cancer, which had returned. However, the team manager had been working from home, offering advice and building stage PowerPoint presentations.

When the race moved south-east into the Mayenne region for the stage 5 time trial between Changé and Laval, Pogačar was well-prepared because Peiper had impressed on him the importance of seeing the 27.2 km route in person, given its blend of country roads, frequent corners and a twisty, technical finale. Four days before the Tour start, the leader rode it twice, helping to inform him whether he could take certain bends on the TT bars or on the handlebar sides. Sufficiently forewarned, he still chose to take a few risks.

'Rain was coming, so I prepared the bike with medium tyres, not the fastest ones. A bit of a slower model, but with higher grip,' Yeyo Corral says. 'We decided to be cautious and be careful of crashes: we were in the first week of the Tour, you [can] lose a lot, no?'

Pogačar insisted on going with the fastest tyres. 'We did that and he won. But it was crazy because it was downhill, it was raining ... my balls were here,' Corral says, touching his windpipe. 'When he trusts something, he goes for it full gas. He trusts himself a lot.'

He had reverted to an older, aerodynamic position used earlier that year for the time trial at Tirreno–Adriatico in March – an indication that he was not afraid to go with his feelings ahead of the raw data. He felt that they had found the right balance between expressing his full power and aerodynamics. 'I started feeling good on the TT bike one week before the Tour because I changed position,' he said afterwards.

The victory was an ideal response to a comment made by Tom Dumoulin in the hours after the seismic 2020 Planche des Belles Filles time trial. Captured in the NOS documentary *Code Geel*, the Dutch star compared Pogačar to someone who sits on a bike like a *mijnwerker* – a miner, implying a lack of style and grace.

Dumoulin's words hurt Pogačar. 'I was going to prove I'm not a miner and I am a proper rider who can keep winning races. Every race I went to, I wanted to prove I am a good rider,' Pogačar told *The Times* in December 2021. 'It doesn't matter how you look, it's about how much power you can generate.'

The answer was clear in Laval: an awful lot. His performance in a flat time trial for powerhouses underlined his lack of weaknesses. With Mathieu van der Poel staying in the race lead by eight seconds, meaning his Alpecin–Fenix team continued to take on greater responsibility in pacing the bunch, the situation for Pogačar could tactically not have been much better.

Rather than wait for a challenge to appear, he pressed home his advantage into Le Grand-Bornand. 'I haven't killed the Tour, there's still a long way to go,' he said afterwards to the media. But he had inflicted the mortal wound and delivered the coup de grâce 24 hours later on stage 9, adding 32 more seconds to his lead with another attack.

Spanish climber Enric Mas described him moving away from other contenders on the road to Tignes as if they 'didn't exist'. This was Pogačar's world and his rivals were living in it with all the impact of non-speaking extras. Nine days into the race, he was five minutes ahead of every competitor, save for the unfancied Australian Ben O'Connor. No one else could compete. After pulling on the yellow jersey, Pogačar laughed and said yes when a journalist asked if he would be his own biggest rival for the remainder of the race.

The 2021 Tour was the tipping point, the full scope of his humongous talent dawning on riders and the wider cycling world. Over the next fortnight, a chorus of resignation came from peers.

Ben O'Connor, AG2R Citroën Team: 'He's just at another level right now compared to everyone else.'

Jonas Vingegaard, Jumbo–Visma: 'He has a really big lead and yesterday he really showed he is probably the strongest here.'

Simon Yates, Team BikeExchange: 'He's obviously got the best legs here by a mile.'

Michael Woods, Israel Start-Up Nation: 'What can stop him now? A crash?'

While Pogačar exuded strength and self-belief, that was not always the case deep down. 'I'm more confident on the bike than in life, where I'm quite a reserved person,' he said in an end-of-season interview with *L'Équipe* in October 2021. 'But I can assure you that I'm far from being the most confident rider in the peloton. Sometimes, I have shit legs and that makes me doubt myself.'

Winning at the top level of the sport is never straightforward, but Pogačar had made it a habit, one he is yet to drop at the time of writing. As immense and taxing as the Tour de France is, it was simply another bike race continuing a sequence, his fifth stage race out of six won in the space of a year – the blip being an event where he had finished third while helping Brandon McNulty.

There was no rider in the sport quite like Pogačar and early in the 2021 season, his contract extension with UAE Team Emirates reflected his value. The six-year deal, running to the end of 2026, was of near-unprecedented length; post-Tour triumph, he added another year on to it. 'I feel really comfortable here, I trust them and they trust me,' he said in a March 2021 press conference before Tirreno–Adriatico. The contract, estimated to be worth €5.5 million a year, helped to make Pogačar one of the sport's highest earners.

None of the victories or their spoils went to Pogačar's head, according to Joseba Elguezabal. 'I've worked with a lot of riders who haven't had a quarter of his talent and they didn't know how to handle success like he does ... I was struck at how incredibly calm he was, which in turn kept the whole team calm,' Elguezabal told *Procycling* magazine in 2021. 'He wanted to show that winning the [2020] Tour had not been a fluke.

'But he'll never talk about that or pretty much anything else like that in public; he's always very cautious. That's part of his character and I think a lot of Slovenians are like that: very warm-hearted in private, but in public almost inexpressive, quite cold.'

His quiet compassion towards Primož Roglič exemplified those traits. The Jumbo–Visma rider had quit the Tour ahead of stage 9, slowed by his crash injuries and preferring to recover to have a chance at winning gold in the Olympic time trial. As the race continued, Pogačar called Roglič several times to see how he was doing. He even held up his race number in tribute on the race's last day.

Roglič's younger understudy at Jumbo–Visma now rose to the occasion. A climber, the 24-year-old Danish Jonas Vingegaard found himself thrust into the vacated leadership role on his Tour de France debut.

While Pogačar had been a rising star from the moment he joined the WorldTour peloton, Vingegaard's route to the top had been more circuitous. He had worked the dawn shift in a fish auction to make ends meet while racing in Denmark. He turned pro at the age of 22 and in his first year with Jumbo–Visma, he lost the 2019 Tour of Poland lead to nerves. Turning over what could go wrong in his head, he barely slept before the race's final stage and didn't eat anything the next morning, his partner Trine Hansen told *L'Équipe* in 2022.

Used to being in the shadow of Roglič and Wout van Aert, Vingegaard showed that he had all the physiological tools and the mindset to compete. Despite losing time, chasing with Roglič on stage 3 post-crash, he finished third in the stage 5 TT.

On stage 11, which included a double ascent of Mont Ventoux before finishing at its foot in Malaucène, he rode Pogačar off his wheel 1500 m from the top of the legendary climb. It was the champion's only show of weakness that Tour, losing 40 seconds rapidly. 'I cracked a little bit and I was dropped,' Pogačar said. The Dane's advantage was nullified on the long descent to the finish, as Pogačar was helped by distanced rivals Richard Carapaz and Rigoberto Urán. In fact, Pogačar was the ultimate winner on the day, as the second-placed Ben O'Connor lost almost four minutes to him. However, Pogačar's brief scare on a sweltering day hinted at a frailty to fix – heat management – as well as the all-consuming rivalry to come.

The Dane's confidence burnished, he was Pogačar's shadow during the race's Pyrenean mountain stages. Vingegaard wore the white jersey of best young rider for the race's final fortnight, although Pogačar led the competition. Finishing second in Paris ahead of Richard Carapaz was a success for Vingegaard. 'He came out and showed his character, he's been racing fantastically,' Pogačar said of the Dane after stage 17. 'Jumbo–Visma had all that bad luck, but in the future I'm sure he can be a Tour de France winner pretty soon,' he said generously – and presciently.

After a week of UAE Team Emirates controlling and riding defensively, Pogačar won back-to-back stages, outsprinting Vingegaard and Carapaz with zippy late accelerations on the Col du Portet and Luz Ardiden, showing his powers of recuperation.

'His biggest trait that I found was his recovery rate was so good,' says John Wakefield. 'At a Grand Tour, if guys drop 10 per cent [during a race], he's dropping 4 or 5 per cent. He's pushing higher numbers because he's recovering better at the end of the Tour.'

If his first Tour victory felt like a shock turnaround, his second triumph had an air of inevitability for the race's last fortnight. There could be no questions about who deserved it. Pogačar's winning margin of 5 minutes 20 seconds was emphatic. This was then the second largest in the 21st century.

More fans also got to know, and like, Pogačar better during his weeks as the Tour's figurehead, regularly in front of the cameras. His persona was of a laidback big kid, popping wheelies in photo shoots and sticking out his tongue behind his compatriot Matej Mohorič, who was then being interviewed after a stage win. Quick to smile, even on the race's toughest climbs, his stubble-free, expressive face is ripe for physical comedy. He even broke the fourth wall, looking into the TV camera briefly on the way to time-trial victory. Winning the Tour is not supposed to look so joyful and chilled-out.

'It's a game for you,' interviewer Sébastien Piquet said to him after stage 18.

'Yeah, of course: it was a game for me since I started. I'm enjoying playing it.'

Even during his rigorous pre-race recon of the Pyrenean and Alpine stages in May 2021, Pogačar found a way to mix a little pleasure with work. He had *directeur sportif* Andrej Hauptman and his friend Žiga Ručigaj in the following car, advising him where to go on the route app VeloViewer.

'He was really hardcore training. After every session, we had a lot of problems – restaurants in France close down after two, three o'clock,' Ručigaj says. 'So you have nothing to eat. A lot of times, we ate fast food like kebabs and hamburgers. He was preparing for the Tour de France on fast food.'

Ručigaj adds that some evenings, they shared a litre of wine between them. 'I think it was really good for him sometimes to be on easy mode, not just everything on training and Tour de France,' he says.

This slightly more tranquil warm-up, which included a meaningful win at the Tour of Slovenia in mid-June, was needed. Because after pulling on the yellow jersey in Le Grand-Bornand, Pogačar had a fortnight as race leader, facing the full gamut of post-stage commitments: the immediate broadcast flash interview, podium presentations (occasionally for three different jerseys, as he also won the young rider and King of the Mountains competitions, necessitating different face masks on the podium), signing dozens of jerseys backstage, a daily press conference of several questions for the written media, and then anti-doping control, all adding hours to his Tour.

Pogačar's toughest examinations came from the press rather than rivals, asking how he would counter those who doubted the legitimacy of his performances.

To believe or not to believe, that is the recurring question. For every Tour winner of the last 20 years, it is a rite of passage to be held to account. In the face of spectacular performances, it is only natural for scepticism to follow given similar showings were subsequently proven to have been achieved through doping. The sport's past casts a vast shadow over the new generation: the Festina scandal of 1998; the Operation Puerto blood-doping investigation in 2006 and Lance Armstrong's seven Tours effaced from the record after his USADA case in 2012.

'I still have the feeling that doping has decreased a lot in cycling,' Pogačar had told *L'Équipe* in December 2020. 'Everyone who wins the Tour is suspect, and that's because of some people's pasts. It's the history of cycling; there have been so many scandals that it's difficult for people to believe. It will take a long time to get out of this and earn respect again. We have to live with it.'

Pogačar's second Tour de France win was also a coming of age for him off the bike: he came to learn that with the yellow jersey, and a microphone in front of him, he was a spokesman for the sport. That went for press conference questions about whether how much partying he did would affect him for the next race or replying to scurrilous insinuations about motor doping.

'I don't know. We don't hear any noise,' he said, looking bemused. 'We don't use anything illegal. It's all Campagnolo materials.'

Whatever the question, Pogačar is a patient and phlegmatic responder. He offers satisfactory answers in several sentences without straying into great expansiveness or deep introspection. A champion of self-control, he rarely gives away much publicly about his mood and little seems to ruffle him. There are never eye-rolls at questions or diatribes.

In private, it's a little different. 'He hates the typical awkward questions, the press conferences on the rest day of the Tour de France,' Joseba Elguezabal told the *Escapa* podcast in 2022, suggesting Pogačar did not like enquiries about doping very much. 'There's always a journalist there looking for morbid curiosity and the awkward question. That bothers him. Otherwise, he's also a very approachable, accessible guy with the media.'

Answering the inevitable questions about the validity of his performance demands a lot more time and rigour than a five-minute press conference can give. There is no possible riposte that can satisfy the full range of observers and critics, it's a complex catch-22. No doped athlete is going to publicly put their hands up and say: 'You caught me'; no clean athlete can possibly prove their propriety beyond doubt.

'I don't know what to do, to do anything else to prove my innocence,' Pogačar complained during the 2021 Tour. He suggested that he would love to share power files or physiological data, but it could be used against him by other teams in the race.

His coach Iñigo San Millán also suggested that, in fact, Pogačar was racing at a lesser level physiologically in 2021 to the previous year, and against weaker rivals. 'It is frustrating people thinking that Tadej has been extra-galactical [extra-terrestrial] this year when he has never achieved the numbers he had last year,' the Spaniard told *Velonews* during the race. 'He hasn't achieved those numbers because he has never been challenged. So he's going slower than last year; the reality is the rest have nothing. Absolutely nothing. They can't even attack.'

He was not up against the top drawer of contenders: Roglič, Thomas, López and Porte all experienced travails, their challenges falling by the wayside; Giro d'Italia winner Egan Bernal was absent by choice. After Pogačar's double salvo in the Alps, Vingegaard, Urán, Carapaz and O'Connor became entrenched in their own battle for the podium.

After winning stage 18 on Luz Ardiden, his third and final stage win of the race, Pogačar was asked in his press conference if he had concerns or worries about his association with Mauro Gianetti.

He was hardly going to throw his team boss under the bus. 'When I met Mauro, he was really great to me and a super-good person. I believe what is in the past is in the past, and this new cycling is a way more beautiful sport than it was, for sure,' Pogačar said.

The Swiss team boss of UAE Team Emirates had a controversial reputation. While racing for French team Française des Jeux, Gianetti collapsed during the 1998 Tour de Romandie and spent 10 days in hospital, several of them in intensive care, close to multiple organ failure.

Two doctors believed he'd been given perfluorocarbon (PFC) emulsions, effectively synthetic blood with enormous oxygen-carrying capacity, and so able to turbocharge a pro cyclist's aerobic engine to help reduce fatigue. PFCs have not been fully approved for human use.

A complaint was made from within the hospital to local prosecutors. Subsequently, the Swiss courts opened an investigation. The investigating judge seized the medical file and blood samples taken from Mauro Gianetti.

Gianetti was later quoted in the *New York Times* saying: 'Yes, I was very ill with an infection, but I didn't inject myself with anything. The investigation is not against me. It is against somebody who could have given me something.' Gianetti refused to share his medical records with the prosecutor.

A 2025 Radio France investigation revealed that the Swiss had filed for damages against the two doctors from the hospital where his treatment took place, who had filed the complaint.

As claimed by Radio France, one of them negotiated with Gianetti's lawyer to get him to agree to drop the charges in exchange for never speaking publicly of the person again. Gianetti did not respond to questions from Radio France's investigative unit.

To some, Pogačar's association with Gianetti is worrisome.

There is no current evidence to suggest any of Pogačar's wins have been achieved with doping. He has never failed a drugs test. 'Taking anything to risk your health is stupid. I tell you now, it's not worth it,' Pogačar said at the 2024 Tour de France.

It is worth noting that several of his peers in the peloton, speaking off the record, indicated that they believe he is a clean rider.

But as one of the greatest cyclists in history, he will inevitably deal with more probing questions, continued scrutiny and occasional speculation. To paraphrase what he said to *L'Équipe*, *he* is the one who has to live with it.

. . . .

Ahead of the Tour's final stage in Paris, the only question on Pogačar's mind was whether to plump for a Big Mac or the McNuggets. On the way to the French capital, the *maillot jaune* and his team stopped off at a yellow arch for a McDonald's. The race was all but won, the daily diet of rice and pasta could be interrupted.

It was essentially immaterial that Wout van Aert won against the clock in Libourne that afternoon, putting a minute into Pogačar, with runner-up Vingegaard also clawing back 25 seconds on him.

Even in a race which Pogačar won without having to fight tooth and nail, UAE Team Emirates received criticism for being a squad reliant on a super-strong leader. Pro cycling followers were used to Team Sky dominating Grand Tours with their unromantic, brutally effective style of racing. Time and time again in mountain stages, their powerful helpers set a fast tempo on the front, dispatching many contenders before leaders like Chris Froome, Geraint Thomas or Egan Bernal accelerated, usually late on the final climb. 'Pogačar's weakness is his team. It has nothing to do with the strength of Sky or Ineos of recent years,' Cofidis manager Cédric Vasseur told *L'Humanité*. For instance, on the lumpy stage 7 to Le Creusot, 24 hours before their leader's Col de Romme rout, UAE Team Emirates spent most of the race's longest stage on the front, chasing a 29-man breakaway and burning precious energy, later leaving Pogačar with just Rafał Majka for support.

Davide Formolo believes Jumbo–Visma, with Roglič and Vingegaard in tandem, were stronger than UAE then. 'It was almost easy for them to isolate Pogačar,' he says. 'But from my point of view, it's much more important to help him to approach the climb in a good position or to stay safe in the crosswinds. Because on the last climb, what can you do?

'OK, the media like to see 10 guys on the last climb with the leader but the reality, what you really need when you're the leader, is just to be in the right place in the right moment. That's it, then it's all about your legs.

'This is new cycling. We were coming from the Ineos era where we see a strong team on the last climb with seven guys in a group of ten. What for? ... Maybe before, it was the era where it was more tactical, playing more with the brain and making other teams stress, to see their strength. Now, Tadej doesn't care, he just attacks.'

Collectively, UAE Team Emirates may not have overpowered the others, but defending the Tour lead was an underrated challenge successfully met for an outfit with no such past experience. 'Without my teammates, without my staff, I would never have won the Tour,' Pogačar told *L'Équipe*. 'On TV, everything seems easy, like playing PlayStation. But in reality, we suffer enormously. The guys bring me water bottles, food; they protect me from the wind, stop with me when I pee or have a mechanical problem. The race isn't just in the mountains; it lasts five or six hours. Most of the work they do is invisible.'

This time round, they could toast another Tour win in front of the Arc de Triomphe with a full complement of eight riders. It was particularly sweet for Pogačar's faithful lieutenant Formolo, who had been forced to abandon mid-race in 2020 with a broken collarbone: 'To see a friend of yours who achieves his goals, that's crazy. We were training and dreaming together, and he reached them. We almost grew up together, we spent many hours together, we suffered so much together.

'He is the strongest rider in the world,' Formolo adds. 'And if I have a problem at five in the morning and I don't know who to call, I'm probably going to ring him.'

Tour de France 2021: general classification

1. Tadej Pogačar (UAE Team Emirates) 82 hours 56 minutes 36 seconds
2. Jonas Vingegaard (Team Jumbo–Visma) at 5 minutes 20 seconds
3. Richard Carapaz (Ineos Grenadiers) at 7 minutes 3 seconds

While apparently resourceful, Pogačar was not indefatigable or invincible. After flying straight to Japan and finishing third in the Tokyo Olympic Games road race, he did not have it in him to take on a second Grand Tour at the Vuelta a España, something which had been planned.

The effects of a draining season were taking their toll. Unusually, he was dropped with 50 km to go in the Bretagne Classic in Plouay after following attacks by Julian Alaphilippe and Benoît Cosnefroy. He then abandoned the race – his first DNF in over two years.

At the back end of the season, he was mixing good and bad days consecutively: at the Giro dell'Emilia in Italy, he also quit the race. Yet

72 hours later, he was on the warpath with a 120-km breakaway at Tre Valli Varesine, leading to fourth place.

Pogačar had the core Tour band back together to help him win Il Lombardia in October 2021. With over 4500 m of climbing around Italy's great lakes, it is the best-suited Monument race for any Grand Tour challenger; suitably, it is the one-day event that has become his fiefdom.

He escaped on the Passo di Ganda, the hardest ascent of the day, 25 km from the finish. Local rider Fausto Masnada used his knowledge of home roads to catch him on the descent and then did a minimal share of the work. The sprint between the pair was no contest, with Pogačar leading out from the front and sitting up to celebrate with 25 m to go.

With two Monument triumphs and the Tour de France among 13 victories that year, his best season to date bore the versatility and voracity hallmarks of Eddy Merckx. Nicknamed 'The Cannibal', the Belgian dominator is regarded as the greatest in the sport's history, with a record five Tour de France and 19 Monument wins among his 525 triumphs during the 1960s and 1970s.

After spending time with Pogačar in early October, the legend told reporters that in the young Slovenian, cycling had at last really found the new Merckx. His words touched the young pretender. 'I'm being very honest when I say that the goal of my career is enjoying the moment and making my family happy: I don't care about the future, about making cycling history, about being compared to the greats,' Pogačar told *L'Équipe*. 'I barely realise what I've achieved over the past two years [2020 and 2021]. But yes, when I hear Eddy Merckx's words, it changes my viewpoint a little. If he says it, I guess I am making cycling history.'

▶ Pogačar was not content to only target stage races. He turned his focus to the sport's most prominent one-day races, including the Tour of Flanders, a Belgian brutaliser up steep, narrow cobbled hills.

11

BEAST MODE

2022 and 2023 One-day Classics

'Fuck you!'

Tadej Pogačar had royally messed up his 2022 Tour of Flanders debut, somehow finishing fourth in a two-up sprint, and he wasn't happy about it.

Those words, shouted breathlessly at rival Dylan van Baarle after the finish, spoke volumes about the standards to which he holds himself. His frustration at the Dutchman's positioning quickly gave way to anger at himself and his own tactical faux pas. He had let van Baarle and fellow distanced challenger Valentin Madouas catch him in the race's dying throes and they subsequently impeded his sprint for victory.

It's a measure of how committed he is: Grand Tour contenders rarely compete in the Tour of Flanders. To do so is likely to lead to, at best, a reality check and a forgettable result; at worst, a stay in hospital after hitting the deck in one of the fights for position before one of its many hills.

The Tour of Flanders is a fiendish event that he had no right to come so close to winning on his first appearance, even being there as a reigning Tour de France champion. Nevertheless, the calm boy-next-door persona wavered as Pogačar's will to win was laid bare.

'His main priority is honestly to have fun and enjoy cycling. And to win as many races as possible, with that. As we know, he has this animal instinct,' his coach Iñigo San Millán told me in 2023 for *Escape Collective*. 'He would not go to any race at all just to prepare and get competition pace. He really goes to every single race to win it, and that's a great, admirable virtue. And if he doesn't win, he will die trying to win.

'Cycling is more than a job for Tadej, more than a pay cheque at the end of the month. Cycling is his passion. He would do it for free, not even paid, because this is what he likes. And he's competitive. When he's out there at the races, he's like an unleashed lion.

'That's his nature as a cyclist. He's quite shy and sometimes more of an introvert, right? But we see this in many areas, in sports as well as many artistic fields, where some people who are more likely to be shy really express themselves in a huge way. Whether it's performing in a concert or in the case of Tadej, attacking on the cobblestones in Flanders.'

Just as well because at April's Tour of Flanders, one of the toughest races in the sport guarantees a literal survival of the fittest, its final half taking riders from wide main roads on to steep, slender cobbled farm tracks, over and over again.

Many of the alpha predators who historically perform best tend to be *flahutes*, Belgian hard nuts who know the lanes inside out, can sniff out the potential for an echelon like a freshly cooked portion of chips several towns over and aren't shy to defend their position with their shoulders or their 80 kg bulk.

No wonder Grand Tour contenders stay away from Flanders and from the ultimate road racing demolition derby that takes place the following weekend, Paris–Roubaix. It takes a certain kind of racer to excel in these cobbled Monuments, ill-suited to lighter riders, who generally possess less muscle and explosive power. Before Pogačar, the last Tour de France champion to finish in the top 10 at Flanders was Eddy Merckx in 1975.

But De Ronde (The Tour) is a Belgian cycling institution which lends itself to the kind of instinctive, all-out racing that suits Pogačar. While he did not race the elite Tour of Flanders in his first three years as a pro, he had done many of its bergs and cobbles as a teenager, sowing early seeds of his attraction.

'We went to the Tour of Flanders in 2018 for the [under-23] Nations Cup, racing for Žiga Jerman: he was the Plan A, better and stronger in those kind of races,' recalls Martin Hvastija, then the Slovenian national team coach. 'But in the end, he had a puncture with 10 km to go and Pogačar was still there. Even if he had been helping Jerman before and keeping him in front, he finished 15th. You can see the quality because he was always there when it was hard, even if the terrain was not for him. Or –' he chuckles – 'we thought it's not for him.'

Pogačar did not believe that Grand Tour winners should avoid the cobblestone Classics, as so many had done before. He had wanted to compete in the Covid-rearranged October edition of 2020 but opted to end his season due to fatigue. His willingness to be on the start line of the 2022 Tour of Flanders in Antwerp more closely aligned with the attitude of cyclists 40 years earlier, where racing all out from February to October in the cycling calendar's biggest events, regardless of the route profile or risk level, was more customary.

Of course, targeting De Ronde or lining up again at March Monument race Milan–San Remo were not tilts at windmills. At 1.77 m tall and tipping the scales at 66 kg, Pogačar had the make-up to be a contender. 'He's not a tall guy, he's not a skinny guy, he's similar to what Bernard Hinault and Laurent Fignon would be in terms of height and weight,' San Millán told me in 2023. 'And back in the day, Hinault was incredibly versatile, he could win the Tour de France and Classics. It's that balance: if you're good, you can be good in many races.'

Hinault, a five-time Tour de France winner between 1978 and 1985, had been the last man to dabble so successfully in such diverse events, winning two editions of Liège–Bastogne–Liège and the Giro di Lombardia apiece – the last reigning Tour winner to do so before Pogačar – and Paris–Roubaix once. Often 'The Badger' had his teeth set in a grimace, acting as the patron of the bunch and ready for a fight on or off the bike; the Breton once walloped a protester who got in his way at the 1984 Paris–Nice. Pogačar is Mr Nice Guy in comparison.

Strade Bianche was not around for Hinault to win in his time, but the Tuscan race has rapidly entered the sport's folklore since its 2007 introduction, producing picturesque scenes of cypress trees, lone cyclists passing hilltop farmhouses and dust kicked up by following vehicles on its white roads.

The 2022 edition was a crash-fest on the treacherous gravel sectors which characterise the race, with world champion Julian Alaphilippe somersaulting over his handlebars on one tract, battered by crosswinds. Pogačar threw caution to them, attacking downhill and on the loose stones with 50 km to go, then riding away. Evidently, there was no such thing as attacking too early. Miha Koncilija was waiting in the crowd at the foot of the Via Santa Caterina, the haul to the finish in Siena. Pogačar high-fived him as he rode past to victory.

By running the gauntlet at races like Strade Bianche and the Tour of Flanders, encountering different terrain, Pogačar also showed his need for different stimuli to keep his career exciting. 'I just want to experience new things, not be bored, always all over doing the same thing,' he said in a 2025 press conference. 'Probably I wouldn't last long [if I did that]. That's the main reason why I change the programme here and there.'

Refusing to limit his desire, being pushed forward by the belief that he can win almost any race, is part of the charm and DNA of Pogačar the bike racer. 'I prefer the idea of being a Classics rider who wins Grand Tours, even if I started off with a victory in the Tour,' Pogačar told *L'Équipe* in 2024. 'I love the Classics, they are pure adrenaline, a shock of a day that has nothing to do with the suffering spread out over three weeks.'

Perhaps no other one-day race gives competitors such a buzz as the Tour of Flanders. The hundreds of thousands of Belgians shouting support from the roadside lend the race a festival atmosphere.

Given its bendy climax through the Flemish Ardennes, taking in the same finishing circuit twice, knowing when to move to the front of the bunch and when to save energy can make the difference for a contender. It helps to have what the experienced Italian racer Matteo Trentin, a UAE Team Emirates rider between 2021 and 2023, refers to as 'the Knowledge', aptly the same name as the exhaustive test for trainee London black-taxi drivers, which requires them to learn over 26,000 streets off by heart.

Trentin cut his teeth in pro cycling on the leading Belgian team Quick-Step, supporting their Classics stars Tom Boonen and Niki Terpstra. As a neo-pro, he learned the lie of the land by staying for a month and a half in Belgium around the spring races. You cannot tell how hard the wind is blowing, how much gravel is on a tight downhill bend or test what racing tyre pressure you need – around 50 psi for Pogačar, incidentally – from a few lines of text in the race book.

Nowadays, the likes of Google Earth and the route software game-changer VeloViewer mean the peloton doesn't necessarily need to see every centimetre of the route. A pre-race recon can go a long way to informing them of key flashpoints. 'It's just having the legs,' Trentin says. 'If you see the last editions we did [2022, 2023 and 2024 Tour of Flanders], it was just MotoGP racing after a little bit.'

Rather than jumping straight in the deep end at the Tour of Flanders after Milan–San Remo, Pogačar needed a sharpener ahead of what he called a 'step into the unknown'. He lined up at Dwars door Vlaanderen, one of several WorldTour races in the build-up to *Vlaanderens Mooiste* (Flanders' Finest), which finishes in Waregem, West Flanders. Even with Trentin serving as his expert guide and all his own positioning nous and horsepower, this was a rude awakening.

He was briefly caught behind a crash before the cobbled Berg ten Houte and left too far back in the bunch as the winning six-man move went with 70 km to go, led by Mathieu van der Poel. 'Somehow we missed it. He tried to get across like thousands of times, but he couldn't,' Trentin says. After again going on the attack defiantly, Pogačar finished 10th in a chasing group.

Trentin describes the post-race discussion back at the team hotel: 'I said "Listen, if you miss the move there, you really need to use the team to get really close to get back in. It's not a mountain stage: even if it's full of climbing, it's a completely different way of racing, a different way of actually carrying on in the race."'

Pogačar might not have made that positional error had he done more Belgian races before. But like the self-taught kid in the training sessions with Koncilija 15 years earlier, he learns fast and rarely makes the same mistake twice.

Trentin could see that Pogačar was a 'smart guy', not afraid to ask when he wanted to know something. 'He has no problem talking to the other guys, not only me, to see what their opinions are and then making his mind up of what he thinks he has to do,' Trentin says. 'He is the only one that can do certain things, like attacking on the Cipressa [in Milan-San Remo] or going away 80 km before the finish in Strade Bianche. He is not asking for validation of his own idea, he is asking because he really wants to know what people think to then make his own idea complete.'

Trentin experienced his strength in training first-hand, occasionally going out with him in their adopted home of Monaco, though he is usually an early bird while Pogačar prefers to start later. 'When he says, "OK, guys, today, I have to go hard," then I don't even look at his back wheel, I just let him go. It's like in the races, he's the kind of guy who doesn't let anything go by chance.

'The amount of quality he has, his versatility, really stood out in every single discipline, if you can call it that,' the Italian adds. 'Climbing, TT, Classics, even sprinting he's not too bad. For sure he's not a sprinter; that's the only thing I can beat him in, actually. Even there it's not like he wants to sit in there and he's going to lose the race because we finish in a sprint. This is the kind of champion mentality [he has]: you don't want to have any weak point.'

The Tour of Flanders would be a rigorous test of his and the team's strengths and tactics. The second half of the Monument, defined by 18 climbs (known as *hellingen*), lends itself to a constantly changing race scenario, as one breakaway move replaces another. It is easy for a competitor to lose an advantageous tactical position and an understanding of where he is in the race and Flanders itself.

Those numerous sharp hills also give plenty of opportunities to shake up the race. Allan Peiper, who lives in the Belgian town of Geraardsbergen, knows the Tour of Flanders inside out and believed Pogačar has the flexible mental approach needed to excel there. 'His playfulness in his racing takes a lot of pressure off his shoulders. He likes to race, he likes to play it up without having a set scenario,' Peiper told me for *Rouleur* in 2021. 'That leaves an open mind for going into racing as fun.'

On a chilly Sunday morning in Antwerp, Pogačar's Tour of Flanders debut started inauspiciously, as he suffered a low-speed tumble 20 km into the race when the road narrowed into one lane. With no harm done, UAE Team Emirates teammates kept him close to the front for the next 180 km, avoiding mechanical problems and more crashes. Ideally placed at the foot of the Oude Kwaremont behind bunch leader Trentin, Pogačar went on the attack, surging through the breakaway detritus, seemingly going at double their speed.

The front of the race regrouped before the Paterberg, with a dozen riders pulling clear on the fast descent, at 50 km to go. Ineos Grenadiers rider Dylan van Baarle and Fred Wright of Bahrain-Victorious broke away during a brief lull in action. Having no more teammates in the chasing group was no problem for Pogačar: on the Koppenberg, the race's single-hardest climb which reduces many to walking in muddy conditions, he punched away again. Only pre-race favourite Mathieu van der Poel and Frenchman Valentin Madouas could join him, the three quickly bridging the gap to the leading duo.

Wright was on the limit, surviving on dwindling energy reserves. 'You could tell Tadej didn't even consider me a threat. And as a result, I was skipping turns [sharing the pace-setting on the front] for the period we were in the group of five together,' he says. 'He and van der Poel didn't care that I was doing that. Normally, if that was me, you'd try and get the guy to come through. They weren't worried about me.'

The Tour of Flanders finale favours strength over finesse, decided by the revisited one-two punch of the Oude Kwaremont and Paterberg.

On the 2200 m of the more gradual first climb, as tarmac turned to *kasseien* cobblestones, Pogačar hit the afterburners and moved away with van der Poel. Leading the whole way up, he tried in vain to suffocate his rival with a sustained injection of pace.

Wright, though, made an error trying to keep up with the superstars. 'I should have just paced myself. You see it time and time again: the guys that try and follow him [Pogačar] end up blowing up. And that's kind of what happened to me … it's hard when there's someone at such a high level. You almost can't think about them or following them, otherwise it's too much – which is strange when the goal of a bike race is to win it. And maybe that's why Tadej has got in everybody's head.'

On the Paterberg, 360 m of infernal uphill which can feel 10 times longer in a Tour of Flanders finale, he stretched van der Poel to breaking point, but there was no separating them. Leading van Baarle and Madouas by 20 seconds into the closing 1000 m, they laid off the gas, freewheeling down the finishing straight in Oudenaarde at 30 km/h – recovery ride pace for those professional cyclists. Van der Poel coasted in the lead, with Pogačar on his wheel. The rookie was readying himself for a shot at the usually faster-finishing Dutchman, banking on the hope that a sprint after 272 km is different to one on fresh legs.

Their idling allowed Madouas and van Baarle to catch up, swamping them with 200 m to go as van der Poel started his sprint to victory. He had the punch to stay ahead, but Pogačar found himself overtaken and briefly blocked by the returning pair. He used his hands to try to budge the sprinting van Baarle out of the way ahead of him, to no avail and threw up his arms in protest 25 m before crossing the line in fourth place.

Ironically for one of the world's most prestigious races where know-how is paramount, his slip-up had nothing to do with lack of experience. It was an error that could have been committed by any cyclist of any age or status. Pogačar was the strongest in that year's Tour of Flanders, but not the smartest.

'It was one of the few times you see him losing in an amateur way,' Trentin says. 'Because – it's sad to say for a guy like him – he should have just pulled and played for second. He was trying to gamble as long as he could and the gamble didn't work because the two guys came back.'

As Pogačar came to a halt, he vented his spleen at van Baarle, who had paused next to him. It was an inadvertent racing incident which was not deemed to break any rules; the second-placed Dutchman appeared to himself say: 'That's what happens in a sprint,' as Pogačar repeated his F-bomb invective. Members of his inner circle – Luke Maguire, Joseba Elguezabal, Alex Carera, Mauro Gianetti and Andrea Agostini – were on hand to pat him on the shoulder, as he shook his head over and over before riding away.

Pogačar was still raging on the team bus. 'But as quickly as he was angry, then it was over,' Trentin says. Laughing, he adds, 'People like him have these kinds of problems: *I lost one year, I'll come back next year and win.*'

Not proud of his contretemps with van Baarle, which was caught on a TV camera, Pogačar later said that it was emotion talking after six hours in the saddle and annoyance at not even having a chance to take on Mathieu van der Poel in the sprint. Quick to cage the beast, he sent an apology to van Baarle over Instagram.

There was no chagrin against the race winner, the immovable object which stopped his force that day. The Dutchman is part of a cycling dynasty, the son of 1980s star Adrie van der Poel, who won the Tour of Flanders and Liège–Bastogne–Liège, and the grandson of Raymond Poulidor, an eight-time Tour de France podium finisher whose rivalry with Jacques Anquetil intoxicated French cycling fans. With such a bloodline, Mathieu was hardly going to become an electrician.

Mixing road racing with the quagmires of winter cyclo-cross, winning seven world titles in the discipline, van der Poel possesses a balletic handling ability, as if the bicycle is an extension of his own body. Long, punchy stages and one-day races are his playground, making him a worthy adversary for Pogačar.

However, there were no more showdowns between the pair in Pogačar's 2022 spring campaign. Betraying a little fatigue, he finished 12th at the Flèche Wallonne and the next day, the world turned on its head: Urška's mother, Darja, died. Tadej and Urška went back to Slovenia, sport now irrelevant.

'Without Tadej, I would not have been able to handle the death of my mother, who fought for almost two years,' Urška recalled to reporters in 2025. 'First against breast cancer, then against oesophageal cancer. It was a long rollercoaster. Tadej was always present. I was once angry with him. I remember my mother getting really mad at me. I thought: *What is this? I'm the one who should be angry.* My mother said: "Urška, can't you see how that boy looks at you? Can't you see how much he loves you? He's the best thing that could have happened to you." I had to make up with him as soon as possible. She really loved Tadej.'

Darja's death was a leading factor in the launch of the Tadej Pogačar Cancer Research Foundation that summer, working in partnership with Iñigo San Millán, UAE Team Emirates head of performance.

. . . .

After racing the Tour de France, Pogačar was soon back to his favoured one-day racing. After abandoning the Clásica San Sebastián in late July and finishing 89th at the Bretagne Classic four weeks later, he showed a return to form at the GP Cycliste de Montréal, impressively outsprinting Wout van Aert in an uphill finish. His peripatetic summer season continued, as he swapped Canada for Australia and the World Championships in Wollongong, finishing 6th in the time trial and 19th in the road race.

The trip also threw up unexpected opportunities to see a couple of his old Ljubljana Gusto Xaurum teammates. Ben Hill linked up with him for a five-hour training ride. 'My brother Sam has a Strava KOM (King of the Mountain) up this hill [Hawkesbury Heights], me and him would race up there every year for our family handicap race. I said to Tadej, "Do you want to go for it?"' Hill says.

'Three days out from Worlds, he said, "I'll just ride threshold" – 470 watts for eight minutes. "Maybe it was a little bit above threshold." Maybe you were just going for the KOM,' Hill smiles. 'And he got it

– by one second.' According to Hill, Pogačar had the good manners to upload his Strava ride as private, so his sibling kept the segment lead.

Hill felt he was still pedalling with the same happy-go-lucky guy who had offered him pizza sticks at the 2018 Tour of Slovenia, barely changed by fame and fortune. His power was different to their Slovenian days though – out of energy, he stayed in Pogačar's slipstream for the last hour or he would have been dropped.

Tim Guy was similarly surprised when a racer from the group of Slovenians doing a recon recognised him riding around the edge of the road race course, shouted his name and chatted with him.

Having organised to meet a former soigneur at the Slovenian team's accommodation, Guy saw Pogačar again hours later as he walked past for dinner and stopped for another conversation. 'Then he'd gone to bed, Boštjan [Kavčnik, his mechanic] came out and they were going to get some other jerseys signed,' Guy says. 'Boštjan rang Pogačar in the middle of the night – this is, like, before Worlds. I'm like "Don't do it, leave him." He comes down and signs them, he was more than happy to do it.' Later, with Guy working as a school teacher in Australia, Pogačar made sure that a signed jersey was left in Slovenia for him to collect on a visit, intended for a cycling-mad pupil of his.

That is the understated generosity and gallantry of Pogačar. Even with all his commitments, he thinks to hand his sunglasses to an awed kid after a tough stage or even to place water bottles mid-race in their hands. He has found novel ways to give back: in August 2023, he donated money to Slovenian flood victims, adding an extra €10 for every autograph or photograph. Over 4500 people flocked to Congress Square in Ljubljana, as Pogačar signed 1793 autographs and took 1214 selfies, raising €30,070.

The World Championships road race Down Under was another sign of the increasingly open style of racing, driven by young stars making bold winning moves far from the finish. Remco Evenepoel took a flyer as part of a 19-man group with 77 km to go, pushed the pace with Alexey Lutsenko of Kazakhstan and left his last remaining companion for a 26-km solo escape to victory. 'They are not afraid, they are always able to do something spectacular,' Pogačar's mentor and UAE Team Emirates *directeur sportif* Andrej Hauptman says. 'It seems to me they compete between them[selves]: "OK, you start at 80 km to go? The next race, I will go at 90 km to go."'

One of the keys to the brave new approach was setting a harsh early tempo with teammates, turning it into a mano-a-mano battle, having ripped off the legs of rivals' most valuable helpers and wearied other contenders. A searing, race-long pace would also help Pogačar's second shot at the Tour of Flanders in 2023, not wanting to leave it to chance or a sprint again.

This time round, van der Poel spent precious early energy after positioning oversights. 'There was a split, then there was a crash where he was behind,' Matteo Trentin says. 'Then Team DSM made a start-stop move on the Kortekeer and he was in the back end of the group because of a pee stop. And then he completely lost his team on the Molenberg [with 100 km to go], so he was isolated pretty soon.'

At that point, Trentin went up the road in a counter-attack to heap on the pressure: 'It was really nice: we had a plan, we profited from every situation, always on the front foot. That was also pretty important: we were never in the scenario where we had to chase. Every part fell perfectly in the puzzle that day.'

Trentin's nine-strong group was loaded with contenders, including Mads Pedersen (Lidl–Trek), Stefan Küng (Groupama–FDJ), 2021 winner Kasper Asgreen (Soudal Quick-Step) and Fred Wright (Bahrain-Victorious), trying to pre-empt Pogačar. As peers on other WorldTour teams freely admit to me, they also plan around the Slovenian star in these races. They would be stupid not to: sitting back and waiting for the second ascent of the Oude Kwaremont, with 55 km to go, usually signals the beginning of the Pogačar-provoked endgame. For most challengers, being behind him at that point is like turning up to a gunfight with a flick knife.

The three-minute lead for the dangerous escape did not stop him. 'I was in potentially one of the strongest mid-race breaks there's ever been at the Tour of Flanders. And still, the favourite came back and dropped us all,' Trentin says. 'I think with this change in cycling, having these superstars with their superpowers, everybody else has to find a way to get around them, anticipate them or hang on as long as you can, then profit from the fact you're already in some kind of sweet spot before other guys. It can be played in several different ways.'

When it looked like the race was in the balance, Pogačar repeated his Kwaremont-Koppenberg combination of late-race blows from 2022, leading van der Poel and Wout van Aert away with him. The Jumbo–Visma star was subsequently distanced on the Kruisberg by a van der Poel acceleration. Having caught Trentin and the six remaining leaders, Pogačar chose the Kwaremont again to drop everyone and tear past the remaining attacker Mads Pedersen, showing impressive power in the saddle. The climb's length and gradient, steepest in the first third before kicking up in a false flat, was ideal for a long, searing attack. Give it a few more years and it ought to be nicknamed the Pogi-berg, given his impact on the race there.

Pogačar has changed the modern racing dynamic of the Tour of Flanders, putting in digs time and time again, twisting it to his own strengths, bending his rivals until they break. Time and time again, he can push 400–500 watts for several minutes, upping it over 600 watts for all-out, two-minute efforts. He combines explosive power with rapid recovery, given his magic mitochondria and lactate clearance capacity.

Van der Poel went off in hot pursuit, but 15 seconds' advantage at the top of the Paterberg proved sufficient. Pogačar could sit up and savour the final 100 m, a stark contrast to his displeasure after the 2022 edition. 'I can say I can retire after today and I will be proud of my career,' Pogačar said post-race after winning number three of the sport's five Monuments. He added that it was one of the victories he has enjoyed the most.

He was only the third Tour de France champion to win the Tour of Flanders after the 1950s doyen Louison Bobet and Eddy Merckx. Il Lombardia and Liège–Bastogne–Liège were in his wheelhouse, but this belonged to an even higher tier, a sign of his adaptability and genre-hopping versatility at the age of just 24.

Runner-up van der Poel showed his sense of humour, with a wry comment on Instagram: 'stick to grand tours please'.

While it could be tempting to pit these two *galácticos* against each other, a Cristiano Ronaldo to a Lionel Messi, the pair are friends. They occasionally train together and exchange messages. Sitting out the 2023 Amstel Gold Race, van der Poel even advised Pogačar days before to attack on the Keutenberg, the race's hardest climb, which he duly did – and he won.

Perhaps their relationship is helped by having sufficiently diffuse objectives. While they clash regularly in punchy stages and prestigious one-day races, Pogačar will surely never stray seriously into cyclo-cross and van der Poel will likely never bother him as a stage race or Grand Tour GC challenger. (Besides, in Wout van Aert, van der Poel already has a career-long nemesis.)

Together, they were winning even more admirers for their panache and front-foot approach to racing. In a category of his own, Pogačar was the exception in the age of the specialist. Although Remco Evenepoel has also won Liège–Bastogne–Liège, he and the seven other Grand Tour champions of the 2020s – Vingegaard, Roglič et al. – have never even raced the Tour of Flanders.

Pogačar has the perfect blend of science and romance, of new-school optimisation and old-school risk-taking. He works in the wind tunnel, weighs every gram of food, feeds up to 120 g of carbohydrate an hour in a race, goes up to altitude to prepare. Then he comes down from the mountain, posts funny memes on social media, blows away competitors with a smile on his face and sometimes tears up even his own plans with long-range moves, daring rivals to follow.

When you're Pogačar, you're taking a calculated risk; for the rest of the peloton, it's hara-kiri. The proof is in the palmarès, and even his closest rivals can only respect him and the Pogi effect.

'I'm proud to be part of this generation of cyclists with riders like Tadej who is going to be remembered for being one of the best there has ever been in cycling,' Mathieu van der Poel told *Rouleur*'s Rachel Jary in 2025. 'I want my legacy to be that I was part of the way that we changed bike racing.'

▶ Rivalries have enriched some of Pogačar's biggest triumphs. Whether vying against Mathieu van der Poel, Primož Roglič or Jonas Vingegaard, the champion needs a worthy adversary to force him to get the very best out of himself.

12

CRACK ME IF YOU CAN

2022 Tour de France

How do you beat Tadej Pogačar? That was the burning question giving the peloton sleepless nights as he ripped through the cycling calendar like a twister, winning race after race. Maybe it helps to be a fellow yellow jersey winner to understand how to break one: during an episode of the *Geraint Thomas Cycling Club* podcast in the 2021 off-season, the eponymous host ventured some answers.

Thomas held forth about how racing had changed because of Pogačar, becoming more aggressive and less controlled. UAE Team Emirates had strengthened, as had Jumbo–Visma, a mark of both their strong recruitment policy and whole teams being coached well collectively, not just individuals doing it mostly on their own. It didn't make winning, or believing you could win, any easier, though.

'You have definitely got to look at different ways of racing. There's no point us riding like we did in the teens [2010s] and just setting a tempo on the front because it's just going to work for him,' the Ineos Grenadiers stalwart said.

What did his guest make of all that? 'They shouldn't be scared of me because I can crack really fast actually,' Tadej Pogačar replied. 'I do a good power on not-so-long climbs. Sometimes the longer climb and high altitude is worse for me: that's what they already figured out. For sure, if it happens that I have a not-so-strong team with long-range attacks, that makes it more difficult for us.

'Just trying to go aggressive from a long way [out] with multiple riders,' he continued. 'Like, Ineos have a lot of leaders, so they can try a lot of things, a different way. I think there can be a lot of things that can crack me or anybody else. It's not that complicated.'

Pogačar's candour cut through their pally banter and prior talk about his background and how he switches off from cycling. A two-time Tour champion discussing weaknesses and ways to beat him is highly abnormal: when at the top of the tree, you don't offer a hand down to rivals reaching from lower branches.

Maybe he was willing to be open with an experienced peer he respects. Or perhaps this was a sign of his confidence – because if this was an invitation to 'crack me if you can', offering the first scribblings of a blueprint, nobody had taken it up in a big stage race for almost two seasons. By the time Pogačar got to the 2022 Tour de France, he had gone 15 months without losing one.

There is only a small chance Jonas Vingegaard and the Jumbo–Visma management listened to the episode. However, they were already hard at work on their own master plan to dethrone the king.

On stage 11 of the Tour, they put it into action – and whether it was coincidence or not, all the elements that Pogačar casually mentioned in that podcast were part of it.

. . . .

The theory was simpler than its execution would be: use Jumbo–Visma's superior manpower to isolate, weaken and beat Pogačar. Merijn Zeeman, their influential *directeur sportif*, realised Jumbo–

Visma needed to be unconventional, to surprise the rest and take risks – 'to drop a bomb', in his own words, recounted by the journalist Nando Boers in his book *Het plan*. Zeeman, fellow DS Grischa Niermann, nutritionist Martijn Redegeld, head of performance Mathieu Heijboer and consultant strategist Patrick Broe were part of a close-knit working group within the squad, akin to the 'Secret Squirrel Club' that helped drive British Cycling to Olympic success, looking for every technological and technical advantage. Over many video calls, sometimes lasting more than three hours, they hashed out the finer details.

As the race neared, the plan was fine-tuned at a training camp in Sierra Nevada in May. The team knew the attributes and capabilities of Vingegaard inside out and believed him to be better in the Alps – at altitude and on climbs longer than 20 minutes – than Pogačar. They also investigated Pogačar's typical racing behaviours, watching every race of his from 2019 onwards, exploring when he deviated from them and in what circumstances. It helped to instil the belief that he could be defeated. Zeeman tied the plan together and sold it to the riders themselves.

No team on the 2022 Tour start line in Copenhagen had a more formidable line-up. Primož Roglič and Jonas Vingegaard were co-leaders, with leading climbers Sepp Kuss and Steven Kruijswijk assisting the two-pronged attack. Tiesj Benoot offered versatile support. Fast-finishing Christophe Laporte was a bodyguard on the flat stages, alongside Nathan Hooydonck. Last but certainly not least, Wout van Aert served as their invaluable cycling Everyman, allowing them to target the Tour's green points jersey as well as yellow. One of the most prolific riders in road cycling at the time, van Aert was able to win on any kind of race course or provide selfless *domestique* help. A natural leader, he often led discussions about strategy on the team bus.

Getting Jumbo–Visma to a position of such strength had not happened overnight. In 2015, the squad had languished 14th of 17 top-tier teams, low on both star quality and fresh ideas. Gradually, Zeeman and managing director Richard Plugge revamped their culture. Inspired by epochal sports teams – especially the Phil Jackson-coached Chicago Bulls and the New Zealand Rugby Team, with their mantra: 'Better people make better "All Blacks"' – they were obsessed with becoming the most cohesive unit in pro cycling, wanting riders to communicate clearly and take ownership of their careers.

Within seven years, the Dutch squad scaled the WorldTour's summit. They recruited intelligently, with new signings taking personality tests; unheralded riders like Roglič, Kuss and Vingegaard would all go from being nobodies to Grand Tour champions.

They made altitude training, that modern prerequisite for maximising the body's ability to carry oxygen, more individual and fine-tuned to each rider. The same went for nutrition, developing their own FoodCoach app, calculating energy requirement per rider, based on training and racing load that day, and adjusting their meal requirements accordingly.

In their quest for improvement, Zeeman even realised that they did not fully understand how to win bike races – they were often following the same predictable tactics as other teams and reacting to situations rather than seizing the initiative.

Stage 4 of the 2022 Tour de France was an early sign of their audacious approach. A dozen kilometres from the finish in Calais, six of their riders led the bunch into the bottom of the final hill, Cap Blanc-Nez. Yellow jersey-clad van Aert blasted away over the verdant top to victory. It was a performance that highlighted the strength of their unit.

For all their versatility, inventiveness and quality, it looked like the big plan might be scuppered by circumstances. The threat posed by their terrific twosome was blunted when Primož Roglič crashed on stage 5 to Wallers-Arenberg. On a day that included 11 cobblestone sectors in northern France, he hit a covered hay bale sticking out on the tarmac and lost 2 minutes 8 seconds (after popping his dislocated shoulder back into place). This dumped him on to the fringes of overall contention, almost three minutes behind Pogačar.

Vingegaard also spent most of the finale in desperate pursuit of the peloton after changing bikes three times in the space of 70 chaotic seconds due to a dropped chain. The subsequent stop-go sequence could have been sped up and put to the whimsical 'The Benny Hill Theme'. Before the next day's start in the Belgian town of Binche, Richard Plugge stood by the team bus, bemoaning their bad luck.

By contrast, Pogačar was enjoying business as usual. He could hardly have experienced a better first week on a route that favoured his all-rounder capacities. Finishing third in the opening time trial around Copenhagen, won by Yves Lampaert, he avoided anticipated crosswind problems the next day and looked at home on the rough *pavé*. Sticking to a move from Belgian Classics star Jasper Stuyven, he gained 13 seconds on Vingegaard and his other challengers.

Confidence buoyed, Pogačar took stage wins on back-to-back uphill finishes at Longwy and Super Planche des Belles Filles, passing the last remaining breakaway Lennard Kämna and an attacking Vingegaard with 50 m to go on a gradient of 24 per cent. His mechanics discovered afterwards that Pogačar's seatpost had slipped down 7 mm that day. In a sport where the smallest set-up shift can put a star off his game, like the Princess and the Pea, he shrugged it off. Evidently, Pogačar is a macro-adapter who could probably do a passable job if handed a bargain-basement bike five minutes before the start.

It looked like being a rerun of the 2021 race. Pogačar's lead over second-placed Vingegaard was a slender 39 seconds entering the Alps, but he had already imposed himself. Was the Tour already done and dusted? Certainly there were pundits who said as much. 'I think it is over, barring a crash, injury, Covid,' Bradley Wiggins said on his eponymous Eurosport podcast after stage 6. 'Tadej has proved himself, he's clearly the strongest. You can't see him faltering physically because we've never seen him falter physically.'

Cracks were showing in the facade of UAE Team Emirates, though. The valuable *domestique* Matteo Trentin tested positive before the race for Covid-19, so the Swiss rider Marc Hirschi – who had himself tested positive at the preceding Tour de Suisse – came back into the line-up. Then, despite the stringent, amplified Covid protocol in their 30-person bubble, riders Vegard Stake Laengen and George Bennett went home due to the virus on stage 8 and after stage 9 respectively.

Key mountains helper Rafał Majka was also positive but carrying a sufficiently low viral load to continue.

Such support would be sorely missed on one of the 2022 Tour's toughest days. The final 80 km of stage 11 had a sawtooth profile, including the Col du Télégraphe and Col du Galibier, the race's high point, before a finish on the unrelenting Col du Granon, 11.3 km at a gradient of 9.2 per cent. The altitude of the route – its last two cols are both above 2400 m – the oppressive heat (35°C) and the race circumstances made it D-Day for Jumbo–Visma to unseat Pogačar. This was the best team in the world versus the best individual stage racer. *If you don't try, you'll never know.*

They set up their ambush in the stage's opening kilometres, with Wout van Aert and Christophe Laporte going up the road as part of a sizeable early breakaway, so-called 'satellite riders' orbiting ahead, ready to impact the race later if needed.

On the first-category Télégraphe, a mere *amuse-bouche* leading to Valloire and the start of the lengthier Galibier, Pogačar was already under siege. Vingegaard's teammates Benoot and Roglič surged, with Pogačar closing the gap from fourth wheel. This was the first of 14 accelerations the yellow jersey either followed or made himself in the remarkable subsequent 25 km, changing the course of the race.

After the peloton regrouped, Benoot set a tough pace and Roglič stamped on the pedals again as they crossed the col. For Jumbo–Visma, it was tactically now or never to utilise their Slovenian as both bait and contender. His condition after the stage 5 crash was an unknown, but while he was positioned 13th overall – a full 2 minutes 52 seconds down on Pogačar – his reputation and deficit created just enough proximity on GC to worry the defending champion. But if Roglič were to wait one more day, he was likely to lose more time, given the stage's severity, and no longer be a viable threat who could be used to draw his rivals out in the same fashion.

Having dropped back from the breakaway to help the next stage of the plan, Laporte linked up with Roglič at the start of the descent and sprinted up to speed. Only the duo and the race's eventual podium finishers – Pogačar, Vingegaard and Geraint Thomas – followed in their wake. The race leader bellowed into his race radio as their advantage grew, but it was too late. Laporte gave his all for five full-bore kilometres before dropping back as the tarmac of the Galibier reared up. He had successfully separated the UAE Team Emirates captain from his helpers, also giving him little chance for refuelling.

A rat-a-tat salvo of attacks started, firing off on the gentler early stretches of the 17 km that make up the Galibier's north side. Vingegaard sprung out of the saddle and up the road, marked by Pogačar. Once the group was back together, Roglič waited a few beats and attacked. Again, Pogačar expended valuable energy, chasing him down before testing them with a burst of speed to see what they had. Wave after wave of attack, as if the finish line was round the bend, not 65 km away.

This was tactically unwise from Pogačar, taking the gap to a sizeable group containing several of his UAE teammates from 40 seconds up to a minute. He should have sat tight and waited for reinforcements, but his impulses were overriding the more lucid parts of his racing brain. Jumbo–Visma's tactics dragged him into action and reaction in the heat of the moment.

Vingegaard and Roglič could play the one-two, taking turns either to attack or to sit on Pogačar's back wheel, making him chase down every move and work a little harder. (Geraint Thomas predominantly kept his own rhythm, not drawn into following every staccato stab of pace, drifting back up to the leaders after the slowdowns.)

Pogačar admitted afterwards that he 'fell into their trap'. His confidence, strength and attacking spirit – often such advantages – were being used against him.

Objectively, there was no need for him to follow every move. He couldn't help himself, also fearing the presence of joker in the pack van Aert up the road and how he could shape the race for Roglič or Vingegaard if he dropped back. 'Riding like that is simply my way of racing, often based on instinct. Sometimes it works out, sometimes it doesn't,' Pogačar told *Cyclingnews* four months later, reflecting on his Galibier tactics. 'But I'm not going to change. I'll always race full gas.'

Pogačar came to expect the next Jumbo–Visma jab, warily looking over his shoulder every now and then on the Galibier's first half. Moments after glancing right, Vingegaard burst up the left side of the road. After the next regroupment, Roglič raised the pace.

For years, they had been leader and learner: morally and physically, it must have been painful for Roglič to race like this, knowing it was probably at the expense of his own chances. The original Jumbo–Visma plan had anticipated Pogačar's teammates chasing and then eventually letting Roglič go. But his compatriot would not give him any freedom and was hurting his own chances more in the process.

'You do 10 sprints alone and Vingegaard and Primož had to do just five, half less than me. I think I killed myself there a little bit and maybe I should have taken more fuel,' Pogačar said afterwards.

Physiologically, he was draining his glycogen reserves at a higher rate. Nutritionally, Pogačar also missed a key feed, according to John Wakefield, leaving him under-fuelled. Without it, he was lacking exogenous carbohydrates and became depleted.

'They knew from an energy consumption side, they had already done all the calculations,' Wakefield adds of Jumbo–Visma. 'So they knew he expends more: this is what he does in the heat and they played that to their best. They simply out-scienced UAE – and they were stronger, overall, as a team.'

Pogačar was feeling the heat. 'Get me water,' he said into his race radio, while the Jumbo–Visma team car behind the group was doling out ice socks and water bottles to Roglič and Vingegaard.

When teammate Marc Soler charged up from the chasing group alone halfway up the Galibier, he was wasting energy. He could have waited: within minutes, the 20-strong group he had been part of caught up as the searing pace in front cooled. McNulty and Majka moved to the front, giving a semblance of control as the group rode through Plan Lachat, over 2000 m of altitude and into the Galibier's steeper, last 7 km.

Rising into thinner air where breathing feels more strained, the Jumbo juggernaut was still going. Benoot came to the front, Roglič accelerated, Pogačar followed and then upped the pace over the top with Vingegaard on his wheel. When the Tour leader tempered his effort and looked behind to see who was with him, four Jumbo–Visma riders briefly fanned out, side by side in the slipstream: Kruijswijk, Kuss, Roglič and Vingegaard. Pogačar must have thought he was seeing double, outnumbered and out-thought.

In the last kilometres of the Galibier, Pogačar put in a couple more attacks to distance Roglič and pressed on with Vingegaard over the summit. While trying to drop everyone made for spectacular racing, he was overreaching.

The other contenders caught up on the descent and the durable van Aert dropped back from the breakaway, first to pace their group and then to do the same for Roglič, dragging them back into contention. This was the fight of the bumblebees: swat one yellow-and-black clad racer away and more seemed to buzz back. Pogačar finally had reinforcements, with Majka rejoining in that bunch, but it was two for UAE Team Emirates against Jumbo's five.

If Pogačar already knew that he was in for punishment, he hid it well. At the foot of the Col du Granon, he spat, smiled and took a performative breather for the adjacent TV camera motorcycle. Breaking the fourth wall further, he mimed a throttle turn with his right hand, implying he was enjoying the full-gas racing.

His tank was about to run empty. Pogačar realised at the beginning of the final climb that he was not on a good day, but it did not show immediately. Majka tapped out a tough pace on the front until there were just seven riders left.

When Vingegaard rose out of the saddle and surged away, with less than 5 km to go, it was one acceleration too many. The telltale sign of Pogačar's emptiness came when Majka injected some speed in one last effort to help him to follow and he was dropped by his own teammate.

Within 1 km, Vingegaard had taken the lead and put 40 seconds into Pogačar. Riding behind him, Geraint Thomas realised quickly that his fearsome rival was not just vulnerable to attack, but wide open.

Now it was his turn to put the boot in. Over the next kilometres, he, Adam Yates (his Ineos Grenadiers teammate) and David Gaudu all caught and passed Pogačar, leaving him to his solitary slog.

His head was bobbing left and right, his upper body rocking. At times, he could barely look up at the corkscrewing road still to climb. His wraparound white sunglasses hid his eyes. Those last 5 km probably felt like they took five days.

In front, Vingegaard had the bit between his gritted teeth, visibly riding faster and full of desire. He clenched his fist and roared as he crossed the finish line to take his maiden Tour stage win. Another 2 minutes 51 seconds ticked by before Pogačar stopped the clock in sixth place, his head hanging so low it was almost on his handlebar stem, as if he could not stand the sight of his bicycle. Pogačar had been beaten many times before, but now he knew what it felt like to be on the receiving end of a convincing defeat.

His unzipped yellow jersey billowing like a cape in the breeze, Pogačar was no longer the Tour's superman or its leader. At the same time that he lost the *maillot jaune*, his cloak of invincibility was torn off.

'I just didn't expect it, Pogačar cracking like that,' Geraint Thomas reflected later on the massage table to Netflix cameras. Almost nobody did, let alone by that sizeable margin. Pogačar had not lost a stage race for 15 months, winning two stages and the overall at his other 2022 stage races: the UAE Tour, Tirreno–Adriatico and the Tour of Slovenia. At times, he had made pro cycling look like literal child's play: on one stage in his June home race, he and Majka played rock, paper, scissors to decide who would get the stage win. (Paper beats rock; Majka finished ahead of Pogačar.) The Granon stage, by contrast, was more like going down a giant serpent in a game of snakes and ladders.

This was the first time that the Dane, his shadow for a Tour and a half, had put time into Pogačar in a Grand Tour road stage. He certainly made it count: while the Slovenian had chipped away 39 seconds over the previous 10 days, Vingegaard made crucial gains in one seismic afternoon.

In a period where many rivals were understandably apprehensive to take the race to Pogačar, fearing it would hasten their own capitulation, Jumbo–Visma's coup was a masterpiece. Their 'total cycling' approach (an expression used by Merijn Zeeman, playing on Johan Cruyff's Total Football) might well be studied at *wielerschools* in the future as a prime example of how a unit isolates and breaks a stronger individual.

Vingegaard's coming of age was simultaneously a loss of innocence for Pogačar. It showed the rest of the peloton, including his own teammates, that the top dog was beatable. 'I was a little shocked: I didn't believe it, to be honest,' Pogačar's teammate Mikkel Bjerg told me in 2023. 'But that just shows that everybody can have a bad day, even Tadej.'

While on the Col du Granon, Jumbo-Visma *directeur sportif* Grischa Niermann told his riders that Pogačar was finished and they had killed him. The man himself vowed to keep fighting until the end.

The next day's finish on the venerated climb of Alpe d'Huez, Pogačar tested the new race leader with several attacks. Twenty-four hours later on the steep ascent to the aerodrome at Mende, Pogačar's explosive accelerations drew Vingegaard away again, without successfully getting daylight between the two. The men in the white and yellow jerseys shook hands after crossing the line, the best of rivals.

This was the absorbing contest that the Tour needed: two fresh-faced, skinny, twenty-somethings incongruously transformed into fearless, hardy brawlers on bikes, refusing to give an inch.

As the race entered the Pyrenees, the attrition rate took a toll on both Jumbo–Visma and UAE Team Emirates. Roglič left the race, physically and psychologically hurting, while Steven Kruijswijk abandoned after breaking his collarbone in a crash. Marc Soler finished outside of the time limit on stage 16, suffering with stomach illness. Rafał Majka did not start the race the following day, having torn his quadriceps following a chain slip. Their line-up was halved to a four-man class of 1998: Pogačar, Bjerg, McNulty and Marc Hirschi, limping to the finish with a bad knee.

On the road to Peyragudes on stage 17, their fight was unaffected. A heavyset star of time trials, Bjerg rode such a tempo on the second climb, the Hourquette d'Ancizan, to the point that GC contenders were in trouble, as well as Wout van Aert. McNulty was meant to go flat out for 15 minutes on the penultimate ascent, the Col de Val Louron-Azet, and his effort lasted for an hour, setting the pace for Pogačar and Vingegaard until the last kilometre of the final climb.

Pogačar completed the sterling teamwork by outsprinting the race leader at the top.

On stage 18, Pogačar threw in several more attacks to make it another duel with his fellow protagonist. Something, or someone, had to give. The man in second place pushed hard down the penultimate climb of the Col de Spandelles, Vingegaard's back wheel almost skidding out on one corner. Minutes later, Pogačar overcooked one of its bends, slipping in the roadside gravel. After his light fall, averting serious injury, Vingegaard slowed up ahead to wait for him. Sportsmanship in the heat of battle. Pogačar proffered his hand and the two shook on it.

The Dutch team made their strength in numbers count one more time. Wout van Aert dropped back from the breakaway to pace the duo, leading to Vingegaard putting 64 seconds into Pogačar on the climb to Hautacam. After the race's last mountain stage, Pogačar was sanguine. 'There couldn't be a better way to lose the Tour de France than this. I gave it all today thinking of the GC. I'll leave the race with no regrets,' he said. He finished the Tour second, 2 minutes 43 seconds down after losing 9 more seconds to his opponent on the penultimate day and its 40 km time trial.

Tour de France 2022: general classification

1. Jonas Vingegaard (Jumbo–Visma) 79 hours 33 minutes 20 seconds
2. Tadej Pogačar (UAE Team Emirates) at 2 minutes 43 seconds
3. Geraint Thomas (Ineos Grenadiers) at 7 minutes 22 seconds

Having raced with Vingegaard during his time at Jumbo–Visma, George Bennett admits his surprise at how good he became, even if there had been earlier signs of his precocity. 'We did a team Zwift during lockdown [in 2020]. We got to the top of Alpe du Zwift, it was me and him and he just absolutely smacked me in the last few hundred metres,' Bennett recalls.

Vingegaard only grew as a competitor with the yellow jersey on his shoulders. Greater self-belief was a key component of his triumph, given how anxiety had wrecked his challenge in earlier years. 'The morning of Il Lombardia [2020], the year I got second, I had to sit with him and be like "You need to finish this food, you need to eat." I don't know what changed, maybe he just grew up,' Bennett says.

'Tadej never gets nervous ... but whatever that little hurdle was for Jonas, he's clearly over it because now he is also a killer. He doesn't blink twice when it comes to a race now.' Perhaps Vingegaard finally realised how good he is.

He was different as a racer and person, the introvert to Pogačar's outgoing charmer, happier to be out of the public eye, a dyed-in-the-wool stage racer rather than being a man for all seasons.

A sport with a history of compelling rivalries – Coppi and Bartali, Anquetil and Poulidor, Merckx and Ocaña, Armstrong and Ullrich – had its latest humdinger. Pogačar and Vingegaard, UAE and Jumbo, a pair of arch rivals and superteams to push one another and lift their achievements even higher.

In defeat, Pogačar's popularity was boosted. 'I felt more love from the public than after my two Tour victories,' he told *L'Équipe* in October 2022. Because it is not just familiarity, but extended superiority which often breeds contempt from fans. As the balance of Grand Tour power shifted, he showed that he could fight a losing battle magnificently and take defeat magnanimously. A little vulnerability went a long way.

It was a reminder for the watching world, as well as Pogačar himself, that winning the Tour was far from a guarantee. This was the biggest setback of his fledgling career, and a rite of passage.

Pogačar could now let his hair down. A fellow 2022 Tour de France finisher from a rival team, who prefers to remain anonymous, remembers seeing him in Le Duplex, a nightclub that is the go-to Parisian spot for the entire race circus. Just hours after the twilight conclusion on the Champs-Élysées, and under the flashing strobe lights of this subterranean, 2.4-star Google-rated establishment, Pogačar looked like any other 23-year-old partygoer.

'He was there with his Adidas trousers on, a plain white T-shirt and a drawstring bag,' says the pro. 'The most unassuming image of one of the greatest riders there's ever been. And he just looked like a little schoolboy, lost.'

This is not meant to be a pitiful image; the professional cyclist is laughing as he tells the story. 'I think that's one of the reasons he's so successful, it appears he doesn't really think about it too much: he lives quite a simple life – relative to his stature, how great a bike rider he is.'

In various interviews that autumn, Pogačar framed second place as 'like a victory' or indicated he didn't take it as a defeat (he had won three stages, he pointed out). He spoke of lessons gained and a new hunger, a new motivation driving him forward.

His soigneur Joseba Elguezabal believed he emerged mentally stronger from the defeat. 'I see him with a greater capacity to listen now,' he told the *Escapa* podcast in October 2022. 'He's been winning since the beginning of his career and eventually you get into a bubble where only winning matters. Even within the team, we had talked about it with Matxin: we knew that the day he didn't win would be tough and we would have to be prepared. But I've seen a lot of maturity in him, [he is] calmer, reflecting on what happened and eager to continue growing.'

The performance gave Pogačar a reality check and a chance to interrogate what he or the team could improve. Some insiders believe that UAE Team Emirates were not fully maximising his potential. 'He didn't win the Tour [in 2022], but I really felt like this guy was already the best, the most complete. And he was at 80 per cent,' his 2022 Tour teammate George Bennett says.

'I feel like I'm a rider turning over a lot of stones: altitude, heat [work], diet, training. You know what I mean? There are riders who are really living and breathing it. I felt like: yeah, he loved it, he trained really hard, but he never did VO_2 [max] efforts, he just rode round zone 2 twatting it all day and occasionally some 15-minute efforts.'

That is a nod to his training methodology under coach Iñigo San Millán. A switch of trainer and approach from Javier Sola made a significant difference, but that did not come until November 2023.

Bennett believes there was weight Pogačar could lose and 'so many things' he could improve. 'It was so crazy to see that he could live such a chilled life, he didn't push the envelope all the time and he was *that* good. Knowing this guy has got so much potential when he starts living like Jonas [Vingegaard] – and obviously now, that's happened,' Bennett says. 'It's more just a mindset of 0.1 percenters, which wasn't around then [for him]. He was essentially a kid that just loved riding bikes with his mates and loved racing. It was all fun and games as opposed to live or die by this.'

Joining UAE Team Emirates at the end of 2021 after seven years on Jumbo–Visma and its different incarnations, Bennett had seen the Dutch outfit grow and develop from a 'shit' mid-table team to one of the sport's super-squads first-hand. So, in terms of science, aerodynamics and the people at UAE Team Emirates, what stood out as special or cutting-edge to him?

'I was underwhelmed in some ways,' Bennett says. 'They had some really great people, like my coach Kevin Poulton, but they weren't the people with the power, making decisions. It wasn't rivalling Jumbo for the science, unfortunately.'

'It was good,' he qualifies. 'They were able to develop a good [Colnago] TT bike which they didn't have before. But ultimately, Jumbo were ahead of them. And coming to Israel-Premier Tech [in 2024], Israel is ahead of them as well in that regard.'

Another former UAE rider, Sven Erik Byström, is also unsure whether the team examined the minutiae before Pogačar finished as runner-up.

'I left the team [before 2022], so I can't say I know everything. But I felt up to that point, Tadej was just this greatest talent ever who won these races. It wasn't really because he had the best nutrition, best equipment or whatever. But when he got second, then they had to look into every small little detail to change that.'

Becoming the sport's richest team in the world with an estimated budget of €50 million, UAE Team Emirates could keep investing in quality on and off the bike to address their deficit. They notably added stage race contender Adam Yates, experienced Belgian road captain Tim Wellens and climber Felix Großschartner during the winter of 2022.

This was about much more than just the Tour, outshining Jumbo–Visma and procuring stellar support for Pogačar. Having a formidable roster, blending youth and experience – riders like Yates and young talent João Almeida would feasibly lead any other team – also put them further up the path to being the sport's leading team. Top helpers would have their own opportunities to co-lead and win other races while committing wholeheartedly to 'the Boss', as Yates has taken to calling Pogačar, in his objectives.

Often employed in the mountain train, riding at 6.5 watts per kilo for as long as possible, Bennett enjoyed the team atmosphere and being a *domestique* for Pogačar. 'He's charming, he's not an asshole. You're prepared to hurt yourself for a guy like him,' Bennett says.

However, such was Pogačar's strength, bike-handling ability and positional nous, Bennett could feel superfluous at times. 'It got to the point with Tadej that he wins so much, sometimes I felt like he could have won with me or without me as a helper. And I loved riding for Tadej, he's a great guy, a mate. But did he need me? Probably not,' Bennett says, with a little laugh. The New Zealander left the team at the end of 2023.

That same year, there was another more consequential departure. Allan Peiper had stepped back from the team in 2021 as he underwent further treatment for prostate cancer. In January 2023, the man that Pogačar viewed as a mentor and wise head returned briefly as a race analyst, but he and UAE Team Emirates could not agree on terms and his role was brought to a close. Afterwards, Pogačar called it a pity, suggesting that 'he would still be an asset for the team'. The pair still exchange occasional messages with each other, more about life than cycling.

'They were super close. I fully believe Tadej trusted him 100 per cent,' John Wakefield says. 'Allan brought incredible stuff. I don't think I'd be where I am today knowledge-wise if it wasn't for Allan. For me, there was a big gap left when he left the team. A big part of me left when he did . . . it definitely left a hole in the team. And if it left what it did for me, I feel it left similar for Tadej.'

Wakefield left for Bora–Hansgrohe at the end of 2022, sensing a plateau in the team's performance. 'Nobody is perfect. I don't know if this is right to say, because they are winning [now] but when they got really good and the level was high, it was [a case of] "OK. This is what we're doing, we just keep doing it."

'I don't think it's like that now, but in my last year [2022], that was also one of the reasons I felt I needed to move because I kind of felt a bit stagnant . . . the team got better, better, better every year. And then I felt like we got to a point where it kind of stayed the same.'

The statistics do not necessarily bear that out – UAE Team Emirates have won more races every season inclusive from 2021 through to 2025.

Wakefield also saw a marked change in Pogačar: still chilled and chirpy, but no longer the callow neo-pro he had first encountered four years earlier: 'He became more of a leader, he knew what he wanted, definitely on a big maturity progression. Physiologically, I won't say there was a big jump but he had improved.'

Pogačar remains someone who wants everyone around him to thrive and helps to naturally build a team around him. 'He never changed as a person,' Wakefield says. 'You'd be at a training camp, eating breakfast alone at a table, just because. He comes down, sees that you're there alone and he'll sit and talk with you.

'It's almost like "This person is alone, let me keep him company." Then when someone [that I know] comes down and sits with me, then he knows that it's fine and he leaves. That says a lot about the guy's character.'

▶ Pogačar has become modern cycling's centre of attention with his aggressive style of racing. His success has brought him fame and fortune, though they come with their own pros, cons and commitments.

13

THE POGAČAR EFFECT

January 2024

Dusk is falling across the dark curves of the Al Hudayriat Island cycle circuit, and so are Tadej Pogačar's eyelids.

Clad in black jeans and white-collared team-issue shirt, the toast of UAE Team Emirates has flown into balmy Abu Dhabi as the surprise guest at the launch of the 2024 eSports World Championships.

Pogačar watches from the front row as an eight-person panel, including UCI president David Lappartient, UAE Team Emirates president Matar Suhail Al Yabhouni Al Dhaheri and team principal Mauro Gianetti speak for almost 40 minutes about the October event. The racing will take place using the MyWhoosh platform – and that's why Pogačar is here, as the UAE-based indoor cycling app is a prominent sponsor.

If he is tired, it is forgivable: he has flown straight from a Spanish training camp, hopping a couple of time zones, and had already been for a bike ride that afternoon. Lappartient chatted with him and took a selfie video as they rode together on the front, looking across at the city's glinting skyscrapers.

On their wheel is a 40-strong peloton of fans, MyWhoosh employees and media, keen to get close enough for a photo without getting in the way. However fatigued he is, the playful side remains too. During a pause, Pogačar taps one kid's left shoulder, then moves to his right. As the boy looks over the wrong flank, he rolls off with a wave.

Duty calls. After the press conference winds down, he is on his feet, posing for photographs with luminaries and selfies with kids from the Abu Dhabi Cycling Club. He spends 10 minutes answering questions from a huddle of journalists about everything from his season goals to 'Tadej, are you the cycling Instagram meme lord?'

This is a sponsorship obligation for Pogačar. MyWhoosh are one of his personal sponsors, as well as being a main backer of his squad. The *Gazzetta dello Sport* estimated that Pogačar earned €2 million from nine personal partnerships in the 2025 season, and that's on top of his estimated €8 million annual contract from UAE Team Emirates-XRG.

His agent, Alex Carera, is at the centre of his business empire, deciding which brands he partners with and carefully managing his schedule. The Italian has had a long-term plan for Pogačar since his early days as a pro. 'There are three important steps,' he told me in 2021. 'He's already done number one: become a champion in his sport. Number two: become famous in general, worldwide sport. And number three, transcend sport.' Carera is clear that cycling comes first: exceptional performances and greater longevity are enabled by handling everything off it with sufficient care.

It's a fragile balance. Away from the races and training camps, which run to a more defined schedule, life comes at Pogačar faster than a speeding peloton. His week can involve a flying visit to the UAE, photo shoots for a Tuš supermarket sandwich brand, an appearance for the Slovenia Tourism Board as an official ambassador, collecting a prize at an award ceremony, appearing in one of his favourite Slovenian rapper's music videos, even posing for a sponsor's bee products.

Being the best means constantly being busy, requiring a different stamina to racing the *bergs* of Flanders full-pelt. In the relative blink of an eye, Pogačar's reality has transformed: the young man who would play League of Legends into the evening, and found his first post-race press conference as Tour leader 'too big', now pedals up the Nice foothills with Formula 1 stars Carlos Sainz and Ollie Bearman or meets Slovenia's president in Congress Square, cheered on by thousands of compatriots celebrating his latest win.

Especially at bike events, Pogačar is the centre of attention, serenaded by cries of 'Pogi! Pogi! Pogi!' and surrounded by a moving sea of extended mobile phones. He is grateful for his fans and often goes out of his way to acquiesce to the requests of children in the crowd. Of course, there are limits to his time and patience: sometimes the selfies get too much for him; he doesn't always like doing photo shoots; and he can find the daily routine of post-race media interviews and press conferences exhausting.

Pogačar does not get to have bad days publicly – at least, not without creating headlines. During his media dealings, he has to think carefully about what he is saying and do it with a patient smile on his face. Then, there is the drifting flotsam and jetsam of social media opinions.

Being under the microscope is 'difficult. It was more difficult in the past,' Pogačar said ahead of the 2025 Tour de France. 'People always have opinions, no matter what you say, no matter what you do. You can never please everyone. Since I stopped following a lot of media and stopped being too much on social media, not paying too much attention to that, my life's been better.'

Urška is his calm in the craziness, the integral pillar in his life. Together, they enjoy the highs and commiserate over lows; together, they go training or on coffee rides. If talk ever turns to sport psychologists, Pogačar shrugs: well, he has Urška as his mental support – and life partner. They got engaged in September 2021.

They have a special understanding of each other's personalities and lives, as well as the sometimes eccentric demands of professional cycling. Try explaining three weeks away at an altitude training camp or sweating in a scalding bath for 40 minutes as heat work to a partner with a regular office job.

As a person, Pogačar is more spontaneous and adaptable; Urška sees herself as a perfectionist more prone to worry. They complement each other: she helps him with nutrition and training advice, and is also an excellent cook. On some training rides, she even checks his blood lactate values with a personal meter, pricking his earlobe and reporting back to the coach to help fine-tune the next sessions.

Behind closed doors together, he can be his most normal, mundane self, watching Netflix or putting together carbonara for dinner. Cooking a relaxed meal for each other is a relative luxury in what is a long-distance relationship for much of the cycling season – populated by weeks on end of being apart in different hotels and countries, snatching minutes on video call during massages, or rushed moments wishing each other good luck at starts. Their teams regularly let them attend respective summer training camps, affording a little more in-person time. Otherwise, during busy months or Grand Tours, they can count the days spent together on one hand. Pogačar regards not seeing Urška and family as the biggest downside of his chosen career.

After finishing a race, it is a time trial to get to his phone and message Urška. If she is competing at the same time, he will ask Luke Maguire or a soigneur about her performance or even be told about it over race radio mid-event. Occasionally, it is a treat for Pogačar to watch her race while he warms down or on the team bus.

On the rare occasions when Urška is present and emerges from the crush of media, cameramen and race officials post-race – usually the only woman there – Pogačar's body language visibly softens. In their regard and embrace, there is an unspoken, private understanding of what they have been through together. 'Urška is a really, really big part of my life. She wouldn't say [it], she sacrifices so much more than she would admit for my career. And I'm so happy that I have a person like her next to me,' he told Eurosport after the 2024 World Championships, voice wavering and close to tears.

When Pogačar can reciprocate, he does. He has been at numerous leading Women's WorldTour races; if he had carte blanche, he'd probably get in a campervan and follow the women's Giro for a week. At the 2025 Women's Tour de Romandie, he rode his bike around, supporting Žigart and wearing a bespoke white jersey emblazoned across the front with upper-case red letters: 'Please do not disturb', and a circled camera logo with a red cross through it on the sleeves – sending an apparent message about how often he is solicited.

After all, fans stop him in the supermarket aisle and on the street. 'Sometimes you are just walking quietly and you see someone discreetly taking pictures next to you,' Urška told *Le Parisien* in 2022. 'You know you can't say anything because it would give a bad image. But at the same time I just want to be with him for five minutes.'

The demands can come from unexpected sources. Pogačar has been stopped while driving by police officers. Rather than apprehending him for any perceived offence, they just wanted a few autographs.

It is not difficult to see why Pogačar – whose Instagram following is larger than his home country's population – so readily captures the imagination. Not just because he's the best, but because of the entertaining, happy-go-lucky way he goes about it.

This Gen Z champion posts regularly on social media; whether it's an insight into his life, plugging a sponsor partnership or simply lip-syncing to Borat, the king of the cycling castle uses it more than most other sports-leading athletes. It makes him more relatable, a vehicle for his natural sense of humour.

During the 2023 Tour de France, a 24-second video on Pogačar's Instagram page of him riding along on a rest day and munching a baguette from his jersey back pocket, set to Plastic Bertrand's 'Ça Plane Pour Moi', got 450,000 likes. The next day, he uploaded a video of himself doing a backflip into a swimming pool. It's a good metaphor for his approach to life – jumping straight in with a splash, not taking it too seriously.

Pogačar has regularly called cycling 'a game', and his playfulness is one of his biggest draws. His *joie de vivre* seems as untameable as the tufts of hair standing to attention through his helmet, which have become his calling card, even if he must conceal much of the stress and strain publicly. Winning in elite sport is a serious business, of selfishness and suffering; he chooses to accentuate the lighter side. As he has improved, the expectations on Pogačar have narrowed to a point where anything other than a victory in an achievable goal is a disappointment.

'I know what he has to sacrifice for it. Getting to the top is one thing. Staying at the top is much harder. Everyone looks at you and expects only the best. You should not underestimate that pressure,' Urška said in 2025.

A leading rider has to keep doing the same work and training that got them to the top in the first place – or even more of the same – just in order to stay there, at a time when the demands have multiplied, perhaps even five-fold. Pogačar has learned to be more discerning with those surrounding him.

'When he was no-one, no-one wanted to support him,' Andrej Hauptman says. 'He remembers who his friends were before. Now, he has a lot of "friends,"' he says, emphasising the word. 'It's difficult because you never know why someone is around you. Maybe because he is really good [at cycling]? Everyone has an interest to be your friend.'

On his rare returns to Slovenia, he sometimes stays with the Hauptman family in the countryside, happy to cook pasta and stay down to earth. 'For him, it's best when nobody bothers him at the restaurant or he's with friends from the past. He's normal because he's still young. This is the goal: to be as simple as possible,' Hauptman says.

Pogačar feels he can channel his status and privilege into positive social change. His Tadej Pogačar Foundation spreads awareness and raises money for charity with events, auctions, donations and a portion of his merchandise sales. He has also done fundraising work for tech company Plume. 'It feels like I need to do something, not just to sit on my sofa and enjoy the success because that's not the point, because not everyone gets the same chances that I get,' he told *CyclingTips* in 2022.

Meanwhile, his Pogi Team, run by Miha Koncilija, aims to help the next wave of young cyclists in Slovenia. His old friend Blaž Debevec is also a coach there and filmed some short videos with Pogačar for their Instagram account in December 2024. Larking around at the club HQ in Vikrče, he saw the same easy-going guy he has known for over a decade. 'We had pre-written some script so that we didn't waste his time, but he just kept adding stuff, improvising all the time. It was a really nice moment to have him like this after a long time. It was just like back in the old days.'

Don't count out a venture into acting after the bike racing is done. 'He's a multi-talent: he would also be good at that kind of stuff,' Debevec says.

It would be impossible to be unchanged by the wins and wealth, but Pogi the persona and Tadej the man at the root of it are still very close together. 'He can maybe do some acting, but on the other hand, I don't think he's acting much in life,' Debevec adds. 'That's the way he is as a person, always nice. If you ask anyone who knows him personally, they will all say he's an incredibly nice person. I really laugh when I maybe see some comments under some [online] posts about him, writing that he's cocky and stuff like that. They just don't know him.'

While there is always another race, another goal, another sponsorship obligation to attend, having fun is what propels Pogačar forward. On training rides, he still races to be first to town signs with his friends, and meets up with Urška for coffee.

'I created my life around the bike,' Pogačar said in 2025 after winning a Tour de France stage on Peyragudes. 'I found my closest friends on the bike, my fiancée on the bike. So the point is that you need to enjoy the moment, enjoy the little things, not just the victories … what you're sacrificing everything for, and live in the moment.'

▶ Pogačar rarely abandons any bike race and had never experienced a broken bone as a professional cyclist – until the spring of 2023, when he had to overcome a new challenge.

14

THE FALL

2023 Tour de France, Col de la Loze

The race radio crackles into life. 'I'm gone. I'm dead,' Pogačar says.

After 16 days of fierce competition, his regular sparring partner Jonas Vingegaard is up the road and out of sight. Making sure of his second Tour de France victory and giving Pogačar the most emphatic defeat of his career in one fell swoop.

Dropped by the group of favourites 8 km from the top, stage 17 has become a battle between Pogačar and himself on the Col de la Loze. White jersey open, turning the pedals slowly, earpiece ripped out, he is peaky and hollow-eyed, on the limit. His body is saying stop.

As he wends his way past the Folie Douce restaurant on the last hairpin before the straight push to the top, the watching cycling fans can relate to its name: seeing Pogačar crack like this is sheer madness.

His teammate Marc Soler rides ahead of him, setting the pace and looking around at regular intervals with all the solicitousness of a mother hen for its chick. He screams at him to keep going, that he has to suffer.

When Francis Bacon said 'the greatest art always returns you to the vulnerability of the human situation', he could have been talking about professional cycling. Pogačar is a pitiable sight, getting pushes from spectators on the Col de la Loze. After the respite of a short descent, he inches up the final 300 m on the runway of Courchevel Altiport, a cruel, arrow-straight gradient of 17 per cent.

For once, Pogačar – Plan A – has been left behind. Having stayed ahead in the lead group to pursue the final spot on the podium, his super-*domestique* Adam Yates squints at the big screen beyond the finish line, joined by Rafał Majka, who had supported him on the climb's finale. Their chests heave as they catch their breath 2300 m above sea level.

They share a brief look of disbelief. Yates had expected that his leader might lose a minute, not 5 minutes 45 seconds. There are parallels to the horror written on the faces of Primož Roglič's teammates Tom Dumoulin and Wout van Aert in the 2020 Tour, watching atop La Planche des Belles Filles as the Tour win that had seemed to be in the bag fell through an unseen hole. The wheel turns quickly.

Pogačar felt like he had let his teammates down. 'I'm sorry,' he said four times to Yates after stopping beyond the finish line, the last apology a rasping whisper. His body language was defeated; shaking his head but trying to smile, he said he was 'fucked' in the post-race flash TV interview. 'If I didn't have such a great support around me, I was already thinking of losing the podium today,' he added.

He was not used to feeling these emotions: devastation, anger, guilt. From that day on, the Col de la Loze, with its cycle path road barely wider than a normal car and regular gradient changes, took on a special significance for Pogačar. The 2023 Tour's highest point became an emblem of a sporting nadir and his worst day on the bike. In that moment, it was no laughing matter, though he and teammates would later joke about Marc Soler's intense, scary eyes staring into his soul as he encouraged his forlorn leader.

His challenge to Vingegaard over, Pogačar's comeback Tour had turned into the comedown Tour. Road cycling's most complete rider was now further away than ever from winning another edition of the sport's big race.

. . . .

Pogačar could pinpoint his downfall back to the exact day, minute and geographical location – a pothole in the middle of the N826 main road outside the rural Belgian town of Bertogne.

Three months earlier, 85 km into Liège–Bastogne–Liège on 23 April, he was riding behind teammate Vegard Stake Laengen on one side of the bunch, saving energy, when Mikkel Honoré hit the crater and both his tyres exploded. The pothole threw off the Dane, Laengen moved right and as Honoré and his bike somersaulted, Pogačar braked, but had nowhere to go. Next, he was on the ground.

For a few minutes, he sat on the grassy verge. His elbows were bloodied and cut, his buttock had road rash, his right hip was sore, his wrist ached. Imbued with that pro cyclist's resilience, which would make Monty Python's Black Knight look like a quitter, Pogačar called for his Colnago and set off for a couple of hundred metres before realising he could not hold the handlebars.

The X-rays confirmed he had broken two bones in his left scaphoid. It was a sour end to the spring campaign of his wildest dreams: Pogačar had won 12 of 20 possible races leading up to cycling's oldest Monument, starting with the Jaén Paraiso Interior one-day race and three stages of the Vuelta a Andalucia, as well as the overall.

Every one-day race posed the same challenge for rivals – catch a ride on the Pogi Express and hang on for as long as possible. At the Amstel Gold Race, he first attacked with 80 km to go. He led a small group away, 30 seconds ahead of the bunch. After a slow puncture left him waiting for a bike change, he smoothly rode back to the leaders, then reduced the group to Tom Pidcock and Ben Healy before leaving them behind for a 28-km solo win. 'I'm living the dream this season,' he said after downing his half-pint of beer on the podium.

His coach Iñigo San Millán had feared he was overtraining, but realised he had simply gone up another level. He was better, bolder and seemingly more confident than ever.

'I've never seen anyone that can ride like this,' teammate Mikkel Bjerg told me for *Escape Collective*. 'He trains really, really hard but he can keep doing it for weeks on end. All big GC guys have a really good recovery [rate] and I think I just never saw anyone on this level before … and then I guess, mentally, nothing can throw him off course.

'I think he trusts a lot in his own abilities,' Bjerg adds. 'So he's not really afraid of anything. Sometimes, I can get a bit stressed, like "Ah, I really need to perform today." He's just really calm and knows if he does his best, it will be fine. Even if he doesn't win, he will have created a spectacular race and probably finish on the podium.'

Seeing Pogačar's tranquillity under pressure helps him to relax. 'Like if they lose five positions, some guys take their hands off the handlebars, try to force their way through the peloton or start to scream. Tadej never says anything [bad] to anyone, he just passes them. He has this class about him, not getting too stressed about this fight for position or the crosswinds.'

While he can exude a laissez-faire attitude, there is little left to chance in modern cycling or UAE Team Emirates' approach, and that goes for tactics too. Bjerg describes 'a constant dialogue' ahead of a race or every Grand Tour stage, with Pogačar 'vocal about what he wants and how he wants the final to be ridden'.

He likens their approach to a military mission. 'He always asks us, "What do you guys think?" And then with the plan, it is like what I can imagine happens in the army or something. There is one plan and only one goal, and everyone in the group respects that.

'That's such a special feeling because normally in a team with two or three leaders, somebody has their own ambitions … And then once Tadej wins, everybody is so happy because they all really felt part of the plan. That's what really makes it special: that he is so good that you can do your best and nine out of ten times, he wins.'

Not quite that much, but with a win ratio of over 50 per cent that spring, comparisons to Eddy Merckx were back with a vengeance. His wrist-shattering crash on the pockmarked road to Liège had robbed him of potentially doing something nobody, not even the Belgian colossus, had done: winning the Ardennes Classics trio and the Tour of Flanders in the same year.

When Pogačar crashes, the shockwaves are felt beyond sport too. The deterioration of the road was discussed in the Wallonia national government and the offending scar on the tarmac was patched-up within 48 hours.

If only Pogačar's injuries could have been mended as quickly and easily. After undergoing wrist surgery to treat his fracture, he faced a new challenge in his pro career: an injury lay-off. Fitted with a chunky cast, he could not even play his beloved video game, FIFA. He was initially worried about his chances of lining up in Bilbao for the start of the Tour de France just 10 weeks after his fall, aware that it would be a race against time to be adequately prepared.

Once in a brace, he went swimming, hiking and cross-training, running up and down the hillside steps in Monaco, as well as riding on the turbo.

'The home trainer is good, but it's not enough. He lost three weeks of training and he could only do three good weeks in June,' his coach San Millán told *L'Équipe*.

Getting back on the road earlier than the doctor's orders, Pogačar went to altitude at Sierra Nevada. He enjoyed a successful return to racing, winning Slovenian national titles in the road race and time trial in mid-June. Even so, he started his fourth Tour de France in an unfamiliar position – as an underdog unsure of his form, with nothing to lose.

Jumbo–Visma had no desire to let their biggest rival settle back into action, and Pogačar and Vingegaard were trading attacks on the lumpy opening stages in the Basque Country. Into the Pyrenees, the Tour's defending champion left Pogačar behind on the Col de Marie-Blanque, putting 1 minute 4 seconds into him by the finish of stage 5 in Laruns. It was a blow to his challenge, but Pogačar kept his perspective after hearing that Urška had been concussed. 'I'm more sad to hear my girlfriend crashed in the Giro, that's a bit more sad than losing 50 seconds [64 seconds] to Jonas,' he said.

Smelling blood, the Dutch kings of calculation wanted to finish Pogačar off early and wrench control of the race. The next day, the team rode hard on the penultimate climb of the day, the Col du Tourmalet. Vingegaard attacked with Pogačar in his slipstream.

Wout van Aert, an early breakaway member, was there to set the pace when they reached him, but the familiar strategic ruse had a surprising ending. As a fan wearing polka dots and wielding a red flare ran alongside the two contenders midway up the finishing climb of Cauterets-Cambesque, the Slovenian showed his sporting pyrotechnics, getting out of the saddle, and accelerating past Vingegaard. The Dane tried to follow, but a couple of seconds turned into 24 seconds by the finish. Ever the showman, Pogačar bowed as he crossed the line by way of victory celebration. 'You can never underestimate him,' Jumbo–Visma *directeur sportif* Arthur van Dongen muttered in the team car behind, filmed in Amazon Prime's *All-In* documentary on the Tour with the Dutch squad.

Pogačar and Vingegaard were already in a league of their own, as incumbent yellow jersey Jai Hindley 'got his ass handed to him', in his own words, finishing among the closest rivals over two and a half minutes down.

The race's opening fortnight was the Vingegaard-Pogačar duel at its best, constantly leaving spectators – and likely both the protagonists themselves – guessing at who was stronger.

Jumbo–Visma continued to set a hard tempo with their dream team, aiming for death by a thousand cuts, trying to whittle away at Pogačar's explosivity and fatigue him. On stage 9, finishing on the Puy de Dôme, Vingegaard had one of the best days of his career, breaking some of his power records, and yet he still lost eight seconds to Pogačar. Five stages later on the Col de Joux Plane, Vingegaard fought back after being dropped and outsprinted Pogačar for eight bonus seconds on the climb before a 12-km descent to the finish in Morzine.

Exchanging cordial fist bumps on the start line, and metaphorical fisticuffs on the race's hardest mountains, the pair are not close friends who send each other messages or train together, as Pogačar has done with Mathieu van der Poel. There is too much at stake in their Tour exchanges to drop their guards when racing one another so intensely year in, year out.

The enterprising way Pogačar raced made it easy for spectators to forget his recent adversity. Finding it difficult to fully bend his wrist, he had ridden with a carbon brace until the Slovenian national championships and was still secretly wearing it at nights during the race's first week. 'It was a big issue. I was not ready physically and mentally for the Tour,' Pogačar reflected a year later, wondering whether he had overtrained in the rush to be ready.

The race entered its final week on a knife-edge. Ten seconds separated *maillot jaune* Vingegaard and Pogačar, and it looked like every single one might count.

The stage 16 time trial between Passy and Combloux, concluding with the 6.3-km Côte de Domancy, pried open this closed Tour. The outcome beggared belief, as Vingegaard beat Pogačar into second place by 1 minute 38 seconds and put 2 minutes 51 seconds into Wout van Aert in third. It was a rout; Jumbo–Visma staff members were high-fiving and hugging by their team van afterwards.

Having started the time trial two minutes behind Pogačar and glimpsed his following team car near the finish, Vingegaard was shocked to be so far ahead. 'It was one of my best days on the bike ever. I think at one point I started doubting my power meter because it was showing so high a number,' he said afterwards.

Pogačar's decision to change from his TT bike to his lighter road bike for the punishing climb added a few more seconds to his deficit, but it would not have changed the result.

An image behind the podium taken by leading cycling photographer Pauline Ballet captured the mood: Vingegaard on his feet, signing yellow jerseys with Pogačar sat behind him, his elbows bent and resting on his thighs. Slightly turned away, he is lost in thought, a despondent expression on his lips. 'It's normally the other way round,' his 2023 Tour teammate Matteo Trentin says. 'It doesn't really happen, to have this kind of bad day – which wasn't a bad day, because he was second … that's also part of growing up. I think his TT stepping up is 99.9 per cent because of that smashing he got in the TT by Vingegaard. He is not too used to getting smashed like that and he doesn't like it. He went more into TT stuff straight away at the end of the Tour and you can see the results.'

The beating was a hint of the impending capitulation. Pogačar had a cold sore on his lip, a physical sign of a tired body in overdrive.

'People close to me already said after the Joux Plane and the Grand Colombier [at the end of the second week] that I didn't look really good,' Pogačar explained later.

There were other omens that hinted he was not on song: on stage 17 the next day, Pogačar had crashed on the day's first climb, the Col des Saisies, bloodying his knee and right elbow. He stopped short of using this as an excuse later, but his team rode defensively all day.

It was a day to fear, containing over 5000 m of climbing, concluding with the *hors catégorie* 28-km Col de la Loze and a finish at Courchevel – a day too far for Pogačar's challenge.

With 9 km of the Col de la Loze left – its steepest parts still to come – the pallid Pogačar dropped back, finishing a distant 22nd. Vingegaard attacked on the climb's upper reaches, putting 5 minutes 45 seconds into his adversary, though he could not catch breakaway stage winner Felix Gall.

Why, then, did Pogačar lose so much time? Jumbo–Visma's relentless tempo had paid off, believing the high altitude and long climbs en route would favour Vingegaard. There was also a hint of overfuelling: UAE Team Emirates nutritionist Gorka Prieto-Bellver later suggested Pogačar's stomach had shut down. His body could not process everything he took in. Experiencing the sensation that none of the energy food or drink he consumed went into his legs, Pogačar felt empty at the foot of the Col de la Loze.

Another reason was his lack of consistent training. He had missed a crucial May block of sessions on the road. Pogačar could deliver his best power and numbers for only two and a half weeks, not the whole shebang.

A few champions never recover from such a pasting. Taken in conjunction with Vingegaard's Col du Granon coup in the 2022 Tour, it also gave the impression that Pogačar cracking is as spectacular as Pogačar winning: he loses by minutes, not mere seconds.

Pogačar was struck by the sadness of those close to him after stage 17. Having left the Tour that morning, Urška was considering returning to pick him up and take him home. His soigneur was crying, his father's stomach was in knots as they embraced at the finish. 'Tadej told us he was OK. He was comforting us, not us comforting him,' Mirko Pogačar said at that year's Slovenian Athlete of the Year ceremony, as reported by Slovenian website *Aleteia.*

His teammates tried to lift his spirits. 'Of course he was disappointed, as is normal,' Matteo Trentin says. 'But by the time we came in the team bus, it was me and Rafał Majka telling him: "Tadej, we're like this every single day. And most of the time, it's because of you. So welcome to our world – normal people feel like this normally in a Grand Tour. We don't attack up every climb, we just get dropped. Now you know how we feel." We just kidded and laughed [about it].

'Especially when somebody shows he's stronger than you,' Trentin adds. 'He didn't make any mistakes. And he was coming with a wrist injury behind him. At the end of the day, the sadness didn't last very long.'

There were reasons to be cheerful. UAE Team Emirates had enjoyed one of their best Tours as a team, Adam Yates spending four days in the *maillot jaune* after winning the opening stage. (Pogačar punched the air crossing the line in third place, celebrating his teammate's success as if it were his own.) The Briton went on to finish third in Paris, meaning that the squad achieved the rare feat of having two riders on the podium.

After stage 20, when asked during a TV interview for his best memory from the 2023 Tour de France, Pogačar replied that it was the atmosphere in the team bus, where he and his teammates would shoot the breeze on the way to the team hotel or have a dance to high-tempo tunes while getting ready to race.

When Pogačar is down, it is never for long. On stage 20, the race's final mountain-stage finishing on the climb of Le Markstein in the Vosges, he outsprinted Gall and Vingegaard for a stage victory that left him visibly relieved, pumping his fists in the air. 'All you want to do is to feel good, and it was pretty shit when I didn't feel good. Today I was feeling like myself again. That's why I have my smile back,' he said afterwards. It was far from Pogačar's most emphatic victory, but to strike back in that fashion after such a profound setback makes it one of the most underrated triumphs of his career.

His spirit as an inveterate racer was unaffected. Even on the cobblestones of the Champs-Élysées a day later, Pogačar went up the road in a short break, policed by Vingegaard's teammate Nathan van Hooydonck. Such was his strength, the Dutchman admitted he only had the power to come past and help him to set the pace once, riding 432 watts for 11 minutes.

Another lost Tour – the only one of Pogačar's career where he did not wear the yellow jersey – did not equate to a bad season, but the Tour score between him and Vingegaard now stood at 2-2.

'I have huge respect towards him and I think we have a good future together. A-ha, now I feel like we're a couple,' he said to laughter in the press tent. 'In the future, we will still battle it out.'

Pogačar could crack a joke, but the defeat was a source of frustration and anxiety. He was starting to feel the passing of time, aware that he would stand on the podium in Paris to take the best young rider's jersey for the last time, given his age would make him ineligible in 2024. 'Then I'm not a young kid any more,' he said.

Tour de France 2023: general classification

1. Jonas Vingegaard (Jumbo–Visma) 82 hours 5 minutes 42 seconds
2. Tadej Pogačar (UAE Team Emirates) at 7 minutes 29 seconds
3. Adam Yates (UAE Team Emirates) at 10 minutes 56 seconds

▶ A sporting career at the very top does not get better by chance, it gets better by change. As Pogačar headed into the 2024 season, he focused on maximising every little possible gain like never before.

15

LIMITLESS

2023 and early 2024

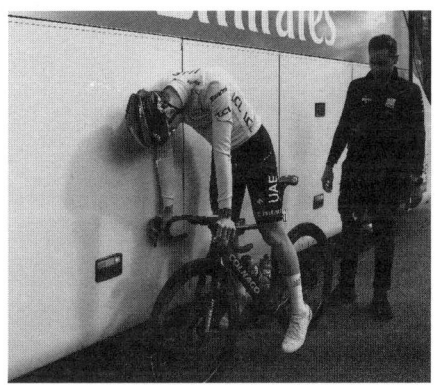

Having the capacity and hunger to win almost any top-level race between February and October, regardless of its route profile, can be a good thing and a bad thing. For Tadej Pogačar, there is always the temptation of one more victory to chase. But how much is too much?

At the 2023 World Championships in Glasgow, only two weeks after the Tour de France finish, he found the answer. Finishing third on an explosive road race course to winner Mathieu van der Poel, he took post-race TV interviews in a chair, later describing his tiredness level as '10 out of 10'.

Days later, Pogačar finished 21st in the time trial, 3 minutes 5 seconds down on champion Remco Evenepoel, his lowest one-day race result of the entire season. 'Maybe it's just too much for my body going full gas all year. Today, I probably paid the price,' he told Eurosport.

Looking washed out, with bags under his eyes, he was a man in need of a break.

The toll of a long 2023 season was clearest at Il Lombardia, his last race. Used to making a clean break with one attack, he made his move on the Passo di Ganda and was followed by four rivals. Showing his bike-handling skills, he improvised and made the winning gap on the descent instead, seizing the moment.

Thirty kilometres from the finish, Pogačar suffered cramps in both thighs, having to push through, 'punching the shit' out of it and with the help of a vinegar and salt drink. His 17th win of the year, more than any other rider in the men's sport, yielded 800 important UCI ranking points, helping to ensure UAE Team Emirates stayed ahead of Jumbo–Visma in the Road World rankings. Five years earlier, Gianetti and Fernández Matxin had first outlined their goal of being the number one team in the world, which became a driving force. Now, they had done it. It was not just the Pogačar show; 17 different riders on the team also won races.

There was no resting on laurels for 2024. By the time their first camp of the new season in Abu Dhabi rolled around, their talisman had already told the team management of his desire to race the Giro d'Italia. 'When I proposed this, they immediately said yes ... I could feel they also want me to try something else, not to repeat the same every year,' Pogačar said at a press conference in December 2023.

It was the first part of his bid for cycling's 'triple crown'. Only Eddy Merckx and Stephen Roche had won the Giro, Tour and a World Championships in the same year, achieving it in 1974 and 1987 respectively.

The challenge of racing for Grand Tour wins in May and July, then competing for a rainbow jersey on a hilly course around Zürich in late September, meant exercising more restraint. His spring calendar was pared back: there would be no UAE Tour (or January altitude training camp before it), no Tour of Flanders, Flèche Wallonne or Amstel Gold Race title defences, which meant missing out on several of the races where he has the most fun.

Less could be more. With only Strade Bianche, the Volta a Catalunya, Milan–San Remo and Liège–Bastogne–Liège on his schedule before the Giro d'Italia, Pogačar felt he could be excited for each race separately.

Just as his schedule underwent its most drastic overhaul since he turned professional, so did his training sessions. Iñigo San Millán moved to leading Spanish football team Athletic Club to head their high-performance department. Pogačar was ready to try something new.

'We had a good relationship, his training was super good for me, but maybe sometimes you need a change of pace, different stuff, a different style of training,' he said in May 2024. 'After five years or so with Iñigo, it was a little bit enough of the same training.'

One of five trainers divided around the team's 30 riders, his new coach Javier Sola discovered he would be tasked with helping to improve Pogačar's game only when his name appeared on the list given to him by Matxin, like any other rider. It would be a step up. He had previously worked with the likes of Domen Novak, Vegard Stake Laengen and Sjoerd Bax after joining the team at the end of 2022.

Bax describes him as kind, friendly, calm and patient. 'That's also what you need as a rider because sometimes you're doubting yourself and then you don't need someone who makes you stress even more,' he says.

As well as monitoring sessions in real time with TrainingPeaks software, Sola was in regular communication with Bax, to hear his opinion and what could be tweaked. 'Every day was funny – directly after the ride uploaded, within five minutes, you always got a text on WhatsApp: "How are you, man?" *Every* day, sometimes even if it was just a normal one-hour ride,' Bax says. Sola also regularly attended the year's key training camps to work together in person and measure blood lactate.

A tall Seville native with a side parting, Sola is a discreet figure – besides, when it comes to discussing the training which sharpened Pogačar's edge, it behoves him to be circumspect.

However, in a rare interview, Sola recognised Pogačar's 'supernatural' qualities. 'He's exceptional, but what's even more striking to me is how quickly he gets in shape,' he told *El País*. 'The numbers – watts, VO_2 max, lactate [threshold] – are spectacular, yes, but you see that he's been training for four weeks and you go, wow this guy improves faster than the others. And he also assimilates nutrition better.'

Sola adapted Pogačar's training, adding more variety and interval work. His zone 2 sessions included working on fatigue resistance, and doing longer tempo work (moderate-to-hard efforts, in zone 3) with a lot of VO_2 max work. While not a drastic change, it was like putting premium/super unleaded petrol in a sports car which was used to standard unleaded.

'We did zone 2 and then always 10 minutes at 6 or 7 watts per kilo, it was always a bit the same intervals,' Bax says of their old training work before Sola. 'I think with Javier Sola, he [Pogačar] trained more specifically. He also did more sprints: when I did the Classics with Pogačar [in 2023], he was three kilos heavier, focusing more on the shorter efforts. He really did more polarised training and more focus in the preparation, I think.'

Bax adds that these methods were nothing particularly special, but that Pogačar's ability to assimilate a greater training load than the average pro cyclist made him even better.

His training in the winter of 2023 incorporated more functional strength work. UAE Team Emirates head of performance Jeroen Swart and his colleagues could see deficits in his mean maximal torque (newton-metres per kilo of body mass), making it an area for small gains. Having done lots of training volume, they could work on improving it with low-cadence workouts.

Incorporating more high-intensity training work was a crucial piece of the puzzle too, helping to stimulate adaptations.

The higher the intensity of the effort, the greater use of fast-twitch muscles and subsequent burning of glycogen, with an ultimate, paradoxical benefit of increasing his muscles' glycogen stores.

'It [interval training] increases capillarisation of muscle,' Swart told *The Cycling Podcast* in 2024. 'It increases mitochondrial mass, increases lactate buffering, hydrogen buffering, increases lactate redistribution. All of those mechanisms have been hyper-stimulated by more high-intensity training together with strength training and the other methods he was already using.'

. . . .

In pursuit of maximal power and efficiency, Pogačar also switched from 170 mm cranks to 165 mm. It would make him marginally more efficient and aerodynamic, allowing him to get lower on the bike and giving him a more functional hip angle while pedalling. Though lessening the load on his leg muscles, he put in more dedicated strength work off the bike to ensure optimal physical comfort for the slightly elevated pedalling cadence caused by this change.

A professional cyclist is as finely tuned as his *avant-garde* machine: tweak one element and it can put something else out of whack. In 2023, Pogačar started working with Alexandre Baccili, a Brazilian sports physiotherapist and kinesiotherapist. Based down the road from him in Monaco, he had worked with Chris Froome on recuperation from his career-threatening 2019 crash.

He helped Pogačar in his recovery from his wrist injury as well as injury prevention. They worked on exercises for specific muscles, depending on the training he was doing. Strengthening his core and stabiliser muscles would also help Pogačar's explosivity when needed in the one-day races of spring.

More activation work, stretching and lunging with colourful body-weight bands, was incorporated into his pre-race warm-up, increasing blood flow and readying his muscles for the efforts he was about to make. He was also firing up the quads and glutes, which stabilise the hips and knees, a key part of the pedalling process.

His off-the-bike work with Baccili and team physio Victor Moreno would also complement power output and comfort in his aerodynamic position on the time-trial bike, a particular winter focus for improvement. The 1 minute 38 second time loss to Vingegaard in the Tour de France time trial to Combloux and his 21st place finish in the World Championships time trial had been eye-openers for Pogačar.

The search for aerodynamic optimisation had yielded a position that was too aggressive, leaving him unable to express his best against the clock consistently. 'Honestly, it ruined my glutes and my head, so since then, I put it a little bit less aggressive,' Pogačar said in May 2024 at the Giro d'Italia. 'I worked on my physique, it's improving. Every training that I do, it's better; I'm really satisfied with the direction and the improvement of my body, my position, my legs, my motivation.'

In the ongoing quest for optimal CdA, they had examined narrowing his cockpit and riding a smaller frame, going from 50 cm to 48.5 cm, and studied his position in the bunch in relation to slipstreaming, how many watts he was using and the energy he was expending. (The team even gamified that on a couple of quieter 2023 Tour de France stages, seeing which rider could spend the lowest kJ/watts per kilo, ie. race as efficiently as possible.)

Pogačar might win some races by a couple of minutes, but that does not mean skimping on the milligrammes to be saved and microseconds to be won.

At their January camp, UAE Team Emirates made their regular pilgrimage to the Velodrome Luis Puig in Valencia, examining different stem tilt and handlebar angles and discovering how Pogačar performed with different bikes, components and positions. Biomechanist David Herrero had been to the UK's Silverstone Performance Hub the previous year to test helmets, bikes, wheels and apparel.

Going to the limits of the UCI rules, Pogačar also had an aerodynamic time-trial base layer just 1 mm thick, fitting around the arms, shoulder and back. The garment was designed to redirect airflow, giving continuity and avoiding stagnancy at the back, helping CdA.

Pogačar even had different pairs of socks, made of breathable material to reduce wake and lower leg drag in different ways.

The team's eagle-eyed focus on equipment quality was a paradigm shift from when he joined in 2019.

'Six years ago, it was totally different. If I compare this year to my first year at the team, it was almost amateur,' Pogačar said in 2024. 'Back then, I thought everything was professional, but we moved on really fast. Every team pushes each other to reach new limits with technology, with nutrition, with training plans, with altitude camps. Especially Visma and UAE, Ineos, Lidl–Trek and Quick-Step.

'The bikes are also so much faster, especially the tyres,' he added. 'The tyres make the biggest difference from what we had six years ago.'

The team had moved from Campagnolo to Shimano groupsets in 2023, also partnering with Enve wheels and Continental tyres. He had a bespoke Prologo saddle and was racing Colnago's top-range V4Rs. Pogačar also used a bespoke 55-tooth chainring from Carbon-Ti, designed especially for him, at Milan–San Remo and Liège–Bastogne–Liège in 2024. Every aspect of performance was focused on precision and quality.

Internally, the team's ability to monitor riders and prevent overtraining helped to improve them too. Jeroen Swart considers this the biggest change he has seen during his time on the team.

'They were missing that optimal cycle between training and recovery, adaptation and improving,' Swart told *Bicycling* in 2025. 'Many of them weren't improving; and some were even going backwards, because they were getting progressively fatigued throughout the season.'

Another hint of weakness from previous Tours was performance loss in intense heat and at altitude: the Col de la Loze and Col du Granon performances came on scorching days – around 35°C in the valley. Pogačar himself felt that he had struggled when it was very hot.

He did heat training, having hot baths or riding on the indoor trainer in the sauna to replicate temperatures of 40°C. In 2024, Pogačar raced regularly with a sensor from Swiss brand CORE to continuously measure core body temperature and regulate heat, helping to alert him when he was going into the red.

Pogačar knuckled down nutritionally, admitting that he had taken time to learn to stick to a more balanced diet and eat less at times he needed to eat less. 'When our nutritionist joined the team a year after me, it was really hard for me to follow his plan. I needed four years to start really focusing on it,' he said in mid-2024. 'It's not easy mentally to follow such nutrition.' The Snickers or Mars bars which might appear in the feed bags in his early years were far less prevalent as he got more serious. Pogačar was slightly leaner for much of the 2024 season: having not added more muscle for an intensive spring Classics programme in 2024, he turned up to the Tour at 64.5 kg, trimming 1.5 kg off his already slim frame.

Running the numbers on kilojoules expended and carbohydrates burned, team nutritionist Gorka Prieto-Bellver had developed his own app assessing what had been spent and what was needed to eat. The team chef would then cook a meal tailored for each rider's requirement.

Pogačar was also exploring mental gains. He started working with Stijn Quanten, a Belgian self-styled brain coach, in January 2024, after being introduced by friend and fellow rider Eddie Dunbar. He had worked with clients such as F1 star Sebastian Vettel, Wout van Aert and footballer Wayne Rooney.

From analysing a client's brain, Quanten gave training methods to improve performance. It is often about firing the central nervous system, intensely stimulated by pro cycling, which requires a mix of split-second decision-making, gimlet focus and reaction at high speed.

Working from a mental plan with various games and tests, Pogačar reportedly did them every single day through the winter of 2023 and into 2024, staying up until midnight sometimes. Pogačar shattered numerous records and reported exceptional performances mentally, scoring highly on the stress resistance parameter.

'Everyone can see how effortlessly he rides and lives. But no matter how funny, jovial and instinctive he comes across, there's always a plan behind it. He knows exactly what he's doing,' Quanten told *Het Nieuwsblad*.

The gains all added up: overall, Swart had identified several that winter, each of an estimated 1 per cent, but indicated they had also seen an improvement of 6–8 per cent on some metrics for Pogačar. 'That was a surprise,' he told *Bicycling*. 'You think you're at the limit, but you don't actually know where the limit is.'

Pogačar's all-round manner impressed Andrej Hauptman. 'I remember in December/January after the [2023] season, we all saw in the team, "Wow, he's still good,"' Hauptman says. 'A bit from the [training] data and especially here,' he says, tapping the side of his head with his index finger. 'His way of thinking. I cannot explain exactly how, but you know when you see someone is different, that he is more mature.

'Maybe sometimes, even if you lose the Tour, it's good for you. Every experience helps you to grow mentally. Sometimes just when you see his way of thinking or behaving [compared] to another, you see that something is changing.'

Turning up to Strade Bianche in early March, Pogačar even looked different, rocking a fresh frosted tips blonde haircut, courtesy of Urška, who normally cut his hair at home.

Pogačar had never started his season as late as he did in 2024. On a Strade Bianche route that had been extended to 215 km, he raced like a tiger unleashed from its cage.

He followed through with his pre-race tease of attacking on Monte Sante Marie, the race's longest gravel sector, with 81 km to go. There were echoes of Muhammad Ali predicting which round of the next fight would feature his knockout.

For anyone else, it would have been fanciful, borderline absurd, especially jumping away on to a long tarmac section into a headwind. According to Hauptman, the agreed plan with the team had been to attack 40 km later on the Le Tolfe sector, hoping that the team car could get behind him for the forthcoming rough road. His *directeur sportif* was nervous as he drove behind Pogačar.

'Sometimes he changes the plan,' Hauptman says. 'He always has this "feeling". Because a lot of times we can really prepare tactics, but in the end, when you come to a certain point in the race and see the situation as a rider, you see: "Wow, this is the moment to go." Tadej is really good at that.'

Pogačar was simply improvising: adapting his race to a Strade Bianche which had been unexpectedly intense, the lead group whittled down by a hard pace, hailstorm and deluge. 'I knew if I didn't make the difference there, it would be hard to get away solo,' he explained. 'It was a moment of decision, it was horrible weather and [at] the moment I decided: "Let's push it, let's see if somebody comes across or not."'

Nobody did, worn out by the race and demoralised by the premature move. As he pulled his lead out to over three minutes, Pogačar was impressively, unusually present. He waved at fans and gave a thumbs up to one spectator carrying a tray of drinks. At the top of Via Santa Caterina, he beamed for photographers. He was winning by a country mile and loving it. 'After today, I gained back all the confidence that I maybe lost after the [2023] crash,' Pogačar said in his post-race press conference. 'I got the confirmation that all is good.'

Strade Bianche 2024

1. Tadej Pogačar (UAE Team Emirates) 215 km in 5 hours 19 minutes 45 seconds
2. Toms Skujinš (Lidl–Trek) at 2 minutes 44 seconds
3. Maxim Van Gils (Lotto Dstny) at 2 minutes 47 seconds

In contrast, the rest of the bunch trailed into the Piazza del Campo, faces turned pale by the dirt of the white roads, haunted by Pogačar. He had made his rivals feel like they were backmarkers racing in the last-placed group.

'What the fuck?' said fourth-placed finisher Tom Pidcock in reaction to their drubbing. It would be a regular sentiment expressed at Pogačar's supremacy that season.

▶ Italy has played a big part in Tadej Pogačar's career. He had wanted to race the Giro d'Italia for many years. In 2024, he got his opportunity and didn't let it go to waste.

16

RETURN OF THE KING

2024

'These guys are not your friends,' Allan Peiper said to Tadej Pogačar about his rivals during the 2020 Tour. 'They are going to cut your throat whenever they have the opportunity. And you need to remember, the day when they're on their knees, that you need to do the same thing.'

The words of his battle-hardened mentor made Pogačar sit up and listen then. Four years later, he raced the entire season as if those words were imprinted on his being.

His attacks were being launched from further out, the gaps to the rest were getting bigger and Pogačar was seemingly getting even better. Those close to him could see his self-belief was back. 'He wasn't sure of himself [last year],' Urška told *Sporza* in July 2024. 'I think this is why this year they've done everything they could so that he went confident into all races, and not doubting himself.'

His rivals were the ones questioning themselves even more. There was a sense of realism – defeatism, even – settling in among them, struggling to find a way to beat him, whether in Grand Tours, one-week stage races or one-day races.

'They race so hard in that traditional pre-emptive period that nobody *can* get away. If you do, you end up getting burned out front and inevitably throwing away your own race,' Ben Healy told me ahead of the 2024 Liège–Bastogne–Liège. 'Everyone's kind of in this frame of mind: how do you beat him? And nobody wants to take that gamble.

'I think you end up racing his race,' added the Ardennes Classics contender. 'In the Classics, UAE take it up after an hour of racing and slowly grind everyone down. And then he'll attack with 50 km [to go] and if you can't follow him, that's the race over.'

In a couple of sentences, Healy had essentially predicted how the Monument would be won and lost. The Irishman, EF Education-EasyPost's breakaway specialist, was the man on Pogačar's wheel on La Redoute when he moved away. Healy, van der Poel et al. did not need to be rocket scientists to work out that Pogačar would choose to blast off, 35 km from the finish, on the race's most renowned climb; they could have done with rocket power to catch him, though.

His ride to victory finished off the job started by his teammates 230 km earlier. Every UAE teammate had his own personal finish line where his work concluded, some of them hours before the endpoint on Liège's Quai des Ardennes. They felt like the ones in control, making their own plan for how to win the race rather than strategising around other teams. 'It's strange: a lot of the time at UAE, it was textbook,' Sjoerd Bax says.

On a wintry mid-April day, Bax worked for several hours in the race's first half and beyond to keep the day's breakaway within easy reach while others ensured that Pogačar was layered up and fuelled. Into the first of the nine punchy climbs populating the last 100 km, Finn Fisher-Black, Diego Ulissi and Domen Novak took turns on the front of the bunch to set a hard tempo, hurting the legs, squeezing the pace over the top and on to the descent.

On hill after hard Belgian hill, many helpers from other teams melted away. By the time the crucial fight for position came, touching 85 km/h downhill before La Redoute, only 50 riders remained in the group. Riding like a man possessed, Novak surged forward at the climb's foot for one final effort and as he peeled off, Pogačar took flight.

While he carved out a gap, punching up the race's green, forested hills and flowing down them, the chasing pack were like punch-drunk fighters, many in survival mode after six hours of suffering, with insufficient resources or teammates left to make a dent in the deficit. UAE had numbers, with João Almeida and Marc Hirschi helping to disrupt the chase on occasion. Checkmate.

Pogačar's winning margin of 1 minute 39 seconds over Romain Bardet was the biggest in race history since Bernard Hinault's solo through the snow in 1980. It was a poignant moment, pointing to the sky with both arms as he crossed the line. He was riding for Urška's mother Darja, two years after her death.

Liège–Bastogne–Liège 2024

1. Tadej Pogačar (UAE Team Emirates) 254.5 km in 6 hours 13 minutes 48 seconds
2. Romain Bardet (Team dsm-firmenich PostNL) at 1 minute 39 seconds
3. Mathieu van der Poel (Alpecin–Deceuninck) at 2 minutes 2 seconds

Having passed every test of his spring campaign with flying colours, Pogačar's Giro d'Italia debut was long overdue: he had wanted to race it in 2020 before switching tack to the Tour. The *corsa rosa* traversed a country close to his home and his heart. He had raced, or trained on camps, over the border since his early teens. Now he was competing for an Italianate team with many Italian partners, had an Italian agent and numerous, close Italian friends and teammates.

'What can I say, they make good pasta and pizza,' he added, after winning Strade Bianche. Frankly, Pogačar was fortunate to be let into the country by border agents after joking his favourite toppings were kiwi, hot dog meat and chocolate sauce at the start of the season. At least he didn't include pineapple.

This was the moment he came full circle. Almost 10 years to the day before lining up for the start in Venaria Reale, a 15-year-old Pogačar had been part of a small group of talented Slovenian cyclists from the national youth team in Trieste, watching as Luka Mezgec sprinted to the country's first Giro stage win. This 'unforgettable moment' inspired the young dreamer, who then went around the team buses, getting water bottles from his heroes.

A decade later, he would share the bunch with the grand old man of Slovenian cycling. Shaven-headed sprinter Mezgec has seen a transformation in his compatriots' results and the wider public's attitude to the sport since 2013, when he started in the WorldTour.

In the few years that it took for Slovenia to go from being ranked 20th in the UCI's rankings to number one, drivers on the nation's roads went from giving him the middle finger to a hearty thumbs up while out training. Thanks to the Roglič and Pogačar effect, Mezgec can't get away from the previously niche sport.

'It's actually annoying. During the Tour, I open Slovenian web news and you have five articles on the first page about cycling coming up. I want to read something else during the race,' he says, laughing.

Well aware of the quicksilver nature of cycling success, Mezgec had sought out a young Pogačar in the bunch after his flying first year with UAE Team Emirates and said: 'Look, in 2014, I had quite a good season with five WorldTour wins. Man, remember this feeling when you're winning – it's so good, it can stop quite soon.' He laughs at his own words: the success has not abated for Pogačar.

'He's a killer when he needs to become a killer. Before that when there's, say, five riders left, he is a kind, little guy. But then in the end, when he needs to go, it's no mercy,' Mezgec says.

Pogačar was already putting rivals to the sword on the Giro's second day, despite a small scare. Approaching the final climb to the finish at Santuario di Oropa, he hit the deck turning a bend, caused by a front-wheel puncture. What could have been a broken collarbone ending his race and shortening his season became a forgettable footnote. Uninjured and paced back to the front by his UAE teammates, he surged out of the saddle with 4.5 km to go, shoulders and bike rocking metronomically. His success in spite of struggle was redolent of Marco Pantani, the troubled Italian hero who tore up the same road from the back of the field to first place after suffering a mechanical problem at the 1999 Giro.

Fellow contender Ben O'Connor blew up after trying to follow Pogačar's acceleration, later dubbing himself the 'dumbest' guy in the race. 'I did some pretty good numbers there, by far the best attack I've ever launched in my whole life,' the Australian said to me for *alvento* in 2024. 'I think it just showed how good "Pog" was. He still won that very clearly and impressively, but he had more impressive attacks later in the race.' Pogačar pulled on the leader's *maglia rosa* and joined the select club of cyclists who have won stages in all three Grand Tours. It was a sign of things to come.

Pogačar avoided the pitfalls dotted around the race's high mountain stages – a hectic finale into Andora off a high-speed descent, a testing day through Tuscany containing three gravel sectors, an attempt from rival teams to form echelons on a pan-flat stage. Then, there was a comprehensive post-race media protocol of interviews and a press conference which Pogačar called, in a rare public show of irascibility, 'the only exhausting part of having the pink jersey … basically needing to repeat [answers to] four questions ten times.'

Even in the heat of a Grand Tour and fighting for position, Pogačar could handle himself in the peloton. He had a team at his disposal, but he did not always need them to place himself well. 'That's the biggest thing with him,' Mezgec says. 'A lot of GC guys have whole trains on the side, taking the risk out by being in one line in the front. He's just chatting in the middle of the bunch. His bike-handling ability and skills riding in the peloton are so good as well, he can save so much energy because he can ride like that.

'You see other Grand Tour contenders and they are under stress, burning energy, trying to follow teammates' wheels, always half in the wind, just to not crash.'

On stage 7, the 40.6-km time trial between Foligno and Perugia, Pogačar beat Filippo Ganna by 16 seconds. He now had cold, hard confirmation on the results sheet that his hard work – on the track, in the wind tunnel, stretching with resistance bands, riding his TT bike on the rainy Riviera roads – was all paying off. Pogačar made particularly fearsome inroads on the climb to the finish, putting a minute into the two-time world time-trial champion Ganna to overturn the powerhouse's early virtual lead. It was the Giro stage win that gave him the most satisfaction. Given the four time trials on the 2024 Giro d'Italia and Tour routes, he wanted his aero position to be fully dialled in: he warmed down on his Colnago TT1 aero bike after numerous Giro road stages too.

By the end of the race's first week, Pogačar was already almost out of sight, over two and a half minutes ahead of closest rivals Geraint Thomas and Daniel Felipe Martínez. He was keeping observers guessing as to how he would win: 24 hours later, on Prati di Tivo, he sprinted to the stage win against his fellow GC contenders.

Cycling is both professional sport and moving society on two wheels, competitors and team managers remembering favours – and grudges – from one year or race to the next. Occasionally, the simple act of a race leader's team not chasing a breakaway hard and letting them fight out the win can go a long way. Taking every last crumb of success could harden riders against Pogačar, figures whose help he might need one day.

After three stage victories in eight days, he had some peers in the bunch asking him why he needed to go for another stage win. 'One hundred per cent some guys are annoyed,' Pogačar said about his dominance. 'But I'm racing for the team that pays me, the riders are here for me. They work their ass off just to come prepared for the Giro, they work super hard so that we can come as a group, show that we are strong and can win. If you don't win, hard work doesn't pay off.' While not here to make enemies, the idea was anathema for Pogačar: you can't expect a Real Madrid striker to miss an open goal in *El Clásico*, even if 3-0 up against Barcelona.

Mindful of the Tour ahead, Pogačar learned to make the most of the race's few less-eventful days to recoup his energies, but his racer's instinct was irrepressible. He popped up in the hectic finale of stage 9 into Naples, charging to the front to lead out Juan Sebastián Molano, who finished third, with the kind of reciprocal act of support that Grand Tour leaders rarely make for teammates.

His supremacy was confirmed when the Giro moved into the Italian Alps. On the queen stage to Livigno, Pogačar made his move with 15 km to go on the penultimate climb, the Passo di Foscagno. Aside from a half-hearted, brief acceleration from Martínez, there was not even a flicker of reaction from a rival; it was as if he was competing in a different race. Without Jonas Vingegaard, Remco Evenepoel or defending champion Primož Roglič at the Giro, he had horsepower to spare. He made up a three-minute gap to the leader Nairo Quintana, hoovering up jettisoned breakaway members like a pink Pacman in the process.

His closest challengers finished 2 minutes 50 seconds down, settling into their race for the lower podium spots. 'He's riding in a different world,' Geraint Thomas told *Cyclingnews* in Livigno. 'He could win by five minutes or a minute, our group didn't seem to be bothered. It was about racing each other.'

Pogačar followed it the next day with another victory on a rain-sodden day to Monte Pana, accelerating away in the dying stages while still seated in the saddle.

Pogačar took his sixth and final stage win on stage 20, helped by a dazzling display of teamwork. A day with two ascents of Monte Grappa saw the familiar sight of his helpers in white and black marshalling the bunch. Tall *rouleurs* Mikkel Bjerg and Vegard Stake Laengen set a tough pace on the first climb, before Felix Großschartner and Rafał Majka ramped up the pace on the second ascent, leaving only three rivals left in his wake before Pogačar's unanswerable attack.

Pogačar is never shy to acknowledge his team post-race with those simple magic words: thank you. 'You can really hear that he means it, it's really from his heart,' Bjerg told *Escape Collective* in 2023. 'So it's really easy to then say, "OK, I'll do the same tomorrow to get the same acknowledgement from him."'

The willowy Dane is one of the jokers on the team who helps to bring the squad together. Just like Pogačar himself. 'He's a funny guy, who makes everybody laugh around the table,' Bjerg adds. 'You really feel like you're friends with him. Let's say even if you're new in the team and never spoke to him before, he would treat you like any of the guys he's known for 10 years. He really manages to bring everyone together and create a really nice space to be in … he's really down to earth, you don't feel like he's a cycling superstar.'

The light-heartedness is still there when he races too. On stage 2 of the Volta a Catalunya in March 2024, Pogačar and Domen Novak went up the road and stopped for a pee. They then hid in the bushes for 'a little bit of fun', leading the bunch to believe they were still ahead, on the attack. Three hours after the ruse, he was tearing the race apart, winning by 1 minute 23 seconds: no laughing matter for his rivals.

Having ridden as a teammate of both Mathieu van der Poel and Pogačar during his career, Sjoerd Bax sees parallels between the two prolific entertainers of modern cycling. 'They both have a bit of a childlike way of looking at the world, making a lot of jokes, having fun. And I think it's also the only way to keep it fun for yourself: to not take everything too seriously,' Bax says.

'Tadej chooses a bit the guys he wants for the races, the guys that give 100 per cent for him,' he adds. 'As a helper, he is the best leader you can imagine, super friendly and interested [in you]. The day before the race, he asks if you want to go for a coffee, he really wants to create a group. And he's not even trying: that's really the way he is.'

When Bax broke his femur in a mid-race crash at the 2023 Il Lombardia, Pogačar publicly said afterwards that his victory was also for the injured Dutchman. 'Even after he won, he messaged me the same day asking how the surgery went. I was like "Wow, in between all the press conferences, this guy thinks about me."'

By the end of the Giro, the whole cycling world had Pogačar front and centre of their minds. The most successful Grand Tour of his career was a demolition job: he had won 6 stages, spent 19 stages in the lead, and his margin of victory was the largest of his professional career and the broadest seen at the Giro since 1965.

Hoisting the Trofeo Senza Fine in front of the Colosseum, he could reasonably have asked the line made famous by Maximus Decimus Meridius: 'Are you not entertained?'

2024 Giro d'Italia: general classification

1. Tadej Pogačar (UAE Team Emirates) 79 hours 14 minutes
   3 seconds
2. Daniel Felipe Martínez (Bora–Hansgrohe) at 9 minutes
   56 seconds
3. Geraint Thomas (Ineos Grenadiers) at 10 minutes 24 seconds

There were 33 days between the finish of the Giro and the start of the Tour (its *grand départ* due to take place back in Italy, ironically, and in the Tuscan city of Florence). Enough time to allow Pogačar to have a takeaway or two with Urška during a precious week of holiday before knuckling down for an altitude camp at Isola 2000. Staying a stone's throw away from an important stage finish of the forthcoming Tour, he rode the climb 15 times, getting to know every hairpin.

His time there did not go as expected: his grandfather France passed away at the age of 81 and Pogačar briefly returned to Slovenia for the funeral. While training up at altitude, he also tested positive for Covid-19, a detail he matter-of-factly revealed during his pre-Tour press conference, bringing a surprise revelation to what is usually a festival of circumspect, anodyne quotes. 'That was a bit of a question mark, but I recovered really good from that,' he said, likening the experience to a cold that passed quickly.

Surprisingly, the 2024 Tour de France was the first time that modern cycling's box office 'Big Six' ever raced together: Pogačar, Evenepoel, Roglič, van der Poel, van Aert and Vingegaard.

After a horrific crash at the Itzulia Basque Country in mid-April, the defending champion Vingegaard considered that being on the start line was its own victory, having spent eight days in intensive care with punctured lungs, a fractured sternum and collarbone, and seven broken ribs.

The cycling shoe was now on the other foot: 12 months on from being disadvantaged by his own injury, Pogačar did not hesitate to test Vingegaard's legs and nerve. Stage 4 over the Col du Galibier and down to Valloire was the first significant challenge.

If Visma–Lease a Bike had edged the duel between the warring superteams in previous editions, UAE Team Emirates' catch-up game appeared complete. On the final climb, Visma called back a rider from the breakaway to help the isolated Vingegaard as four men in white and black set a punishing pace into the headwind. With Yates, Almeida and young Spaniard Juan Ayuso on song, Pogačar's team possessed one of the most fearsome combinations of climbing *domestiques* ever seen at the Tour.

Pogačar attacked in the final few hundred metres and an advantage of 7 seconds over the lofty Alpine climb's summit turned into 50 by the finish, exploiting the Dane's slower descending on technical, wet roads. The result gave Pogačar great confidence that he could go on to take the win.

Not everything was smooth behind the scenes though. Four kilometres from the top of the Galibier, and after doing a pace-setting turn, Ayuso had dropped to the back of the group, seemingly taking an unexpected break from the grunt work to save energy, eliciting shouts and waves from Almeida on the front for him to come through.

Afterwards, Pogačar was quick to waft away any whiff of controversy. 'When you go full gas, even if you just want to say to one guy: "I love you", you need to shout. When there's so many people around you going 200 [bpm] heart rate, there's not ever normal conversation … I don't think he was angry about anything, we did a really good race.'

Almeida did not appear to be expressing his undying affection, though. In Ayuso and Pogačar's first-ever stage race on the same team together, those moments caught on television hinted at insubordination.

Four years younger than Pogačar, Ayuso is a stage-racing prodigy cut from the same cloth, combining excellent climbing and time-trial ability. A third place finisher in the 2022 Vuelta a España at the age of 19, Ayuso has made no disguise of his ambition. 'One day I would like to be better than him [Pogačar], because he is the best rider in the world. I dream of being like him, so to do that I would have to beat him,' he said in December 2024. 'Of course I don't want this to create a misunderstanding because Tadej is not a rival, but my yardstick. He sets the bar and you have to try to reach it.'

Privately, Ayuso's move did not go down well within the team. Part of the family feel and straightforward functioning of the champion-packed squad was the understanding that Pogačar was the alpha and omega, requiring would-be contenders to be fully at his service. 'I think Ayuso just wanted to go for his own result,' Sjoerd Bax says. 'They were not too happy with him in the end … if Tadej is there, he's the one clear leader. Ayuso also wanted to be the leader.'

Ultimately, Ayuso bowed out of the race on stage 13 after testing positive for Covid-19. He was set to leave the team at the end of 2025 for Lidl–Trek after a mutually-agreed early termination of his contract.

Emotions can run high on the Tour. Pogačar was caught on Netflix cameras telling Vingegaard: 'Fuck you, man' when the Dane would not work together with him and Remco Evenepoel in a short-lived breakaway near the stage 9 finish in Troyes. On a chaotic stage containing gravel sectors, it was a chance missed for them to collaborate and move closer to securing the podium places. Speaking to ITV Sport, Evenepoel talked about Vingegaard 'not having the balls' to attack and work together.

2024 Tour de France: general classification after stage 9

1. Tadej Pogačar (UAE Team Emirates) 35 hours 42 minutes 42 seconds
2. Remco Evenepoel (Soudal Quick-Step) at 33 seconds
3. Jonas Vingegaard (Visma–Lease a Bike) at 1 minute 15 seconds

It was down to Evenepoel and Vingegaard to take the race to Pogačar. On stage 11, Vingegaard showed his chutzpah, catching up Pogačar after he broke away and then pipping him in a sprint at Le Lioran in the Massif Central. Even losing by centimetres, the race leader was quick to step back and appreciate the show. 'If I was a fan watching on TV, this would be one of the best stages ever,' Pogačar said.

'We can go a little bit on the defensive, but maybe still take a stage win if we can, not spending too much energy because we have a comfortable lead,' Pogačar had remarked ahead of the race's mountain-

stuffed last week. Don't believe everything he says: the opposite was true, as Pogačar enjoyed the most remarkable week of his career, starting with winning stage 14 on Pla d'Adet. Pogačar improvised, telling his surprised teammate Adam Yates to launch an attack when the original plan had been to set a hard pace. He then bridged across to him with 5 km to go and left his rivals behind.

'I get so many messages, every single interview with you guys [the media], everybody saying don't waste energy,' Pogačar told ITV afterwards. 'But I think I will never change. I will try with an attack if I feel it, and today was the same. Today worked, the other day [on stage 11] it didn't. It's life. I love to race, I love to try.' Not every spectator seemed to appreciate his spectacle, with one roadside individual disruptively chucking crisps into his face midway up the final climb. 'Our nutritionist is super angry, as we're not allowed to eat those,' Pogačar joked later in his winner's speech. Compared to Eddy Merckx, who was punched in the kidney near the finish of a Tour de France stage in 1975, he got off lightly.

Every subsequent mountain stage was a metaphorical slap in the face to his rivals. On Plateau de Beille the following day, the Pogačar show continued, when he dropped Vingegaard with 5 km to go and beat him by 1 minute 8 seconds. On a sweltering day, Pogačar had his supreme moment of the Tour. It yielded not just his 'best feeling' of the whole season, but also some of the highest power numbers in cycling history for such an effort, riding at a monstrous estimated 6.98 watts per kilogram for the 40-minute duration of the Pyrenean climb.

'I think I'm a little bit better than old me. I'm more experienced, I don't make too many mistakes,' Pogačar reflected in his stage 19 press conference. 'Sometimes, if you're anxious in the race, this is super bad and this year, I was never under stress, I was always in control of my own mind.'

Momentum is a precious, precarious thing in pro cycling and Pogačar had a ton. He felt a better, positive energy around him at the 2024 Tour and found it to be the first Grand Tour where he was totally confident every day.

Having gone over three minutes faster than Marco Pantani's record time for the Plateau de Beille, he was well on his way to following the Italian as the eighth and next man to achieve the hallowed Giro-Tour double.

When the race concluded in his backyard close to Monaco, with finishes on Isola 2000 and the Col de la Couillole, he won both stages, one with a longer-range move, the other with a devastating sprint against Vingegaard.

In the race-ending time trial between Monaco and Nice over La Turbie and Col d'Èze, he took the downhill *corniche* road back to the city full bore. It would have been easy, sensible even, to take his foot off the gas, but then that wouldn't be Pogačar. He put over a minute into Vingegaard and Evenepoel by the finish on the way to stage win number six. His dominance was absolute.

2024 Tour de France: general classification

1. Tadej Pogačar (UAE Team Emirates) 83 hours 38 minutes 56 seconds
2. Jonas Vingegaard (Team Visma–Lease a Bike) at 6 minutes 17 seconds
3. Remco Evenepoel (Soudal Quick-Step) at 9 minutes 18 seconds

A third Tour de France win took him level with past winners Philippe Thys, Louison Bobet and Greg LeMond, and was his most meaningful triumph yet in cycling's flagship race. 'The first Tour was the hardest to win because I only won it on the last day,' he told *L'Équipe*. 'But I think this one is the biggest for me because, after two years in second place, after so many ups and downs, [being at] the Tour last year unprepared because of my broken wrist.'

With little sporting intrigue to be had in the race's last week as Pogačar romped to stage wins, external focus had turned to his peerless power numbers and smashed record times on mountains (a near-meaningless metric, given that bikes, tech and aerodynamics improve over time and every mountain features in a stage with differing preceding routes over the years). A Tour de France winner had not claimed the last three stages of the race since 1930 and Eddy Merckx was the only Giro-Tour double doer to achieve it in similarly prolific fashion. Pogačar laughed off continuing comparisons. 'A cannibal? He eats human flesh. I eat sweets at the finish and gels and bars on the bike,' he quipped to *Sporza*.

Pogačar also fielded questions about carbon monoxide rebreathing, a legal, but controversial technique, given that it involves a poisonous gas. It was used to measure key values such as haemoglobin levels in blood during his altitude training, helping to assess its impact.

'It's a two or three-minute test. You breathe into a balloon then out for one minute, then you see the haemoglobin mass, then you need to repeat it two weeks later … it's not like we are breathing in exhaust pipes every day from the cars,' Pogačar said.

It is usually carried out at the start and end of the camp, when the number of red blood cells have increased. (The rebreather device can also be used to inhale carbon monoxide for the purpose of performance enhancement, though there is no evidence of WorldTour riders doing this.)

Vingegaard also used the method as a diagnostic tool, but the man in first place was fielding the most questions. The Slovenian knows he will never be free of suspicion. 'Cycling was damaged so much in the past, before my time. In any sport and situation of life, if someone is winning, there's always jealousy and haters,' Pogačar said in his post-race winner's press conference in Nice's Palais des Congrès. 'If you don't have haters, then you're not succeeding … I think this is one of the cleanest sports, of all sport in general because of what happened so many years ago, because there was so much abuse.

'But I tell you now, it's not worth it, taking anything to risk your health,' he added. 'It is super stupid because you can cycle maybe until 35 and it's a long way [to go] to enjoy life. It would be really stupid to throw this away and risk your life for stupid racing. It's just a game – yeah, it's fun and all, you want to win, but it's not everything. The most important thing is that you're healthy. And we're already pushing ourselves so much in the races, there's no reason to push the body even deeper.'

Exuding the joy of six stage wins, Pogačar was on a high that could not be dampened – not even by a post-podium brush with the fountains in Place Masséna, dunked in there by a mischievous UAE party which included Marc Soler and Joseba Elguezabal.

There was one last scurrilous rumour from the Tour press pack following Pogačar around – that he wound up at McDonald's in Nice, happy if a little worse for wear, in the early hours of the morning after his emphatic triumph.

. . . .

Given his transcendent form, it was a shock when Pogačar pulled out of the Olympic Games, citing 'extreme fatigue'. He had been scheduled to compete in the road race in Paris, taking place a fortnight after the Tour ended. While the Tour had taken its toll, Urška's surprise non-selection in the Slovenian team was a potential factor. 'It's not the main reason, but for sure it didn't help,' Pogačar said to *NOS*. 'I think she deserves her spot. She's the double national champion in road race and time trial.'

However, it meant he could grab more respite and build up more gradually for the World Championships in Zürich, the only race between him and the triple crown.

He had heaped pressure on himself for a 274-km course that centred around seven laps of 27 km of an up-and-down finishing circuit. All the uphill damage could be done in its first half, containing the 800-m, punchy Zürichbergstraße climb, with a section at 17 per cent gradient, and longer, more gradual Witikon.

A mix of youth and experience teamed up in the radioactive green kit of Slovenia, including father figure Luka Mezgec; Pogačar's pal from adolescent racing, Jaka Primožič, his UAE teammate Domen Novak and fellow contender Primož Roglič. Such is the peculiar nature of World Championships: raced by national teams, fierce rivals can become teammates with united goals for one day a year. Speaking his mother tongue, cracking old jokes and talking fast cars with Primožič, Pogačar felt at home.

The lyrics of his favourite song, 'Lose Yourself', by Eminem, were no doubt playing through his headphones and spooling through his head: *This opportunity comes once in a lifetime* and his had arrived.

After Belgium and Slovenia set a high early rhythm, Slovenia's Jan Tratnik slipped into a 10-rider move with 127 km to go, which included Magnus Cort (Denmark), Pavel Sivakov (France), Laurens De Plus (Belgium), Florian Lipowitz (Germany) and Stephen Williams (Great Britain). It was a dangerous group – no out-and-out stars, but plenty of firepower.

Without a rider up front, Spain and the Netherlands were on the back foot. Yet inertia reigned in the peloton, quickly finding itself almost three minutes down.

'We had all the plans to burn everyone, to set a faster pace every lap,' Luka Mezgec says. The intention was for Pogačar to wait until the final one, with 27km to go, and make his bid for glory. 'Then he just smoked [them] with four laps to go, with no real plan. He just improvised.'

With 100 km to race, after an exploratory Roglič surge had been squashed, Pogačar accelerated on the Witikon climb. Ben O'Connor tracked his attack, then thought better of it. It seemed far too early; there was a cross-headwind over the top and the finish was so far away. Even Pogačar later derided it as a 'stupid move'. His rival Remco Evenepoel opted for another s-word: *suicide*.

He was racing on instinct, but there was also a little strategic method to his apparent madness. The versatile Dutch team were not chasing, despite not having a rider in front. Belgian and Slovenian riders were working, but running low on numbers. 'Just Roglič remains with Tadej,' explained Andrej Hauptman. 'If Belgium stopped [riding] because they have a rider [De Plus] in front: OK, we had Tratnik up there but if it goes to three minutes, imagine what happens. Be sure that Tadej was thinking like this, calculating everything.'

The dangerous 10-rider group could have stayed away if the favourites and their teams got into a tactical Mexican standoff, akin to the 2022 World Championships. Pogačar did not want to wait too late and be left wondering.

He was constantly looking around, observing who was with him and processing the size of his advantage. Andrea Bagioli (Italy) and Quinn Simmons (USA) strained to follow his initial move, though they could last only a few minutes in his wheel.

Competing in an event without rider race radios, there was no rapid communication of time gaps or information to be had. Up ahead, Tratnik came to the rescue with some quick thinking. He noticed the gaps coming down on the time board shown by the motorcycle pilot and asked what had happened. Once he heard Pogačar was in no man's land, he dropped back to pace him up to the group. 'Tadej knew that it was early. But in the end, we were lucky that Tratnik waited for him and helped him another lap,' Hauptman reflects.

Back with the breakaway, Tratnik headed straight to the front with Pogačar on his wheel, pushing the pace. It reinforced his leader's belief in the viability of this audacious attack. 'At first, I was like "This is so stupid." Then I saw Jan waited for me. OK, let's go,' Pogačar reflected afterwards. If anyone could make a breakaway stick 100 km from the finish, it was him.

It was essentially one man, getting next-to-no assistance from his fellow breakaways, against many from different teams behind. Pogačar daring the rest to adapt their plans, chase him and burn through helpers while pushing his own training, willpower and capacities to the limit.

When he surged again on the Bergstrasse climb, only French rider Pavel Sivakov could follow. It was another World Championships oddity: his trade-teammate at UAE Team Emirates, paid to give his utmost for Pogačar all season, was competing against him for the only time that year. There was some collaboration between the pair of friends, as Sivakov gave Pogačar the occasional turn on the front and a welcome rest. In his view, staying with Pogačar furthered his own chances of a medal, though he could keep up for only another lap before fading away.

'The guy in front always has an advantage,' Sivakov told Eurosport. 'At the World Championships, Pogačar told me: "They'll look at each other, let's go." He was right.' The implication is that there would be sufficient prevarication behind, with rivals not wanting to risk using up men early and being left isolated.

Pogačar had 50 km to race alone, but the manpower behind was also dwindling. The Belgian and Dutch teams had burned through several helpers, chasing hard. Every lap, the group's size reduced and attacks took the rhythm out of the chase. Remco Evenepoel and Mathieu van der Poel both made bids to escape. The bunch could go fast enough to hold the deficit at 50 seconds, but made few inroads: Pogačar described it later as being held 'on the leash'.

That fragile time gap was the difference between victory and defeat, genius and foolishness. Pogačar fretted, wondering how much he had left in the tank compared to the chasers. They were in dribs and drabs, attacking one another, hesitating and then reforming in groups. Ben Healy and Toms Skujiņš made a dangerous move on the penultimate lap.

As Pogačar's lead briefly dropped to 35 seconds on the last lap, he looked on the brink of a collapse on the final ascent of the Witikon.

He was dying inside, counting down the metres to the top of the climb.

'In the last hour or two hours, I went through all the emotions possible. I just couldn't give up, for everything that happened or will happen. I pushed through,' Pogačar said afterwards.

When he hit the downhill on the circuit's second half, he knew that the triple crown was his. Crossing the line, Pogačar was world champion. Joining Eddy Merckx and Stephen Roche in history – and how!

2024 World Championships road race

1. Tadej Pogačar (Slovenia) 273.9 km in 6 hours 27 minutes 30 seconds
2. Ben O'Connor (Australia) at 34 seconds
3. Mathieu van der Poel (Netherlands) at 58 seconds

Seconds later, he was engulfed by his teammates, who had abandoned the race earlier and were waiting just beyond the finish line. They slapped him on the back and lofted him on their shoulders. 'You think he cannot surprise you any more but still he's got something there to show,' Mezgec says. 'We all *do* cycling, but he's just playing cycling – the only guy.'

The flood of feelings from winning in a sprint finish usually trumps a long solo escape, but these World Championships were different. The emotional weight of his astonishing breakaway showed. After dousing himself in water, Tadej ran towards Urška – no mean feat in cycling shoes – post-race, parting the mass of media, his hands aloft before lifting her in an embrace. They were in their own little world, seemingly shutting out everyone else. They both knew how much he had given to that race and what the outcome meant – not just to him, her, their friends and family, but to his country.

After all his victories and achievements, Pogačar could still surprise himself. 'I cannot believe what just happened. After this kind of season, I put a lot of pressure on myself today,' he said, adding later: 'This is dreams come true. I didn't even dare to dream to have the rainbow jersey when I was a kid, so it means even more now.'

Slovenia was on top of the world. Pogačar's teammates waited on the team bus until he had finished his post-race obligations. Partying on a Sunday night in Switzerland was a challenge, with their strict closing hours; Team Slovenia went back to their hotel after midnight to keep the drinks flowing and the party going. 'We were all completely dead,' Jaka Primožič says. 'But hey, it only happens once in a lifetime.'

Reduced to being bit-part players to the main act, his rivals were exhausted and stupefied again. A Pogačar attack to victory was no surprise, but the manner in which he did it was akin to changing the trick they all saw coming – as weighty as expecting the conjurer to pull a rabbit out of the hat, and a rhinoceros trotting out instead.

The 2024 World Championships road race encapsulates what makes Pogačar so engaging. Modern sporting success might hinge on data and infinitesimal gains, but fans also love emotional connection, romance and jeopardy. Usually, the strongest does not need to be the most daring. Pogačar chose to gamble and confound expectations, putting everything on the line, when he could have waited longer, calculated and still won.

Good things come in threes – fours if you count his season-ending win at Il Lombardia. There was a symmetry to his Strade Bianche victory: he finished the year in the same country where his season had started, performing the same celebration, lifting his Colnago bicycle aloft after crossing the finish line. With his unstoppable solo moves, Pogačar had redefined one-day racing again in 2024.

Tadej Pogačar's one-day race results in 2024

Strade Bianche – 81 km from the finish, solo attack – 1st place
Milan–San Remo – 7-km attack – 3rd
Liège–Bastogne–Liège – 34-km solo attack – 1st place
GP de Québec – 4-km attack – 7th
GP Cycliste de Montréal – 23.3-km solo attack – 1st place
World Championships road race – 100-km attack, 51.1-km solo
   – 1st place
Giro dell'Emilia – 38-km solo – 1st place
Il Lombardia – 48-km solo – 1st place

In all, with his Giro, Tour and Volta a Catalunya stage wins and GC titles included, he had taken 25 victories in 58 race days, an astonishing rate of 43 per cent. As an individual, he won more races in 2024 than all but five WorldTour teams in the sport. He had double the UCI ranking points of all but one man, Remco Evenepoel.

Whatever Pogačar achieves in the future, his 'perfect' triple crown year will be very difficult to surpass. He enjoyed not just one race in a state of grace, but a whole season.

▶ Pogačar and Mathieu van der Poel seem to be in their own contest to see who can accrue the most Monument one-day race wins. The 2025 Milan–San Remo was a classic instalment in their duel.

17

THE PUZZLE

Pavia, March 2025

The old man sips his cappuccino as raindrops trickle down the bar window. 'Cycling is tough,' he sighs. 'Football players are little kids.'

Beyond the red table cloths with flowers on them, the first team buses roll down the Viale Giacomo Matteotti for Milan–San Remo. It is building into a miserable Saturday to race for seven hours.

One of the punters says his grandfather did an amateur edition of Milan–San Remo in the 1930s. Talk among the three old-timers turns to how fast they will go, who the favourites are and who will win. 'Pogačar, but he has to attack,' the bar owner weighs in from behind the counter.

When everything else in pro cycling seems to come easy to its Slovenian subjugator, Milan–San Remo is the stone stubbornly stuck in his cycling shoe, the marathon Monument which continues to elude him.

He has not done any other race so many times as a pro and failed to win: his sequence of results heading into the 2025 edition went 12th,

5th, 4th and 3rd, with the victor in sight every single time. 'Milan–San Remo is the one that is going to send me to my grave … I'm getting so close but so far, it's unbelievable,' Pogačar told podcaster Peter Attia in 2024.

The great French cycling journalist Philippe Brunel dubbed it a Promethean race for its intense emotional pulls. It builds slowly in energy and intensity, like an Italian balladeer strumming his guitar in one of the cafés off San Remo's pedestrianised main strip. He may start off slowly, but by the end of the song, he'll be up off his seat, playing fast and wild, the music so loud that nobody can hear themselves think.

The race has changed little in 40 years, decided by the coastal climbs (*capi*) which are as short and sharp as their names – Mele, Cervo, Berta, Cipressa and, lastly, the kingmaker, the Poggio before a corner-strewn descent into the Ligurian city. The protagonists go so fast up the final 3-km climb that they brush the walls and have to brake for the corners. 'Six hours training and then a test in the end,' Pogačar said, tongue-in-cheek.

For a man who just needs a protracted stretch of steep road to cause havoc, there is enough elevation gain to make a difference, but the hills are not hard or long enough to get rid of everyone, requiring a top-end five-minute power that attracts many different contenders.

This fickle race possesses almost as many possible eventualities as its 289 km. Alongside Pogačar's name as a pre-race favourite are those of Mathieu van der Poel, *puncheur par excellence*; Jonathan Milan, the muscular, nodding-dog sprinter; and Filippo Ganna, the hulking beast of time trials. The craftiest sometimes beats the strongest or fastest finishers with an opportune attack into San Remo. 'It is like a sudoku where you can't make an error,' Ganna said in the *Gazzetta dello Sport*'s pink pages on race day. 'If you slip up, the damage is done and it's goodbye hopes.'

How Pogačar knows it. He has ridden the finale many times; the Poggio is only 55 km from his Monaco front door, almost visible down the coast, eternally blowing him a raspberry.

Impromptu race preview done, the Pavese café clientele insist on paying for my coffee and *cornetto alla crema* and the proprietor tells me he'll see me here again next year. There will be no similar acts of sporting generosity for Tadej Pogačar today.

· · · ·

Outside in the mizzle, the cicada click of freewheels passes as competitors go to sign on ahead of the race. Rival *directeurs sportifs* shoot the breeze, their breath rising into the cold morning air like cigarette smoke.

The UAE Team Emirates–XRG team bus is the very last in line on the Viale Giacomo Matteotti. Most of the mechanics, assistants and soigneurs have black beanies on to go with their black jackets and white trousers.

At half past nine, 45 minutes before the start, mechanic Boštjan Kavčnik is fastidiously wiping down slightly damp wheels and bikes with a navy blue towel.

Every bike has a sticker on its stem, bearing key route and feeding info. On Pogačar's rainbow-liveried steed, the race's two feed zones are in a blue background; the four final climbs stand out in white, with their distance and average gradient; and there are five marked points in green, informing him where helpers with nutrition are and what to eat. Before the beasting comes the necessary feasting: he is set to take on approximately 120 g of carbohydrates every hour, split between bottles with 60 g and 30 g, plus energy gels and water.

Most eye-catching is the baby Hulk sticker above the stem notes, snarling with its left fist raised ready to smash. His past frustration at San Remo near misses can be used as fuel. 'I hold back anger when I'm normal Tadej. And then I put that anger on the bike,' he said in Netflix's series *Tour de France: Unchained*.

His inner circle watches on. Luke Maguire is ready to shepherd him around the mixed zone for one final lap of the microphones and TV cameras. The super-agent Carera brothers talk business. Andrej Hauptman performs a race radio-check. Joxean Fernández Matxin pours himself a coffee from the team bus' machine and poses for a selfie with a fan. 'This isn't hard. Footon was hard. That's where you learn – and you invent,' he says, referring to his time in 2010 as *directeur sportif* of the lowest-ranked team in the ProTour.

Inside the barriers, three rows of fans and VIPs are positioned around the team bus door, wielding mobile phones. As the team's sign-on time approaches, they twitch expectantly with every swish open of the white separating curtain. A mechanic emerges. *Not Pogačar.* Nils Politt clip-clops down the steps in cycling shoes. *Not Pogačar.* Then the man of the moment does appear – 'Grande Tadej!' someone shouts – and here he is, blending in with the rest of the bunch in a black rain jacket version of the rainbow jersey.

A scab on his right hand is one of a few vestiges of Pogačar's literal field day at Strade Bianche a fortnight earlier. He rag-dolled into a patch of brambles in a high-speed crash while leading the race with 45 km to go. After re-emerging, sunglasses askew and skinsuit torn, he caught escapees Tom Pidcock and Connor Swift and dropped them for another solo victory. Evidently, Pogačar likes to win the hard way; this one hurt even more than usual. A Dutch journalist shows me a photo: some jokester has already printed out an A4 piece of paper in a plastic leaflet and put it on the crash site. It reads, *Pogačar è stato qui* – Pogačar was here.

Of course, the longest one-day race in professional cycling doesn't care that you hit the deck hard at Strade Bianche and spent time in a hyperbaric chamber to help heal the injuries. Pogačar has spent days doing final tune-ups on the race route, joined at times by experienced teammate Tim Wellens.

'[One day] Tadej trained six hours, also behind the moto and I joined him for one and a half hours … he did Cipressa-Poggio three times and I did it once,' the Belgian rider tells me at the team presentation the day before the race.

His application is another reminder of what it takes to stay number one. 'Of course Tadej has talent, but to keep the motivation and the work going even if you win so much, for me it's quite impressive. After a travel day, he does two hours on the rollers and then the ice bath, this and that. He's always thinking about the bike.

'It's not easy if you're on top to continue working as hard as necessary to stay there. He's the best rider in the world, but I'm pretty sure he is one of the riders in the world who works the most.'

I walk behind Pogačar as he leaves Pavia's Piazza della Vittoria after the presentation. He is clad in a baggy, long-sleeved rainbow jersey – Gen Z fashion, which also wards off the March chill. Professional cyclists usually stroll languidly, as if trying to save every kilojoule of energy; he struts with speed and purpose, arms swinging, a fragile-looking but powerful bird of prey. A chorus of 'Ta-dejs' comes from behind the barriers, a few camera flashes light up the gloom.

He has already done his signings and selfie session before taking to the stage. He adorned with a swirly T and P signature a colourful poster held aloft by 15-year-old Luca Colombo and his 12-year-old brother Andrea. It is not hard to tell who they are supporting: their placard has three upper-case 'POGI's in pink lettering, yellow lettering and rainbow colours respectively, recognising his triple crown.

Before the riders roll out for the race on Saturday morning, I spot the same poster again. These kids from Varese are just two of tens of thousands of youngsters who are fans. Time was when Italian children had a number of homegrown champions to choose from, but the pull of Pogačar is too strong.

'Because he makes such a show. It's always him in front, on the attack. When he breaks away on the climbs, it gives so many emotions, it's beautiful to see him race,' Luca tells me.

His favourite exploit was the 2024 World Championships. 'Or Strade Bianche, after he crashed, got up and managed to do something atypical and *epico*.'

The young duo, clad in the red, white and blue jersey of their local club, are doing their first bike races of the season tomorrow. Maybe one day, they could be in the same bunch as their idol. As the peloton cycles past, it is not a particularly enviable place to be: most are wrapped up in rain jackets, leaving Pavia to a caterwaul of screeching disc brakes.

The rain stops after three hours, the layers come off and the race wakes up when it hits the coast. Alpecin–Deceuninck helper Silvan

Dillier does the lion's share of the work on the front of the bunch, while Isaac del Toro goes back to the team car for gloves mid-race, ferrying them to team leader Pogačar.

Triumph in Milan–San Remo comes down to a meticulous management of nutrition, concentration and resources, while profiting smartly from the expenditure of others.

UAE Team Emirates' seven-point plan for the race led to a Pogačar attack on the Cipressa.

The talk since their winter training camps had been the need to do the 5 km hill in under nine minutes, giving it all the athletic cachet of a Bannister-era four-minute mile. Go fast and hard enough as a unit and a Pogačar attack would torpedo the hopes of all but the punchiest contenders, left hopelessly behind with next-to-no fresh helpers. His point of attack was pinpointed down to the corner.

So, they sit further back for most of the day, saving their energy rather than getting involved in the chase of the break. 'It's better we take a risk. Because otherwise, if we lose one more guy for nothing, this plan is caput,' Pogačar said on the team bus in their pre-race briefing.

In Alassio, with 55 km to go, ahead of the Capo Berta, Vegard Stake Laengen and Domen Novak come forward, moving Pogačar into the bunch's front rows.

From this point to the Cipressa, the peloton is a seething, frothing mass, fighting for every inch of tarmac. 'The most scary moment [of the year] is the last 30 minutes before the Cipressa. One small mistake and you can finish your career easily there,' Pogačar reflected, weeks after the race.

Three kilometres from the foot, four UAE Team Emirates–XRG riders were in a line on the left of the road – Nils Politt, Tim Wellens, Jhonatan Narváez and Pogačar. As waves battered the rocks beneath them, they were churned back in the sprawl. Wellens was their only rider in the bunch's top 20 on the right turn on to the Cipressa, with favourites van der Poel and Ganna sitting pretty in the first five. Pogačar was 20 riders back, having to spend precious energy to move up the snaking line with Narváez.

'Any small detail through the day can change everything in the race,' Pogačar had said on its eve. Here was one: Wellens set a blistering pace on the first half, as planned, but Isaac del Toro, who was supposed to be involved in that effort in the climb's first 4 km and finishing off with a 25-second *à bloc* effort, was nowhere to be seen. This race is built on plans as fragile as sandcastles, requiring hasty rebuilding.

Narváez took over from Wellens and as the headwind turned to tailwind round one corner, he gave his all. The coruscating, inevitable burst came from Pogačar, sprinting in the drops out of the saddle, baring his teeth like a wild hyena. Ganna clawed his way on to his wheel with van der Poel; Frenchman Romain Grégoire was there momentarily, feeling the burn and dropping back. The rest could only watch them disappear out of sight.

'It was no secret what he was going to do, but knowing it and following it are two different things,' his friend Michael Matthews, who has come close to victory in San Remo even more times than Pogačar, told *Cyclingnews* at the finish.

Three was company. By the top of the Cipressa, the gap between Ganna, Pogačar and van der Poel and those behind was 30 seconds; at the end of the descent, as the heavyweights shared the workload, it was a minute. Many observers had believed that detonating the race on the Cipressa was unlikely. Think again: the race's dogma had been rewritten with Milan–San Remo's longest winning breakaway since 1996.

After a fast descent, the leaders flicked right on to the Poggio's freshly laid tarmac and Ganna was unshipped by a third Pogačar acceleration. As the duo in front slowed, Pogačar sprinted out of a coiling corner again, but van der Poel refused to budge, making the most of the slipstream effect on the shallow gradients. Another half-acceleration came, then a sixth and final one, wringing everything out. It wasn't enough: van der Poel made his own attack close to the summit, putting two bike lengths into Pogačar, to show he was not on the ropes.

The last five helter-skelter kilometres downhill into San Remo are as fraught and fast as a police car chase. With the leaders in sight after every turn, Ganna closed the gap painstakingly and caught them with 500 m to go.

A prior reputation of having a fast finish counts for a lot less after six and a half hours in the saddle; it is principally about who has the most left in their sore legs. Van der Poel called his rivals' bluff by starting the sprint early, with 300 m to go. At the back of the group, Pogačar had made the mistake of laying off by a few lengths and never got past Ganna, let alone van der Poel.

The charged seconds of electricity over, the Via Roma fills with finishers, officials, soigneurs and media. As Pogačar turns back and rides towards the podium, he shakes his head to Michael Matthews. By now, it is more surprising when Pogačar doesn't win a race as favourite, not when he does. 'Third place. I couldn't do more,' a stony-faced Pogačar mutters to the just-finished Isaac del Toro. His friend Žiga Jerman, a soigneur at UAE Team Emirates–XRG, walks next to him as they inch down the congested road. He drains a bottle of cherry juice, a recovery aid. As Tudor Pro Cycling rider Matteo Trentin dissects the race with teammate Julian Alaphilippe, he asks the passing Pogačar if he won. 'No? You can try next year then!'

Speaking to media, Pogačar declared himself proud of how the team fared, doing everything to make for an explosive race. They took a fresh approach, one tailored to Pogačar's capabilities which will likely be seen again. For all his ability to clear lactate rapidly and accelerate viciously and repeatedly, Pogačar can still only work with the given route.

'I would prefer the Poggio to be 5 km long at 10 per cent, but it is what it is. It's a really hard race for me to make the difference. The laws of physics are at play here and you cannot do magic,' he said to Eurosport. Frighteningly for the rest, Pogačar also hinted that he was not at his best, missing peak power and a few extra watts.

For his great Dutch rival, it is not just a Monument win, but a Monument win in front of Pogačar. His brilliance and dogged resilience stopped the world champion from breaking his duck.

While waiting for the podium ceremony backstage, the duelling deities gushed over the attack-packed finale as if they were two club cyclists sat in the café, dissecting their sprint for the local town sign.

'When you go over the top [with your attack], I thought, *Ah fuck*,' Pogačar said, slapping his left hand over his eyes like a facepalm.

'I thought that I could break you, but no,' van der Poel said.

'It was really close.'

'Yeah, but I was so on the limit.'

Clad in his oversized world champion's jersey again, looking like a school kid who has not fully grown into his uniform, Pogačar walked out and stood on the wrong rostrum step – in second place, before being politely redirected by prizegiver Vincenzo Nibali. As Ganna and van der Poel turned for the Dutch national anthem, Pogačar seemed distracted by his thoughts and fatigue, staring straight ahead.

He had isolated the rest, attacked *six* times in total – and still no Milan–San Remo trophy. Victory does not require magic, just perhaps better positioning.

'I think maybe he could start the Cipressa a little bit more in front,' his team boss Mauro Gianetti said afterwards. (The same could be said of teammates Narváez and del Toro.) 'But it's chaotic, he would not take too many risks, and he was 10, 15 seconds too far behind. When you need to close 10 seconds at the start of the climb, you miss those 10 seconds at the top.'

Part of what makes Milan–San Remo such a difficult race to win is only having seven team members, a considerable factor for the insane positional fight ahead of the Cipressa. Burn his three top helpers there and Pogačar is shorn of numbers to set a more punishing tempo and reliant on a fatigued chase. Could UAE Team Emirates–XRG make the pace hellish from even further out? All *ifs*, *buts* and *maybes* in this fiendish puzzle.

The longing and plan refining starts again. Another near miss gives the gift of Pogačar coming back as a protagonist in the future. One March day, everything will surely slot into place and every past near miss will sweeten the glory. In the unlikely event that Pogačar never cracks 'La Classicissima', he will be in good company, alongside cycling greats Peter Sagan, Philippe Gilbert and Tom Boonen.

At ten past six in the afternoon, a baggy white hoody under his black team jacket, Pogačar emerges from the team bus and is ushered through the waiting throng into a grey Audi sports car, driven by Žiga Jerman. Urška nimbly weaves through the crowd and into the back seat and they accelerate away.

The old man in the café was right: cycling *is* tough, even for Pogačar. But the rest of the spring Classics await and the bitter taste of defeat will not last long.

▶ It is never easy to string together season after season of scintillating performances. Expected to win almost every race he starts, could 'Pogi' become a victim of his own success or ennui?

18

THE WEIGHT OF GREATNESS

2025

As he closed on a fourth Tour de France victory, everything and everybody around Tadej Pogačar was getting on his nerves. The 'pain in the ass' air conditioning in the post-race press conference room. The 'annoying' attacks from Visma–Lease a Bike in the race's opening half. The whole Tour 'mess'.

He was counting down the kilometres to Paris, seemingly worn down by the fastest edition in the Tour's history and the hoopla around it. 'I ask myself: why am I still here?' Pogačar said in Courchevel, when three days away from victory. The weight of greatness had never been more evident.

On the bike, he displayed both control and maturity, winning four stages and never being distanced at a finish by closest rival Jonas Vingegaard or emerging challenger Florian Lipowitz. However, he lacked verve and vigour in the race's final week, unusually not winning a stage.

Pogačar was partly a victim of his own past positivity. After five and a half Tours of swashbuckling moves and generally upbeat moods, a week of more measured racing and behaviour stuck out like a Spanish climber on the cobbles of the Tour of Flanders. Damned if he dominates and wins too much, damned if he defends and doesn't win at all.

Ennui appeared to have sunk its beige claws into him and even a fortnight after the Tour, Pogačar talked to RTV Slovenija of 'counting the years until retirement.'

Though lacking in wrinkles, grey hair and frown lines, he seemed old before his time. After bringing up his 100th win as a professional on a rolling day into Rouen on stage 4, following an explosive classic in miniature, he was beaming. 'I think maybe every year I have less fun on the bike ... a day like today was pure racing,' he said.

Visma–Lease a Bike peppered him with attacks in the race's first week, trying to use contenders Matteo Jorgenson and Jonas Vingegaard. However, serious damage was done to the two-time champion's challenge by underperforming in the stage 5 time trial. As world champion Remco Evenepoel won, Pogačar was second, 16 seconds down, recovering from a blip against the clock in the Critérium du Dauphiné. Vingegaard lost 1 minute 5 seconds to him. On the punchy finish at Mur-de-Bretagne on stage 7, Pogačar outsprinted Vingegaard for a second stage win, gradually distancing him further.

The decisive difference-maker came when the race entered the Pyrenees for stage 12 to Hautacam. Jhonatan Narváez set him up at the final climb's foot as if they were sprinting on to the Cipressa, not a 13.5-km ascent. Pogačar rode the *hors-catégorie* mountain in the lead, putting 2 minutes 10 seconds into Vingegaard, his closest challenger. The Tour de France was effectively over as a contest after this jaw-dropping display of excellence.

'I feel at the best moment of my career,' Pogačar said. 'I'm riding in the rainbow jersey, I ride with an amazing team, so it's like a fairytale for me. I think once this fire goes out, I will probably decline in performance but I'd say that now is the peak of my career, and I'll try to hold it for as long as I can.'

This Tour, Pogačar seemed to be reckoning with his own transience at the top of the sport. On the Champs-Élysées, ITV interviewer Matt Rendell asked Pogačar how he keeps his head and stays true to the kid who likes racing his bike. His reply: 'It's not getting easier. The older I'm getting, the less of the kid there is in me. The pressure and just everything around you for these big three weeks is more surreal. When you were young, you don't care, you go for it,' he said, smiling and shrugging. 'Now, slowly I need to think: "I cannot do this forever" and enjoy the moment.'

2025 Tour de France: general classification

1. Tadej Pogačar (UAE Team Emirates–XRG) 76 hours 0 minutes 32 seconds
2. Jonas Vingegaard (Team Visma–Lease a Bike) at 4 minutes 24 seconds
3. Florian Lipowitz (Red Bull–Bora–Hansgrohe) at 11 minutes 0 seconds

Five months earlier, before his first race of 2025 at the UAE Tour, Pogačar stood like Moses parting the Red Sea, a picture of energy. Having posed for the pre-race publicity photos with five fellow stars in front of the gleaming, glass-windowed Colnago Abu Dhabi flagship store, Pogačar and his tracksuit-wearing peers were left stranded when the automatic doors stubbornly refused to open. Looking in at the expectant guests and media, it was getting awkward. Then the world champion stepped forward, waved his arms in a conductorial flourish and they sprung apart. Is there anything this guy can't do?

He was in control of the moving orchestra when they pinned on race numbers too, winning the WorldTour event's two mountain stages and the overall. There was no stopping Pogačar or marking him out of affairs. Nobody could beat or contain him on a long climb; might as well try to bottle lightning. At every stage race, a Pogačar victory felt inevitable. It was not a question of whether he would succeed, but by how much.

'When you see him on the start line at the moment, we already know we're racing for second place,' his friend and former teammate Davide Formolo says. 'I grew up seeing Ferrari win all the Formula 1 titles. He is like Michael Schumacher, maybe lapping the guy in second place.'

All the doors really were open for him. Pogačar made a late decision to tweak his programme and take part in April's cobblestone classic Paris–Roubaix for the first time. It was quite a U-turn: Pogačar had previously suggested that he would race the 'Hell of the North' for fun at the end of his career, carrying a few extra pounds given that it is not made for riders of his build.

However, he had flirted with the idea over the years, having done recons of the cobbles several times, including the day after his 2022 Tour of Flanders debut. Now, it was a case of *why not*? Time to use his flying form before it was too late. Of the five Monuments, Paris–Roubaix is the least suited to his capabilities and would be his biggest sporting challenge, a surefire way to keep tedium at bay for him and the sport's followers.

'I just want to do whatever keeps me interested in cycling and not lose motivation and just give up because it becomes boring, every year the same,' Pogačar said ahead of the Tour of Flanders. 'I want to get through all the experiences, to get the most out of cycling so when I retire I will not have any regrets, and say I did my best in every aspect of cycling. That's my goal.'

Paris–Roubaix was set to be the next thrilling Monument duel between him and Mathieu van der Poel. A week earlier, Pogačar had bludgeoned his way to a second Tour of Flanders title, and there had been little subtlety about his tactics: he launched a first attack on the penultimate time up the Kwaremont, with 55 km to go, and weakened his rivals with acceleration after acceleration until they wilted.

Early in the race, UAE Team Emirates ratcheted up the pace, creating as much fatigue as possible to play to Pogačar's abilities, squeezing the life out of the rest. It also made for a reduced front group in the endgame, meaning less complications or risk of crashes. Rivals Stefan Küng and Filippo Ganna tried to pre-empt with a long breakaway, but Pogačar simply rode across to them and tore straight past.

Winning Paris–Roubaix would be far less straightforward, though. His participation was the talk of the sport because modern Tour de France champions simply don't do this flat, mercurial 'bullshit' (to quote Bernard Hinault's descriptor). He was the first reigning champion since Greg LeMond in 1991 to start it. The others preferred to avoid jeopardising any title defence in one of the many crashes on this sadistic obstacle course. UAE Team Emirates–XRG boss Mauro Gianetti had indicated his preference that Pogačar didn't try Paris–Roubaix in 2025, but stopping the headstrong racer when his mind is set on something is like trying to bridle a galloping wild bronco.

There was a certain amount of interest about how Pogačar would fare. Without a hill of note to make a difference on the route, he was physiologically on the back foot, as higher absolute power matters more than the relative power (watts per kilogram) that is so important in the Tour de France's mountains. At 65 kg Pogačar is hardly lacking in power, but someone weighing 75 kg, like Mathieu van der Poel, has a natural advantage.

Pogačar knew that there was also the possibility of falling in a high-speed crash, but pointed out that every race carries risk. 'If you're afraid of racing, then don't expect the best result because fear can take a lot of energy from you,' he said.

As a racer, the key to Paris–Roubaix is breaking it down into manageable chunks. Pogačar rode the first few of the race's 30 *pavé* sectors like an old hand, staying at the front of the bunch, avoiding mishaps or mechanical issues. On Haveluy, the sector before the feared Trouée d'Arenberg, Pogačar drove a split in the group and subsequently led a 15-strong group over the misshapen bumps. It was a performance that was already going some way to honouring the rainbow jersey of world champion – and he was just getting going.

The race began in earnest. Pogačar kept pressing affairs, escaping with van der Poel and his grey-clad Alpecin–Deceuninck teammate, Jasper Philipsen.

It looked like being a battle for the ages between the two Monument gluttons over the last 50 km as the Slovenian's continued pressure got rid of Philipsen over Mons-en-Pévèle, one of the hardest sectors.

However, on the short, innocuous Pont-Thibault sector, Pogačar steamed far too fast into a right-hand corner, and paid the price.

There is a photo that captures the dawning moment of realisation, his mouth wide open in horror like an emoji. 'When you go full gas and motos are in front of you, and then they don't turn? You also think there is no turn. But then suddenly, they're really close to you and you're just standing still,' he said, laughing post-race. 'But I should know there is a corner, so no excuses.'

His fall into the verge was about as gentle as it gets at Paris–Roubaix.

However, in the few seconds he spent on the ground and the dozen more spent trying to put his chain back on before changing bikes, van der Poel and victory went up the road. The Dutchman, who seems to smooth out the cobblestones with his free-flowing style, pressed on for a third consecutive victory, in spite of a late puncture. By then, a rubbing front brake had forced Pogačar to change his steed again.

Having enjoyed his debut, Pogačar waved at the fans in the velodrome as he crossed the line in second place. In terms of power, Paris–Roubaix elicited some of the highest numbers of his career. 'It was definitely one of the roughest, toughest, hardest races I did,' he said, looking broken and drawn afterwards. 'But I think I gained some experience that maybe next time I come here, it would not be so extremely hard as it was today.'

Paris–Roubaix 2025

1. Mathieu van der Poel (Alpecin–Deceuninck) 259.2 km in 5 hours 31 minutes 27 seconds
2. Tadej Pogačar (UAE Team Emirates–XRG) at 1 minute 18 seconds
3. Mads Pedersen (Lidl–Trek) at 2 minutes 11 seconds

The mutual respect between van der Poel and Pogačar was clear after the latest dynamite chapter in their duopoly. 'What he does here in his first Roubaix doesn't surprise me, but it's also not normal,' van der Poel said after winning his eighth Monument.

'He's the only rider who can pull this off. I said after Milan–San Remo that he was the only rider who could actually make the difference on the Cipressa. He's 26 – there's so much more to come. When his career is finished, it will be like Merckx and his career.'

When Pogačar was asked in the press conference about when the next instalment of their rivalry would take place, the bags under his eyes spoke volumes as he gave a reply that is just as applicable to his own singular performances: 'Don't be greedy. Enjoy what we have.'

Any lingering doubts about his capacity to win the gruelling race, or all five Monuments, were done and dusted. The most impressive second place of his career was also another expression of Pogačar's free-spiritedness and a reminder of just how good he is. What had seemed to be romantic folly turned out to be a realistic bid for victory which fell narrowly short.

He seemed to have no fear of falling, of failing, of potentially wrecking his whole season or his team's plans on a farm track in northern France. Year after year, he single-handedly changes long-held conventions in the sport: that the Giro-Tour double cannot be done, that a Tour de France winner cannot win the Tour of Flanders, that you can't win a rainbow jersey with a 100-km attack, that you can't splinter Milan–San Remo on the Cipressa, that a Grand Tour winner ought not do Paris–Roubaix.

However, the strain appeared to show a week later at the Amstel Gold Race. While seemingly on another 40-km lone escape to victory, he 'cracked completely' into the headwind, was caught and Danish rider Mattias Skjelmose pipped him in a three-man sprint finish.

Nevertheless, it was classic Pogačar in the other Ardennes Classics, winning the Flèche Wallonne and then Liège–Bastogne–Liège in a nigh-on carbon copy of the 2024 race. It was the same *domestique*, Domen Novak, doing the damage on La Redoute, almost the same place of attack and the same victory celebration, pointing to the sky for Urška's mother. The only significant differences were his rainbow jersey and the fact he stayed seated this time when he made his unmatchable move, adding to the impression of serenity as he glided away.

Afterwards, in a video posted by EF Education-EasyPost on Instagram, the third-placed Ben Healy asked Pogačar playfully when he was retiring, and received an apologetic smile and this reply: 'I have a contract until 2030. So that's the year, maybe.'

Fellow members of the peloton are already aware they are in the presence of generational greatness. They can tell their kids that they raced with the magnificent 'Pogi'. Even leading racers in this modern 'golden era', to use Pogačar's own words, are inspired by him.

'I just try to learn when I see him race and … I'm not going to say analyse because I'm not that smart, but see how he races and typical styles of his,' Remco Evenepoel told me in a press conference. 'But of course, you have to be focused on yourself and try to be the best version of yourself. That's the only way that I can go and try to beat him, and them [with Vingegaard], for the Tour. He is probably the best rider that there has been since Merckx. It's up to us to go and hunt that position.'

While Pogačar's rivalry with Jonas Vingegaard has burned intensely, the Dane has been second best since his crash in April 2024. He was the last man to let go of Pogačar's wheel on his ride to a couple of Critérium du Dauphiné mountain stages and the title, and it was *status quo* at the Tour de France.

Vingegaard indicated there that he was better than he had ever been, but it still wasn't good enough. He remains the most fearsome rival with the best-organised team, trying in vain to isolate and crack Pogačar.

The pair has gotten a little closer too; in the neutral zone of the race's final stage into Paris, Pogačar and Vingegaard chatted about the incredible battles they have shared over the last five years.

'If I was racing without him, it wouldn't be the same and hopefully he feels the same the other way around,' Vingegaard said ahead of the 2025 Tour. 'I guess it could be kind of boring if you just win every mountain stage with two minutes. So yeah, I actually enjoy having a rival like him.'

For other, lesser riders in the bunch, jealousy or frustration would be understandable emotions, given that they dedicate their whole lives trying to win just one of the WorldTour races that Pogačar habitually conquers with apparent nonchalance.

Suspicion is inevitable, too. One fellow WorldTour peer suggests that the power numbers achieved by Pogačar for his 100-km attack to victory in the 2024 World Championships are 'unbelievable' – but then adds: 'I don't know if I believe it or not. I think it's too difficult to do any kind of serious doping or anything like that, I think it's just complete raw talent. Because, let's face it, if he was doing something, there'd be other guys that would be as good. Logically, all these young talents signed for UAE would be knocking on the door. But actually, nobody is that close.'

Pogačar has somehow become a young, elder statesman at the age of 27 in both his team and the wider peloton. Only one rider – Vegard Stake Laengen – has been on UAE Team Emirates–XRG longer than him. He has grown up around the squad, and he has helped to shape it. They are a transformed team, becoming the supreme force in pro cycling and winning more than 90 races in 2025.

'Tadej really brings everyone up,' teammate Pavel Sivakov says. 'OK, even without him, it is super strong but I think he probably elevates it by taking some pressure off everyone else doing their own thing. When you think about it, all the pressure is on him because what matters in cycling is really the Tour and he is the man winning it. It's pretty incredible how he's able to manage this.'

Racing with him on the same team for the 2024 and 2025 Tours, Sivakov is still in awe of his abilities and exceptional physical talent.

While Pogačar makes it look really easy, it is never as straightforward as it appears. His more defensive approach in the 2025 Tour's last week was also a sign of how difficult the edition was. 'It was harder for everyone, really intense from start to finish. Everyone was just so much more tired than the 2024 race, even him. It was much more demanding, every day was extreme racing,' Sivakov says.

Pogačar is not always as breezy when the cameras are off, and there have been occasional accusations of arrogance placed at the team's door. His teammate Nils Politt was seen shouting at various attackers as they tried to join a breakaway on stage 16 of the race. He was trying to control the bunch for Pogačar and indicated that the attacks happened while 30 to 40 riders were coming back after a nature break, contravening one of the peloton's unwritten rules.

'I hate riders who want to lay down the law under the pretext that they are stronger or in big teams. That's a detestable attitude,' said ex-Tour de France star Thomas Voeckler on France Télévisions.

Pogačar gave such comments short shrift. 'I think a lot of riders would see us as arrogant because we want to control every single kilometre of this race. We tried to calm things down,' he said in a press conference after stage 17. 'We don't try to be arrogant, we just try to make our race as easy as possible. I think – and this will sound super arrogant,' he said with a knowing smile – 'but some guys can stay quiet.'

Discussing Pogačar's popularity and conduct in the peloton with numerous WorldTour riders, on and off the record, they had precious little bad to say about him. He and his UAE Team Emirates team generally do not race disrespectfully or throw their weight around. Above and beyond his palmarès, Pogačar is admired because he gets on with everyone, smiling and not taking things too seriously.

He is also not afraid to step forward when required and take responsibility. At the Tre Valli Varesine one-day race in October 2024, heavy rainstorms led to flooding on the Lombardy course. Pogačar went to the front of the bunch and said they were going to stop racing, speaking to the race director and imposing his will for the greater good. Although the race was cancelled, he subsequently made the classy move of posing for photographs with the trophy and autographed it, to be given away at a local youth race.

Far from using his status to bully the rest of the bunch, as a few past champions have done, he is the one fending them off. During the 2025 Tour, a race in which every melodrama blows up and dies in the space of a day, he called the internet trolls off Tobias Halland Johannessen. On stage 11, the Norwegian rider caused him to crash on the run-in to Toulouse when his back wheel crossed with the race leader's front one. Even hours after a fall which could have ruined his race, Pogačar had moved on. 'People, stop giving him shit. It's all good, race incident,' he said in an Instagram video, his teammate Narváez adding the kicker: 'But keep the line, eh' to laughter around the UAE Team Emirates–XRG dinner table.

▶ After just seven years as a professional cyclist, Tadej Pogačar has a palmarès to challenge any rider in history. He is fast closing on the wheel of the legendary Eddy Merckx.

19

DOMINANCE

There is no doubt that Tadej Pogačar is the best, most complete rider of his generation. There will likely never be another man so dominant in stage races, so hungry and capable in such a breadth of high-profile, diverse one-day races, so creative and dynamic with his ways of winning, so exuberant off the bike.

Pogačar can easily already lay a claim to be cycling's greatest of all time. He is butting heads and palmarès with Eddy Merckx.

What makes someone the greatest? It requires sustained consistency and longevity, prestige of wins, versatility, panache, audacity, personality. Pogačar has that all.

He has the quality and quantity of wins too, passing the hundred mark at the 2025 Tour de France, less than six and a half years after his first at the Volta ao Algarve. The depth and calibre of opposition matters too: succeeding against adversaries like Primož Roglič, Jonas Vingegaard, Remco Evenepoel and Mathieu van der Poel in their primes also adds even more gloss to Pogačar's triumphs.

Pogačar's statistics are dizzying. Up to the end of the 2025 season, he had not lost a stage race for over two years. He had won 13 of his last 15 stage races, finishing in the top three of every one since August 2020 – when he placed fourth at the Critérium du Dauphiné. Even his hardiness is remarkable: he has never abandoned a stage race as a pro rider.

He has turned the hilly Monument races of Liège–Bastogne–Liège and Il Lombardia, the beluga caviar of pro cycling, into his bread and butter. In five visits up to 2025, he has *never* lost Il Lombardia. By November 2025, he had won 10 Monuments from 20 starts, with only Merckx on 19 and Roger De Vlaeminck on 11 above him.

At the Tour de France, he is one title away from joining Merckx, Anquetil, Hinault and Induráin in the five club. Pogačar also sits sixth in the list of all-time stage winners, with 21 from six editions.

The greatness debate is a lot more than a mere numbers game which is just as well, because it is not viable for Pogačar to match Merckx's tally of 525 wins, which included many criteriums – Pogačar only averages 55 race days a season and is not competitive in bunch sprints.

Such is his supremacy, Pogačar can also empathise with the downside of dominance. As Merckx won Tour after Tour, as well as many of the sport's other big races in similar resounding fashion, his popularity outside of his home country became strained. He was a victim of boos, even thrown stones and a punch from roadside spectators. Some viewed him as cold and aloof. Style of racing and perception of personality matter: Team Sky's robotic tactics also went down particularly badly in the 2010s, with urine poured on Chris Froome. Pogačar has avoided such inflammatory reaction, but he received some boos at the Tour de France and Tour of Flanders.

That's simply what happens when a team or rider wins too much. One competitor cannibalising the attention and the opposition unsurprisingly leaves some fans hungry for change. With win after exceptional win, the sheen of novelty and excitement gets gradually worn down. It would be a shame to take Pogačar's excellence for granted, for his pulsating attacks to be seen as normal.

While Pogačar has said that he does not care what people think, there is an awareness that his long-distance sorties are not the most crowd-pleasing. 'I've seen some [of my] highlights but not full races because I don't know how much fun it is to watch a rider ride 50 km alone,' he joked to *La Gazzetta dello Sport* after his superlative 2024 season.

Comparing the Cannibal and his modern successor is a fun and frivolous exercise, with a fair few flaws. Getting to the top and staying there is even more difficult for Pogačar, with the sport far more international now, the talent pool vaster and margins for success narrower than a deep-section rim. Some modern races were not around in 1970 and vice versa – who can say how many Tour of Sardinia stages Pogačar would have won or the number of Strade Bianche editions Merckx would have claimed? Even Tours de France cannot quite be compared like-for-like: the 1971 Tour, which Merckx won, contained a whopping 29 stages, eight more than the modern edition.

So much technology and sports science – time trial bikes, clipless pedals, power meters, Lycra and altitude training, to name just five advances in an endless list – was not around in the era of Merckx, whose sports nutrition extended to a steak before and after a race. Bikes are stiffer, lighter and more aerodynamic, although curiously Merckx and Pogačar both rode bikes from the same Colnago brand.

Though he has been for dinner with Merckx in the past and seen YouTube clips of him racing, Pogačar is no passionate student of cycling's yesteryears. Legacy is not on his mind as he seeks to make his own history.

'I honestly don't like the comparisons with other people,' Pogačar told reporters in October 2024. 'Especially with Eddy Merckx and cyclists from that era when I was not even born and [about whom] I don't know much. I was not close to that moment, I always say I like to go my own road, my own path, my own career and make my own story. I try to live in the moment and not think about the past and history, just live in the present.'

For what it's worth, Merckx believes there is no contest. 'It's obvious that he is now above me,' he told *L'Équipe* after the 2024 World Championships. 'Deep down, I already thought as much when I saw what he did on the last [2024] Tour de France, but tonight there's no more doubt about it.' Curiously, the next day, Merckx recanted that opinion, suggesting Pogačar still had some way to go.

Finding a winner in this debate would be more clear-cut if Pogačar can equal or surpass some of Merckx's marks. His Tour de France overall tally, 34-stage win record and Monument numbers are all reachable. But with Pogačar's career still in progress and his win-rate showing no signs of slowing down, drawing any conclusions is akin to calling a winner when a bike race still has 60 km to go.

Speaking at Italy's Festival dello Sport in October 2024, clad in a Steve Jobs-esque black turtleneck, Pogačar showed that he does not take any of his success for granted.

'I was born under a lucky star to get this chance, this opportunity I have to train hard, work hard and be good. Of course there is a lot of hard work, but without good education, how they raise you at home, you cannot reach far … I'm grateful I can win a lot, that I go from race to race as a favourite, but I also know at one point, there will be no more winning, so I take every chance that I can get. As long as we are winning, then we are happy. Then when we are not winning, we try to find some other thing to make us happy.'

How long his golden spell continues depends on his motivation and enjoyment. 'I want to have fun while making history,' he told *L'Équipe* in 2024. 'It will be a game until I start struggling. As long as I feel good every day on the bike, as long as I don't have any problems in training, as long as I can take coffee breaks with my friends, as long as I have good company, and as long as I go to races excited to see my teammates again, it will be a game. And when all that is gone, I will probably end my career. Until then, I will enjoy every moment … I've reached a point now where I aspire to be the best. I want to be the best in history.'

It is difficult for Pogačar to improve on his own feats, setting himself annual Olympus-high standards. Having helped to drive the change in how races are taken on, he and his team have to keep up and fend off rivals in the ceaseless push for self-improvement. The sporting and commercial pressures on him remain, with a whole ecosystem living and breathing his every race: teammates, sponsors, soigneurs, mechanics, managers.

The powers that be at UAE Team Emirates–XRG likely want him annually at the Tour de France, the one race that transcends the sport and carries the most prestige and commercial weight; Pogačar wants changes to his programme annually to keep him interested and motivated. 'Unfortunately, I'm stuck with the Tour every year,' he said in June 2025, tongue-in-cheek. Something might have to give; a Giro-Vuelta double season could give a welcome fresh break.

Time will also tell how much more he has left to give, mentally or physiologically. Pogačar expressed a couple of times during the 2025 season that he is at his peak.

'I'm at the point of my career where if I burn out, I can finish and be happy with what I achieved,' Pogačar said, microphone in hand after finishing the 2025 Tour de France. 'It could happen.'

With his summer references to retirement, Pogačar seemed like a man more in need of a break than somebody ready to jack everything in. His agent Alex Carera made it clear days later that he intends to honour his contract with UAE Team Emirates, signed in late 2024, which runs until the end of 2030. An estimated €8 million a year is not a bad incentive to keep going.

The estimated €200 million buyout clause is also likely to ward off any suitors. He is worth his weight in gold to the UAE team. 'He doesn't want to leave, he's part of the country. What he's doing for Abu Dhabi is worth more than the races he wins. Pogačar is proud of that,' Mauro Gianetti told the *Gazzetta dello Sport*.

Post-Tour, Pogačar clarified his longer-term thoughts to *L'Équipe*: 'I don't think I'll stop right away, but I don't see myself continuing for too long either. The Los Angeles Olympic Games [in 2028] are one of my goals, which takes me to three years from now. Then I might start thinking about retirement, we'll see.' If talk of a Tour de France start in Slovenia in 2029 comes to fruition, something unimaginable before the Pogačar and Roglič residencies at the top of the sport, he will surely want to be racing for that.

There are still new horizons: Olympic gold, a Vuelta a España triumph, Milan–San Remo glory and a Paris–Roubaix trophy are all on his hit list. Yet, failing to win those races will not alter his reputation. Already, he has nothing left to prove.

There will likely be more moments of ennui and self-questioning during draining seasons, but his natural optimism is a countering mechanism. Pogačar sees life like he does a hilly Monument bike race – there to be enjoyed and attacked to the nth degree.

Bowing out on top would be some achievement because most champions, even those who appear invincible, meet their match. An inflection point will come where he will not be able to perform at the same level physiologically or another incredible specimen will turn up who can put out even more watts per kilo or recover even better.

'There is nobody who can dominate for 10 years in a row who has never been challenged by anybody,' Matteo Trentin says. 'Maybe Tadej, but he has already lost the Tour de France. Of course, he is the one-in-a-million.'

Perhaps the man waiting in the wings is his own teammate, Isaac del Toro. The runner-up in the 2025 Giro d'Italia at the age of 21 exhibits a similar precocity to Pogačar. There are aesthetic parallels: the Mexican is of similar stature and weight; he even has the signature Pogačar style as he stamps on the pedals and leaves adversaries behind. Pogačar has indicated before that he is ready for the day when he isn't the best any more, but saying it before the event and then experiencing it are two different things.

Pogačar's incandescent performances arguably bring the day of his own usurping closer. Because with every 80-km solo attack or Grand Tour masterclass, he forces the next generation of riders and teams to push the boundaries – scheme harder for bolder tactics, attract a wealthy brand which can fund even more meticulous research and data-gathering, save that extra watt or two, recruit more intelligently, revolutionise training. Rather than killing professional cycling, Tadej Pogačar has powered its evolution.

For now, he is out there alone in front once again, racing against himself and his own achievements. As he said at Paris–Roubaix: just enjoy it.

The Boss: Pogačar celebrates the fifth of his six 2024 Tour de France stage wins on the Col de la Couillole.

ACKNOWLEDGEMENTS

Well, that escalated quickly. When I talked to a Slovenian youngster at the 2019 Volta ao Algarve about life as a neo-pro and *Harry Potter*, I didn't realise I was in the presence of greatness.

During that race, his rivals in Team Sky referred to him as 'the young kid' and most commentators couldn't pronounce his surname correctly for months. Suffice to say, nobody has that problem now. He has written a lot more chapters in his story since then – and so have I over the last year.

Much like Tadej Pogačar's triumphs, this book would simply not have been possible without the help and support of a vast range of people behind the scenes.

First and foremost, thanks to Anna for her patience, kindness, understanding and support during this book's creation. What a strange, all-encompassing and often-selfish pursuit it is. I love you, I'm glad I exist.

Thanks to my agent, Kevin Pocklington, for his work behind the scenes and to my editor, Matt Lowing, at Bloomsbury for his unwavering backing, positivity and sage editing advice throughout the process. *Il miglior fabbro* is even better at making the right calls at fraught moments than this book's protagonist, which takes some doing.

The same goes for the brilliant team at Bloomsbury for helping to make this book a tour de force: managing editor Sarah Skipper, copy editor Caroline Curtis, Xanthe Rendall, Katherine Macpherson and race statistics compiler Adrian Besley; Emil and Sian at D.R.INK for their dazzling design work, plus Elliot Chapman for the audiobook.

We can't start the sporting acknowledgements without the main man: my thanks to Tadej Pogačar and his inner circle, especially Urška Žigart, Alex Carera, Luke Maguire, Marjeta Pogačar and Mirko Pogačar.

This is not just the tale of the kindly young king from Komenda, but that too of UAE Team Emirates–XRG, who have taken the cycling world by storm in a matter of years. More gratitude goes to management members Mauro Gianetti, Joxean Fernández Matxin, Andrea Agostini and staff Marco Marzano, Žiga Jerman, Boštjan Kavčnik and Joseba Elguezabal as well as riders Mikkel Bjerg, Tim Wellens, Rui Oliveira, Isaac del Toro, Pavel Sivakov and Florian Vermeersch. Further thanks go to ex-staff Fabrizio Bontempi, Allan Peiper, Rubens Bertogliati, Aurelio 'Yeyo' Corral, John Wakefield, Neil Stephens and Vasile Morari for their contributions.

Pogačar's peers in the peloton elevated this book, as generous with their time and anecdotes as they are with their watts. Thanks to Luka Mezgec, Tom Bohli, David de la Cruz, Davide Formolo, Simone Petilli, Sven Erik Byström, Ben Hill, Tim Guy, George Bennett, Matteo Trentin, Jonas Vingegaard, Remco Evenepoel, Sjoerd Bax, Finn Fisher-Black, Chris Froome, Luke Durbridge, Jasper Philipsen, Oscar Onley, Pello Bilbao, Fernando Gaviria, Mikkel Honoré, Diego Ulissi, Filippo Zana, Luca Colombo, Andrea Colombo, Michael Matthews, Ben O'Connor and the other professional cyclists who spoke off the record or under the condition of anonymity, helping to further my understanding of the phenom.

Writing a book about Slovenia's sporting superstar was also a happy excuse to visit one of Europe's most beautiful countries. *Hvala* to Tomaž Poljanec, Miha Koncilija, the Hauptman family (plus Mars, cycling's best dog in a crowded field), Jaka Primožič, Blaž Debevec, Žiga Ručigaj, Martin Hvastija, Samo Rauter and Radoje Milić. The previously untold stories of young Pogi make this book sing.

Additional thanks go to David Crmelj, Uroš Gramc, Mateja Maučec, Karin Klun, Nina Jerončič, Marjana Grošlj, Karmen Globočnik, Miro Šlebir, Mateja Kavčič, Uroš Križanič, Borut Fonda, Bogdan Martinčič, Vlasta Rudar Nenadović, Darja Lučič, OŠ Komenda and Srednja šola za strojništvo, kemijo in varovanje. Apologies in advance for accidentally omitting any diacritical marks in Slovenian!

The writing process of *Unstoppable* inevitably drew me back into the past features I've written. There was a lot of buried treasure in my notebooks and interview archive.

Thanks are owed to my previous employers, *Rouleur,* for the opportunities which helped this project, as well as to *Escape*

Collective, GCN and *Cycling Plus*. As for my recent Tour de France employers *Velo*: the enjoyable company makes every July for me and I appreciate you putting up with my budget-crippling chocolat liégois habit.

From the global cycling press pack who shared titbits, press conference quotes or simply boosted my morale with Tour de France dinner-time highs and lows: thanks to Chris Marshall-Bell, Rachel Jary, Jonny Long, the whole 'Britpack', Sean Russell, David Powell, Peter Stuart, Edward Pickering, Ian Cleverly, Ned Boulting, Andy Hood, James Startt, Felix Lowe, Hannah Gross, Will Tracy, Jim Cotton, José Been, Fabrice Tiano and the UCI, RCS, Valentina Gnan at FCI Friuli-Venezia Giulia, Elisa Nicoletti, Jacob Kennison, Charles le Fouler, Davide Marta and all at Alvento.

A heartfelt *merci* to Jean-François Quenet for his generous sharing of press conference and flash interview recordings, contributing to hours and hours of valuable listening.

I'm so thankful to Richard Abraham for combing through the book, his conscientious, clear advice making the end product much better. In return, I'll try to get the message to the Fulham first XI to give Leeds six points this season. Many thanks also to Phil Cavell for his spot-on technical and physiological know-how, which helped immensely.

Nando Boers' sublime book *Het plan* was full of useful information about Jumbo–Visma and Jonas Vingegaard's 2022 Tour de France victory.

For information or interview snippets, I'm particularly grateful to *L'Équipe*, *La Gazzetta dello Sport*, *El Mundo*, *El País*, *Cyclingnews*, *Delo*, *Siol* and *Večer*. Pro Cycling Stats and FirstCycling were go-tos for pinpoint statistics, and Prijavim helped greatly for Pogačar's early results.

Away from the world of two wheels, thanks to my family, Nick Christian, Siobhan Fennessy, 'the GC', Hannah, Duncan, Stanley and Bessie, Gimhani Eriyagolla, Susan Tomlinson, John Lunt and Mel Spencer. For my godson Leo and nephew Rowan, I look forward to reading this to you and inspiring a lifelong love for cycling, though I fear this won't hold a candle to Penny Dale's *Dinosaurs!* series at bedtime.

A shout-out to the British Library, a haven of serenity and study in London, helping me to deliver my best work. I recommend frequenting and donating to it.

Last but not least, for keeping me fuelled and over-caffeinated, SW16 Bar & Kitchen, The Westow and Butter Up Coffee were unmatched.

Catch Pogačar if you can. Even the TV motorbike struggles as the superstar races down the Galibier to stage victory in the 2024 Tour de France.

NOTABLE WINS AND PLACINGS

2016 (JUNIOR)

Team: **Radenska**

1st – Junior Peace Race, stage 2b

3rd – Trofeo Guido Dorigo

1st – National Championships Slovenia (Junior): ITT

1st – Giro della Lunigiana: stage 3 and GC

3rd – European Championships (Junior): Road Race

2017 (UNDER-23)

Team: **Rog-Ljubljana**

3rd – Istrian Spring Trophy, stage 2

5th – Tour of Slovenia

3rd – Tour of Hungary

2nd – International Raiffeisen Grand Prix

2018 (UNDER-23)

Team: **Ljubljana Gusto Xaurum**

3rd – Istrian Spring Trophy

2nd – GP Palio del Recioto

1st – Grand Prix Priessnitz spa: stage 3 and GC

4th – Tour of Slovenia

1st – Tour de l'Avenir: GC

1st – Giro della Regione Friuli-Venezia Giulia

1st – National Championships Slovenia: Cyclo-Cross

2019 (PROFESSIONAL FROM 1 JANUARY 2019)

Team: UAE Team Emirates

1st – Volta ao Algarve: stage 2 and GC

1st – Amgen Tour of California: stage 6 and GC

1st – National Championships Slovenia: ITT

3rd – La Vuelta ciclista a España: stages 9, 13, 20 winner

2020

Team: UAE Team Emirates

1st – Volta a la Comunitat Valenciana: stages 2, 4 and GC

2nd – UAE Tour: stage 5 winner

1st – National Championships Slovenia: ITT

2nd – National Championships Slovenia: Road Race

1st – Tour de France: stages 9, 15, 20 (ITT), mountains, youth classification and GC

3rd – Liège–Bastogne–Liège

2021

Team: UAE Team Emirates

1st – UAE Tour: stage 3 and GC

1st – Tirreno–Adriatico: stage 4 and GC

3rd – Itzulia Basque Country: stage 3 winner

1st – Liège–Bastogne–Liège

1st – Tour of Slovenia: stage 2 and GC

1st – Tour de France: stages 5 (ITT), 17, 18, mountains, youth classification and GC

3rd – Olympic Games Road Race

3rd – Tre Valli Varesine

1st – Il Lombardia

2022

Team: UAE Team Emirates

1st – UAE Tour: stages 4, 7 and GC

1st – Strade Bianche

1st – Tirreno–Adriatico: stages 4, 6 and GC

1st – Tour of Slovenia: stages 3, 5 and GC

1st – Tour de France: stages 6, 7, 17 and youth classification

2nd – Tour de France

1st – Grand Prix Cycliste de Montréal

1st – Tre Valli Varesine

1st – Il Lombardia

2023

Team: UAE Team Emirates

1st – Jaén Paraiso Interior

1st – Vuelta a Andalucía: stages 1, 2, 4 and GC

1st – Paris–Nice: stages 4, 7, 8 and GC

3rd – E3 Saxo Classic

1st – Ronde van Vlaanderen – Tour of Flanders

1st – Amstel Gold Race

1st – La Flèche Wallonne

1st – National Championships Slovenia: ITT

1st – National Championships Slovenia: Road Race

1st – Tour de France: stages 6, 20 and youth classification

2nd – Tour de France

3rd – World Championships: Road Race

3rd – Coppa Sabatini

2nd – Giro dell'Emilia

1st – Il Lombardia

2024

Team: UAE Team Emirates

1st – Strade Bianche

3rd – Milan–San Remo

1st – Volta Ciclista a Catalunya: stages 2, 3, 6, 7 and GC

1st – Liège–Bastogne–Liège

1st – Giro d'Italia: stages 2, 7 (ITT), 8, 15, 16, 20, Mountains classification and GC

1st – Tour de France: stages 4, 14, 15, 19, 20, 21 (ITT) and GC

1st – Grand Prix Cycliste de Montréal

1st – World Championships: Road Race

1st – Giro dell'Emilia

1st – Il Lombardia

2025

Team: UAE Team Emirates–XRG

1st – UAE Tour: stages 3, 7 and GC

1st – Strade Bianche

3rd – Milan–San Remo

1st – Ronde van Vlaanderen – Tour of Flanders

2nd – Paris–Roubaix

2nd – Amstel Gold Race

1st – La Flèche Wallonne

1st – Liège–Bastogne–Liège

1st – Critérium du Dauphiné: stages 1, 6, 7 and GC

1st – Tour de France: stages 4, 7, 12, 13 (ITT), Mountains classification and GC

2nd – Grand Prix Cycliste de Montréal

1st – World Championships: Road Race

1st – European Championships: Road Race

1st – Tre Valli Varesine

1st – Il Lombardia

REFERENCES AND SOURCES

Journals and Online Media
24UR
Aleteia
AS
BBC
Bici.pro
Bicycling
Bikeradar
CNN
Cycling News
Cycling Plus
CyclingTips
Cycling Weekly
Cyclist
Daily Maverick
Delo
Družina
El Correo
El Mundo
El País
Escape Collective
Gorenjski Glas
GQ
Het Laatste Nieuws
Het Nieuwsblad
Il Mattino
Knack
La Gazzetta dello Sport
La Vanguardia
L'Équipe
L'Est Républicain
L'Humanité
Le Parisien
Le Soir
MARCA
New York Times
NOS
Noticias de Navarra
NRC
PezCyclingnews
Prijavim
Procycling
Relevo
RFI
RIDE Magazine
RMC

Road.cc
Rouleur
RTVSlo
Runda
SBS
Siol
Smarnagora.com
Sportklub
Sporza
Sticky Bottle
Sydney Morning Herald
The Guardian
The Independent
The Times
Trouw.nl
Tuttobiciweb
Večer
Velo
Velo-Club
WielerFlits
Wieler Revue
Zadarski.hr
Žurnal24

Video channels
Cycling Pro.net
Cyclism'Actu TV
Global Cycling Network
Gregario Cycling
MET Helmets
Oradelciclismo
Pogi Team Gusto Ljubljana
Sigma Sports
UAE Team Emirates
Velon

Podcasts
Castelli Cycling
Cyclist Magazine
Escapa
Radio Sportiva
The Cycling Podcast
The Peter Attia Drive
TriCiclo
Watts Occuring
Watts On

Other resources
AGinsurance-soudal.com
All-In:TeamJumbo–Visma
(Amazon Prime)
Allievi.ciclismo.info
Avto Magazin
BikeChannel
Bikeraceinfo.com
Ciclo21.com
Corvos.photoshelter.com
CQRanking
Eurosport/TNT Sports
FirstCycling
FloBikes
GCN
Getty Images
GreenEdge Cycling
IDLprocycling.com
Instagram
Italiaciclismo.net
ITV Cycling and ITV Sport
Juniores.ciclismo.info
Kolesarska Zveva Slovenije
Lanternerouge.com
Letour.fr
Letourfemmes.fr
MyWhoosh
Netflix
Olympics.com
Parlement-wallonie.be
ProCyclingStats
Ruvid.org
Slovenia.info
Strava
Tadejpogacar.com
Tadejpogacar.org
Tudorprocycling.com
TV2
UAEteamemirates.com
Velon
Vismaleaseabike.com
Wildairsports.com
YouTube
X

Books

Boers, Nando. 2023. *Het plan: hoe team Jumbo–Visma de beste wielerploeg ter wereld werd*, Ambo|Anthos.

Boulting, Ned. 2020. *The Road Book Almanack*.

Clarey, Christopher. 2022. *The Master: The Brilliant Career of Roger Federer*, John Murray.

Cossins, Peter. 2014. *The Monuments*, London: Bloomsbury Sport.

Horvat A. Cameron and Mason, Carolynne. 2022. 'Country Profile of Slovenia: Sport Policy System in a Small State', *International Journal of Sport Policy and Politics*, Vol. 14, No. 4, 743-757, Routledge.

Luthar, Oto. 2008. *The Land Between: A History of Slovenia*, Frankfurt: Peter Lang.

Martin, Dan. 2022. *Chased by Pandas,* London: Quercus.

Rowe, Luke. 2025. *Road Captain: My Life at the Heart of the Peloton*, London: Bantam.

Williams, Mark and Wigmore, Tim. 2020. *The Best: How Elite Athletes Are Made*, London: Nicholas Brealey Publishing.

Witts, James. 2023. *Riding with the Rocketmen*, London: Bloomsbury Sport.

REFERENCES AND SOURCES

Outlets and dates are included in the text or in the reference list below when available. Other sources, including books, national newspapers and broadcast media, are cited below. Interviews I conducted and quotes from press conferences or team press releases are not referenced here.

5 'Why? So they don't have confidence [in me]?' Joxean Fernández Matxin quoted in La Bicicleta Podcast, 2x05, March 2021: https://www.esciclismo.com/actualidad/carretera/65040.html

-https://open.spotify.com/episode/4yCu3EYQtuZGJmpxhNNky-D?si=456e0359810142d2 (the actual podcast) (at 3.50)) 8 "I was going to finish second and I was happy ... ': Tadej Pogačar quoted in Issartel, D., 'Tadej Pogačar, vainqueur du Tour de France : « Tout est à l'envers à l'intérieur de moi »', *L'Équipe*, 20 September 2020 https://www.lequipe.fr/Cyclisme-sur-route/Article/Tadej-pogacar-vainqueur-du-tour-de-france-tout-est-a-l-envers-a-l-interieur-de-moi/1174190

10 'Never give up until Paris'. The reply was one word: 'never': Alex Carera quoted in Schiavon, A., '"È solamente l'inizio"', *Tuttosport*, 21 September 2020

10 'It gave him an advantage. I understood ...': Primož Roglič quoted in Issartel, D., 'Comment Tadej Pogačar a renversé le Tour de France 2020', *L'Équipe*, 1 July 2021. https://www.lequipe.fr/Cyclisme-sur-route/Article/Comment-tadej-pogacar-a-renverse-le-tour-de-france-2020/1267183

15 'I don't know. I think I'm dreaming...': Tadej Pogačar quoted in Letour.fr, 19 September 2020. https://www.letour.fr/en/news/2020/stage-20/tadej-pogacar-actually-my-dream-was-not-to-win-the-tour-de-france-but-just-to-take-part-in-it/1291379

15 'I'll never forget that moment ...': Tadej Pogačar quoted in Issartel, D., « Primoz Roglic a réussi à m'apaiser », affirme Tadej Pogačar, vainqueur du Tour de France 2020, *L'Équipe*, 15 December 2020. https://www.lequipe.fr/Cyclisme-sur-route/Article/-primoz-roglic-a-reussi-a-m-apaiser-affirme-tadej-pogacar-vainqueur-du-tour-de-france-2020/1206141

17 'This guy could go on to be the greatest cyclist of all time ... ': Bradley Wiggins quoted on Eurosport/GCN coverage of 2020 Tour de France stage 20, 19 September 2020

20 'So far history has not presented us with any gifts. We have had ...': Bivsi-predsenik.si, Declaration of Independence of the Republic of Slovenia, Speech by the President of the Presidency Milan Kučan, 26 June 1991. https://www.bivsi-predsednik.si/up-rs/1992-2002/mk-ang.nsf/4f0e6b3d16bb4c8dc-125678c003a80ab/b423eb5960971ca3c-125678c003a4c46?OpenDocument

21 'I think it has to do with our nature: we were born with stubbornness and ...': Tadej Pogačar quoted in Instagram Live interview with Breitling CEO Georges Kern, 16 November 2020. https://www.instagram.com/reel/CHqJi_wAtKv/?hl=en

23 'We always told Tadej that there will not only be successes in life, there will also be defeats ...': Marjeta Pogačar quoted on Sol in Luč radio show, July 2021. https://radio.ognjisce.si/sl/239/oddaje/33386/zakaj-tadej-pogacar-zmaguje-mama-marjeta-in-oce-mirko-o-svojem-sinu.htm

24 'When he was a child, whenever he felt that something went wrong in the family, he tried to cheer us up and he played the clown. Every time; he needed there to be no tension in the family. He tried to break the tension, and he stayed like that': Marjeta Pogačar quoted in McGrath, A., 'Tadej, Tomorrow, Always', *Rouleur*, Issue 104, 2021

24 'We tried to teach them to be honest, hard-working and kind to other people. We wanted our children to participate in a sport activity in order to be a part of a ...': Marjeta Pogačar quoted in McGrath, A., 'Tadej, Tomorrow, Always', *Rouleur*, Issue 104, 2021

24 'If they wanted a toy, we couldn't afford everything because we were building the house and we didn't have much money at this time. ...': Marjeta Pogačar to GCN+, PlaySPORTS Network, October 2023

25 'I'm lucky to have a good family. I owe a big thanks to my parents, my brother and my sisters. They made me who I am': Tadej Pogačar quoted in Farrand, S., 'Tadej Pogačar: I don't think I'm the best rider out there, I just try to do my best', *Cyclingnews*, 21 October 2021. https://www.cyclingnews.com/features/tadej-pogacar-i-dont-think-im-the-best-rider-out-there-i-just-try-to-do-my-best/

26 'If we help children with the smallest obstacles from the beginning, how will ...': Pogačar, M., Veliko o ljubezni in skoraj nič o sinu Tadeju (Pogačarju)', *Delo*, 15 June 2022. https://www.delo.si/polet/veliko-o-ljubezni-in-skoraj-nic-o-sinu-tadeju-pogacarju

28 'Immediately, it was really fun for me. I was enjoying [it], I had new friends. It was a nice challenge. And then every year that passed by, I was enjoying it more. I was thinking, "This is really cool, I want to do this forever"': Tadej Pogačar, Cycling in Slovenia with Tour de France Champion Tadej Pogačar [Podcast], FEEL Slovenia Podcast, 13 June 2022

30 'After my first year on the bike, I wanted to become a top cyclist': Tadej Pogačar quoted in Košir Teran, A., 'Slovenec, ki je na Portugalskem presenetil (še sebe), z novico, ki bo razveselila slovenske ljubitelja kolesarstva', *Siol*, 2 March 2019

https://siol.net/sportal/kolesarstvo/slovenska-sportna-senzacija-z-novico-ki-bo-razveselila-slovenske-ljubitelja-kolesarstva-491528

30 'He always found a way to beat me': Tadej Pogačar quoted in Walsh, D., 'Tadej Pogačar: My brother always beat me – but then one day he didn't want to do it anymore', *The Sunday Times*, 18 December 2021. https://www.thetimes.com/sport/cycling/article/tadej-pogacar-my-brother-always-beat-me-but-then-one-day-he-didn-t-want-to-do-it-anymore-5ffts0fj7

32 'I think we have a good school system to introduce different sports to children. I think almost every kid does one sport when they're young. In the end, you get a lot of different kids doing a lot of different sports so you can find good ones and then talent in this way': Tadej Pogačar quoted in Instagram Live interview with Breitling CEO Georges Kern, 16 November 2020. https://www.instagram.com/reel/CHqJi_wAtKv/?hl=en

33 'When Tadej was 13 or 14 years old, he was very focused on cycling. He was training very hard in this time and he wasn't a difficult teenager...': Marjeta Pogačar to GCN+, PlaySPORTS Network, October 2023

33 'We didn't see how good he was when he was young. All his trainers, Miha Koncilija and the others, said he was very talented. I asked, "How can you say this? I can't see it." Because Tadej didn't win races when he was young because he was very small': Ibid.

34 'Every mistake that he maybe made, he didn't do it again. Everything he did in races and in training, ...': Miha Koncilija quoted in Alderman, E., 'Tadej Pogačar: The Tour de France champion yet to win over his nation', *The Times*, 28 June 2023 https://www.thetimes.com/sport/cycling/article/tadej-pogacar-tour-de-france-2023-l3dt7hzvz

34 'I know that if you do something with a great pleasure, I couldn't remove this sport from my children. Because Tadej would die, perhaps, without cycling. He was really into it': Marjeta Pogačar to GCN+, PlaySPORTS Network, October 2023

35 'What can I say? I know it's dangerous, but I love adrenaline': Tadej Pogačar quoted in Košir Teran, A., 'Slovenec, ki je na Portugalskem presenetil (še sebe), z novico, ki bo razveselila slovenske ljubitelja kolesarstva', *Siol*, 2 March 2019. https://siol.net/sportal/kolesarstvo/slovenska-sportna-senzacija-z-novico-ki-bo-razveselila-slovenske-ljubitelja-kolesarstva-491528

35 'The more you let your child be active, the more he [or she] will learn his own limits ... ': Marjeta Pogačar quoted in Hočevar, M., 'Tadej je od naju pobral samo najboljše', *Delo*, 23 July 2023 https://www.delo.si/nedelo/tadej-je-od-naju-pobral-samo-najboljse

40 'I didn't regret it. In fact, I've kept the same mindset I had when I played with my brother ...': Tadej Pogačar quoted in Issartel, D. and Scherrer, G., 'Tadej Pogačar (UAE-Emirates), vainqueur du Tour de France 2021: « À la télé, tout semble facile... »', *L'Équipe*, 18 July 2021. https://www.lequipe.fr/Cyclisme-sur-route/Article/Tadej-pogacar-uae-emirates-vainqueur-du-tour-de-france-2021-a-la-tele-tout-semble-facile/1271348

50 'Who is leading the chase of the escape? It's Tadej Pogačar again. Tireless, always on the attack. He's taken more wind today than a sailing regatta': Oradelciclismo YouTube channel, 'Gran Premio Valli del Natisone 2016 | servizio completo', 9 October 2016 https://www.youtube.com/watch?v=s-yUn2gveCCI

50 'Whenever he was not doing well in a race, he would first carefully lean the bike against the van at the finish line and then start a volley of curses. The bike was never at fault, always and only him': Miha Koncilija quoted in Cvjetičanin, M., 'Vsa kolesa Tadeja Pogačarja', *Delo*, 16 June 2022. https://www.delo.si/polet/vsa-kolesa-tadeja-pogacarja

56 'I like long climbs and difficult finishes, and I also like time trials, though I'm not very good at this discipline. I think I need to work at this': Tadej Pogačar quoted in Marsault, C., '[Champions de Demain] ITW: Tadej Pogačar', Velo-Club, 6 December 2016. https://www.velo-club.net/route/continentales-interviews/les-interviews/114263-champions-de-demain-itw-tadej-pogacar

56 'We talked about it a lot. I knew that if he went any further, they would want to dope him. That's when it starts': Marjeta Pogačar quoted in Issartel, D., 'Tadej Pogačar (UAE Team Emirates) et l'histoire d'une émancipation', *L'Équipe*, 17 July 2021. https://www.lequipe.fr/Cyclisme-sur-route/Article/Tadej-pogacar-uae-team-emirates-et-l-histoire-d-une-emancipation/1271155

57 'Mothers whose children ride bikes are afraid of two things: accidents and doping. It's true that there have been several cases in Slovenia. I had to personally commit to protect him from that': Ibid.

61 'I can't imagine doing anything else. I would suffer in the office, here I am free': Anica Štebe quoted in Rupar, A., '"Tadeja izročam, da bi zmogel in ostal tak, kot je, prijazen in pošten"', *Aleteia*, 19 July 2021

62 'This is one of the first podiums in my career. I hope there will be many more and it will continue like this. That one day I might even win the Tour of Slovenia and something else of a higher rank': Tadej Pogačar quoted in Lopatič, L. 'Slovenija slavi 18-letnika, ki ga že ta teden čaka zrelostni preizkus', *Siol*, 19 June 2017. https://siol.net/sportal/kolesarstvo/slovenija-slavi-18-letnika-ki-ga-ta-teden-caka-preizkus-zrelosti-443568

62 'Of course, I would like them [my teachers] to look kindly on me, but that's not going to happen. It's very tiring mentally when you have to prepare for school and compete at the same time': Ibid.

62 'a little disappointed, but still very satisfied': Tadej Pogačar quoted in 'Mugerli zmagovalec kraljevske etape, Pogačar tretji', Privajim.se, 11 March 2017. https://Prijavim.se/index_page/news/4525/

64 'Fabrizio, are you still proposing these Slovenian kids to me?' Giuseppe Saronni quoted in Marabini, P., 'Saronni: "Sì, Pogačar è il Merckx di questa generazione. Ma il Giro ha mille insidie..."', *La Gazzetta dello Sport*, 28 April 2024

66 'democracy doesn't belong in sports ... I've never been a democracy': Marko Polanc quoted in Košir Teran, A., 'Kolesarski trener opozarja: Če se ne bo delalo dobro, tudi rezultatov ne bo', *Siol*, 15 September 2019. https://siol.net/sportal/kolesarstvo/kolesarski-trener-opozarja-ce-se-ne-bo-delalo-do-bro-tudi-rezultatov-ne-bo-video-507004

71'I sometimes thought that cycling was making me miss out on all the fun,' Pogačar told Siol in 2019. 'But in the end, it's worth putting so much effort into what you love to do. Cycling has given me a very special life. Without a bike and fellow cyclists, I would probably be bored': Tadej Pogačar quoted in Košir Teran, A., 'Slovenec, ki je na Portugalskem presenetil (še sebe), z novico, ki bo razveselila slovenske ljubitelja kolesarstva', *Siol*, 2 March 2019. https://siol.net/sportal/kolesarstvo/slovenska-sportna-senzacija-z-novico-ki-bo-razveselila-slovenske-ljubitelja-kolesarstva-491528

72 'At first, he was quite shy. It took a while. He was a bit like he is in the media now, serious. But with me, he makes jokes, Tadej is more self-confident, he is relaxed. He is funny, he is a joker': Urška Žigart quoted in Bontinck, J-G., 'Tour de France femmes : «Tadej est relax, drôle, blagueur»... Urska Zigart, la fiancée de Pogačar, se confie', *Le Parisien*, 29 July 2022. https://www.leparisien.fr/sports/cyclisme/tour-de-france-femmes-tadej-est-relax-drole-blagueur-urska-zigart-la-fiancee-de-pogacar-se-confie-29-07-2022-TRNNHSQQCFCTPJ3MOZOPX7ZWSM.php

77 'They [Tilen and Tadej] found friends in the club that they still hang out with today and they found values that they still live by. Let [children] know that with hard work and willpower, they can shake stars from the sky': Mirko Pogačar's message of thanks to KD Rog Ljubljana, quoted in Kališnik, P., 'Otroku naj klub postane drugi dom', Delo, 6 December 2021

81 'to be a representative for the UAE, for a culture to promote a healthy lifestyle [and] to promote the use of bicycles in the UAE': Mauro Gianetti quoted in 'WorldTour race: Two examples of UAE's commitment to cycling', TNT Sports/Eurosport, 27 February 2018. https://www.tntsports.co.uk/cycling/worldtour-race-two-examples-of-uaes-commitment-to-cycling_sto6656959/story.shtml

82 'Rather than working on marginal gains, the staff felt they should stick with their old habits. I suggested getting input from researchers, sports scientists, biomechanics and materials engineers. Equipment, tyres, textiles, nutrition: everything needed to be reviewed. But every time I proposed something the staff got upset ... we were 20 years behind our rivals': Martin, Dan, *Chased by Pandas*, London: Quercus, 2022

83 'Some football teams buy big players, but this is not the goal, it is to create a team': Mauro Gianetti quoted in Jones, M., 'Inside Story: The Italian roots making UAE Team Emirates strong', Sport360, 23 April 2017. https://sport360.com/article/other/cycling/230918/inside-story-uae-team-emirates-borne-out-of-italian-passion-but-finding-a-cycling-home-in-the-uae

84 'I'm always nervous before the new season because I always want to improve. I'm always nervous because what if I stop ...': Tadej Pogačar quoted in Christian, N., 'Introducing… Slovenia's first Tour de l'Avenir winner, Tadej Pogačar', Rouleur, 2019,

https://www.rouleur.cc/en-us/blogs/the-rouleur-journal/introducing-slovenia-s-first-tour-de-l-avenir-winner-tadej-pogacar?srsltid=AfmBOor2_q0-kVZ-MV9w8NbDW21O36sSnmx9prlfgOzaS-FtexeU-EsMvb

86 'OK, he was nervous. But most guys would have been panicking and Tadej didn't panic ... He stayed happy, friendly and compliant because he had to do a load of things, go to the police, go to the bank, organise some things ... it struck me how relaxed under pressure he was and I think that's one of his strongest traits. And that was the first impression I had [of him]': Allan Peiper in McGrath, A., 'Tadej, Tomorrow, Always', *Rouleur*, Issue 104, 2021

88 'This little fat kid showed up from Slovenia and, to be honest, I saw a lot of myself in him – his whole enjoyment of racing ...': Dan Martin quoted, *The Cycling Podcast* [Podcast], 'Time Has Come Tadej', 10 October 2022

91 'I certainly didn't expect anything like this in my first season. I didn't expect such a leap when I moved from the older juniors to the under-23 ranks. It's the same now. I surprised myself this year': Tadej Pogačar quoted in Lopatič, J., 'Tadej Pogačar: Nadarjenemu Slovencu so se pri Arabcih obzorja izdatneje odprla', *Siol*, 17 April 2019. https://siol.net/sportal/kolesarstvo/nadarjenemu-slovencu-so-se-obzorja-izdatneje-odprla-pri-arabcih-495404

95 'When I saw the weather forecast for today, and I read that it would be rainy, I was actually happy because I knew I had it in me to do something special': Tadej Pogačar quoted in 'Vuelta: perfect Pogačar takes extraordinary stage win for UAE Team Emirates', UAE Team Emirates, 1 September 2019. https://www.uaeteamemirates.com/vuelta-perfect-pogacar-takes-extraordinary-stage-win-for-uae-team-emirates/

95 'Attitudes and actions like that confirmed to me how much natural class he has as a rider. You can tell him what to do, but he knows it anyway, and better. He's thinking, moving and acting like a winner': Matxin Fernandez quoted as part of interview with Tadej Pogačar, *Procycling*, Issue 283, July 2021

96 'going with the flow': Tadej Pogačar quoted in 'Go with the flow', UAE Team Emirates YouTube channel, 6 September 2019

98 'As the stages go by, other riders show signs of fatigue; they arrive dead, catabolic. Tadej, on the other hand, is getting better every day': Joseba Elguezabal quoted in Peña Gomez, J., '«Pogačar está sin hacer, tiene un margen de progresión brutal»', El Correo, 1 April 2021. https://www.elcorreo.com/deportes/ciclismo/pogacar-margen-progresion-20210401225314-nt.html

98 'My director radioed that I was going well, but advised me to stick to the wheels,' Pogačar told Procycling weeks later. 'But when I saw that [podium rival] Miguel Ángel López had attacked and made some mistakes, I went for it – all or nothing … I felt like I was throwing a dice.What have you got to lose if you do your best? It doesn't matter what the result is': Tadej Pogačar quoted in Fotheringham, A., *Procycling*, Issue 262, December 2019

99 'At that time it seemed incredible to us that a Slovenian could make it into the top at the Giro or Tour. For me, they were kings. Now Roglič wins almost easily, times are really changing': Tadej Pogačar quoted in Hočevar, M., '»Nisem novi Indurain ali Valverde, marveč Tadej Pogačar«', *Delo*, 23 September 2019. https://www.delo.si/sport/kolesarstvo/nisem-novi-indurain-ali-valverde-marvec-tadej-pogacar

100 'He's like a man from another planet': Tadej Pogačar quoted in Hamilton, A., 'UAE's "Young Gun" Tadej Pogačar Gets PEZ'd!', *PEZCycling* News, 23 January 2020. https://pezcyclingnews.com/interviews/uae-team-emirates-young-gun-tadej-pogacar-gets-pezd-rider-interview/

100 'I'm only impatient when I'm not doing well. When I want the race to be over as soon as possible so I can move on to the next one,' he added. 'I'm the type of cyclist who always goes "into the red", racing all or nothing, just to stay in front. I don't know if I'm distributing my energy well and I don't know where my limits are': Tadej Pogačar quoted in Hočevar, M., '»Nisem novi Indurain ali Valverde, marveč Tadej Pogačar«', *Delo*, 23 September 2019

104 'I don't know what to do with myself for the whole day if I don't ride my bike': Tadej Pogačar interviewed, Številke [Podcast], RTV Slovenija, number 170, 20 November 2020

104 'I hope that we can help each other as much as possible. After all, we don't have many such opportunities to cooperate and we have to take advantage of them': Primož Roglič quoted, 'Roglič ni opustil sanj o zmagi na Touru', *Siol*, 24 May 2020. https://siol.net/sportal/kolesarstvo/roglic-ni-opustil-sanj-o-zmagi-na-touru-526134

104 'Definitely. Slovenians must stick together': Tadej Pogačar quoted in Pe. M., Damjan Medica/Planet T, 'Pogačar se nadeja zavezništva z Rogličem: "Slovenci moramo držati skupaj"', *Siol*, 27 May 2020. https://siol.net/sportal/kolesarstvo/na-pripravah-s-tadejem-pogacarjem-526411

104 'Allan is a very important person for me, he taught me a lot, more...': Tadej Pogačar quoted in Scherrer, G., 'Tadej Pogačar, très probable vainqueur du Tour 2021 : « J'essaye de m'amuser en faisant mon boulot »', *L'Équipe*, 17 July 2021. https://www.lequipe.fr/Cyclisme-sur-route/Actualites/Tadej-pogacar-vainqueur-du-tour-2021-j-essaye-de-m-amuser-en-faisant-mon-boulot/1271132

105 'I was not even thinking about winning it because that felt like it's almost impossible': Tadej Pogačar, 'Tadej Pogačar – The most comprehensive interview', MET Helmets YouTube channel, 24 June 2021. https://www.youtube.com/watch?v=7LvnDPSTLUg

108 'problems, also psychologically': Giuseppe Saronni, appearing on Rai 2HD Tour de France coverage, Rai, 6 September 2020

110 'When he started losing some time, games started to play in his head, I think. When your head is all over the place, the legs are also kind of lost': Tadej Pogačar, 'Tadej Pogačar – The most comprehensive interview', MET Helmets YouTube channel, 24 June 2021. https://www.youtube.com/watch?v=7LvnDPSTLUg

111 'I had mixed emotions. Beforehand, I wanted Roglič to win the Tour. I was a fan of his since his first results. Between the ages of 15 and 20, I would shout in front of the TV for him to win, and then, I was the one who beat him, who stopped him from achieving his dream:' Tadej Pogačar quoted in Issartel, D., « Primoz Roglic a réussi à m'apaiser », affirme Tadej Pogačar, vainqueur du Tour de France 2020, *L'Équipe*, 15 December 2020. https://www.lequipe.fr/Cyclisme-sur-route/Article/-primoz-roglic-a-reussi-a-m-apaiser-affirme-tadej-pogacar-vainqueur-du-tour-de-france-2020/1206141

112 'I know why you are here… you came for him, but Roglič should have won. I cried last night when I saw what they did to him… And I'm afraid he might quit his career now': RFI via AFP, 'Slovenia celebrates Pogačar's surprise Tour victory', RFI, 20 September 2020. https://www.rfi.fr/en/wires/20200920-slovenia-celebrates-pogacars-surprise-tour-victory

113 Five reader comments on Pogačar's win over Roglic taken from RTV Slovenija coverage, 'Pogačar: Po tem Touru je Primož še večji zgled zame' and 'Pariz je slovenski! Pogačar na Elizejskih poljanah okronan za kralja Toura'. 20 September 2020. https://www.rtvslo.si/sport/kolesarstvo/dirka-po-franciji/pariz-je-slovenski-pogacar-na-elizejskih-poljanah-okronan-za-kralja-toura/536600 and https://www.rtvslo.si/sport/kolesarstvo/dirka-po-franciji/pogacar-po-tem-touru-je-primoz-se-vecji-zgled-zame/536656

114 'Because of all the negative noise, I didn't celebrate that victory too much. As a Tour winner, it wasn't the homecoming I had imagined … I feel like I always have to prove myself to some people in my home country': Tadej Pogačar to *RIDE* Magazine, 2023 Tour de France summer issue. https://www.wielerflits.nl/nieuws/tadej-pogacar-nog-steeds-enkele-boze-verhalen-over-mij-in-slovenie/

116 'Because preparing for every race [to win], it's quite hard. But I think I managed this and made some improvements last year. ...': Tadej Pogačar quoted in McGrath, A., 'Tadej, Tomorrow, Always', *Rouleur*, Issue 104, 2021

117 'I think I still haven't quite realised what I achieved. In a couple of years, I'll look at this totally different to now. I take it slowly, but also I don't waste too much time thinking about what it was and more about what is going to be': Ibid

118 'When we were in Tenerife with Kerro, the guys would be close to breaking point. We were given efforts that we just couldn't finish. Tim's philosophy was 'more is better'. So if you did five hours and you could physically do six, then, do six. It was more, more, more': Rowe, Luke, *Road Captain: My Life at the Heart of the Peloton*, London: Bantam, 2025

124 'I personally think that we as a team have made a really big step in this discipline ... I'm not so far behind in the time trial any more': Tadej Pogačar quoted in Košir Teran, A., 'Tadej Pogačar: Vsi smo vedeli, kaj pričakujemo, ampak obrnilo se je tako, kot se je', Siol, 21 November 2020. https://siol.net/sportal/kolesarstvo/tadej-pogacar-sobotni-intervju-539351

133 'I was going to prove I'm not a miner and I am a proper rider who can keep winning races. Every race I went to, I wanted to prove I am a good rider … It doesn't matter how you look, it's about how much power you can generate': Tadej Pogačar quoted in Walsh, D., 'Tadej Pogačar: My brother always beat me – but then one day he didn't want to do it anymore', *The Sunday Times*, 18 December 2021. https://www.thetimes.com/sport/cycling/article/tadej-pogacar-my-brother-always-beat-me-but-then-one-day-he-didn-t-want-to-do-it-anymore-5ffts0fj7

134 Ben O'Connor, AG2R Citroën Team: 'He's just at another level right now compared to everyone else.'
Jonas Vingegaard, Jumbo–Visma: 'He has a really big lead and yesterday he really showed he is probably the strongest here.' Simon Yates, Team BikeExchange: 'He's obviously got the best legs here by a mile.' Michael Woods, Israel Start-Up Nation: 'What can stop him now? A crash?' Quoted from the video 'Can Anyone Stop Tadej Pogačar In The Race For Yellow?', FloBikes YouTube channel, featuring Gregor Brown, 6 July 2021. https://www.youtube.com/watch?v=k-T1VquaZaMU

134 'I'm more confident on the bike than in life, where I'm quite a reserved person … But I can assure you that I'm far from being the most confident rider in the peloton. Sometimes, I have shit legs and that makes me doubt myself': Tadej Pogačar quoted in Scherrer, G., 'Tadej Pogačar : « Je suppose que je marque l'histoire »', *L'Équipe*, 13 October 2021. https://www.lequipe.fr/Cyclisme-sur-route/Article/Tadej-pogacar-je-suppose-que-je-marque-l-histoire/1291897

134 'I've worked with a lot of riders who haven't had a quarter of his talent and they didn't know how to handle success like he does … I was struck at how incredibly calm he was, which in turn kept the whole team calm … He wanted to show that winning the[2020] Tour had not been a fluke. But he'll never talk about that or pretty much anything else like that in public; he's always very cautious. That's part of his character and I think a lot of Slovenians are like that: very warm-hearted in private, but in public almost inexpressive, quite cold': Joseba Elguezabal, *Procycling*, Review of the Year issue, 2021

138 'I still have the feeling that doping has decreased a lot in cycling. Everyone who wins the Tour is suspect, and that's because of some people's pasts ...': Tadej Pogačar quoted in Issartel, D., « Primoz Roglic a réussi à m'apaiser », affirme Tadej Pogačar, vainqueur du Tour de France 2020, *L'Équipe*, 15 December 2020 https://www.lequipe.fr/Cyclisme-sur-route/Article/-primoz-roglic-a-reussi-a-m-apaiser-affirme-tadej-pogacar-vainqueur-du-tour-de-france-2020/1206141

138 'He hates the typical awkward questions, the press conferences on the rest day of the Tour de France...': Joseba Elguezabal quoted in 'Ep. 306 - Los secretos de Pogačar al descubierto - Su masajista lo cuenta todo: "Pogačar sabe que el Tour lo perdió él' [Podcast], *Podcast Escapa*, 6 October 2022

139 'It is frustrating people thinking that Tadej has been extra-galactical [extra-terrestrial] this year when he has never achieved ...': Iñigo San Millán quoted in Stokes, S., 'Tour de France: Tadej Pogačar's coach hits back at doubters, says rivals have yet to push him', *Velo* [originally published as VeloNews], 10 July 2021. https://velo.outsideonline.com/events/tour-de-france/tour-de-france-tadej-pogacars-coach-hits-back-at-doubters-says-rivals-have-yet-to-push-him/

140 'Yes, I was very ill with an infection, but I didn't inject myself with anything. The investigation is not against me. It is against somebody who could have given me something;' Mauro Gianetti quoted in Gains, P., 'A New Threat in Blood Doping', *New York Times*, 18 October 1998. https://www.nytimes.com/1998/10/18/sports/a-new-threat-in-blood-doping.html

141 'Pogačar's weakness is his team. It has nothing to do with the strength of Sky or Ineos of recent years': Cédric Vasseur quoted in various French press, including *L'Équipe* and *L'Humanité*.

142 'Without my teammates, without my staff, I would never have won the Tour. On TV, everything seems easy, like playing PlayStation ...': Tadej Pogačar quoted in Issartel, D. and Scherrer, G., 'Tadej Pogačar (UAE-Emirates), vainqueur du Tour de France 2021: « À la télé, tout semble facile... »', *L'Équipe*, 18 July 2021. https://www.lequipe.fr/Cyclisme-sur-route/Article/Tadej-pogacar-uae-emirates-vainqueur-du-tour-de-france-2021-a-la-tele-tout-semble-facile/1271348

143 'I'm being very honest when I say that the goal of my career is enjoying the moment and making my family happy...': Tadej Pogačar quoted in Scherrer, G., 'Tadej Pogačar : « Je suppose que je marque l'histoire »', *L'Équipe*, 13 October 2021. https://www.lequipe.fr/Cyclisme-sur-route/Article/Tadej-pogacar-je-suppose-que-je-marque-l-histoire/1291897

146 'His main priority is honestly to have fun and enjoy cycling. And to win as many races as possible, with that. As we know, he has this animal instinct … attacking on the cobblestones in Flanders': Iñigo San Millán passages quoted in McGrath, A., 'Why Tadej Pogačar won't win all five Monuments', *Escape Collective*, 31 March 2023. https://escapecollective.com/why-tadej-pogacar-wont-win-all-five-monuments/

149 'I prefer the idea of being a Classics rider who wins Grand Tours, even if I started off with a victory in the Tour ...': Tadej Pogačar quoted in Comte, G., '« J'adore les classiques, de la pure adrénaline » : Tadej Pogačar, Vélo d'Or 2024 et amoureux des courses d'un jour', *L'Équipe*, 17 December 2024

151 'His playfulness in his racing takes a lot of pressure off his shoulders. He likes to race, he likes to play it up without having a set scenario. That leaves an open mind for going into racing as fun': Allan Peiper in McGrath, A., 'Tadej, Tomorrow, Always', *Rouleur*, Issue 104, 2021

153 'Fuck you! … that's what happens in a sprint': Pogačar and Van Baarle quoted from the video 'Tadej Pogačar Confronts Dylan van Baarle After Flanders Sprint Finish', FloBikes, 4 April 2022. https://www.youtube.com/watch?v=OgceBBiG_MI

154 'Without Tadej, I would not have been able to handle the death of my mother … She really loved Tadej': Urška Žigart quoted in 'The love, grief and ambition in the life of Urška Zigart', www.aginsurance-soudal.com, 10 March 2025

158 'I'm proud to be part of this generation of cyclists with riders like Tadej who is going to be remembered for being one of the best there has ever been in cycling … ': Mathieu van der Poel quoted in 'The star and the cyclist: how Van der Poel balances fame and focus', *Rouleur*, 2025. https://www.rouleur.cc/blogs/the-rouleur-journal/the-star-and-the-cyclist-how-van-der-poel-balances-fame-and-focus

160 'You have definitely got to look at different ways of racing… not that complicated': Geraint Thomas and Tadej Pogačar passages, 'Tadej Pogačar', *Geraint Thomas Cycling Club (Watts Occuring)* [Podcast], 9 November 2021

161 'to drop a bomb': Merijn Zeeman quoted in Boers, Nando, Het plan: hoe team Jumbo–Visma de beste wielerploeg ter wereld werd, Ambo|Anthos, 2023

164 'I think it is over, barring a crash, injury, Covid. Tadej has proved himself, he's clearly the strongest. You can't see him faltering physically because we've never seen him falter physically': Bradley Wiggins quoted in 'The Tour is over as Tadej Pogačar takes yellow | 10 years since Brad wore the maillot jaune', *The Bradley Wiggins Show* by Eurosport [Podcast], 7 July 2022

166 'Riding like that is simply my way of racing, often based on instinct...': Tadej Pogačar quoted in Farrand, S., 'I race on instinct and I'm not going to change – Tadej Pogačar interview', *Cyclingnews*, 17 November 2022. https://www.cyclingnews.com/features/i-race-on-instinct-and-im-not-going-to-change-tadej-pogacar-interview/

168 'I just didn't expect it, Pogačar cracking like that': Geraint Thomas quoted in Netflix, Tour de France: Unchained, Box to Box Films and Quad, season 1, episode 4

169 'Pogačar is finished, we killed him': Grischa Niermann quoted in 'Hoe Jonas Vingegaard de Tour de France Won | All In: Team Jumbo–Visma' film, Amazon Prime Video, 2023

170 'There couldn't be a better way to lose the Tour de France than this. I gave it all today thinking of the GC.' I'll leave the race with no regrets:' Tadej Pogačar, Letour.fr, https://www.letour.fr/en/news/2022/tadej-pogacar-the-best-way-to-lose-the-tour-de-france/1307881

171 'I felt more love from the public than after my two Tour victories': Tadej Pogačar quoted in Scherrer, G., 'Tadej Pogačar répond aux questions des abonnés: « J'ai beaucoup appris cette année », *L'Équipe*, 26 October 2022. https://www.lequipe.fr/Cyclisme-sur-route/Article/Pogacar-repond-aux-questions-des-abonnes-j-ai-beaucoup-appris-cette-annee/1361444

172 'I see him with a greater capacity to listen now …': Joseba Elguezabal passage quoted in 'Ep. 306 - Los secretos de Pogačar al descubierto - Su masajista lo cuenta todo: "Pogačar sabe que el Tour lo perdió él' [Podcast], *Podcast Escapa*, 6 October 2022

178 Iaria, M., 'Pogačar, un 2025 da 12 milioni di incassi. E il marchio vale doppio', *Gazzetta dello Sport*, 13 October 2025

180 'Urška is a really, really big part of my life. She wouldn't say [it], she sacrifices so much more than she would admit for my career. And I'm so happy that I have a person like her next to me': Tadej Pogačar quoted after 2024 World Championships road race in interview to Anders Mielke, Eurosport/TNT Sports coverage

REFERENCES AND SOURCES

181 'Sometimes you are just walking quietly and you see someone discreetly taking pictures next to you. You know you can't say anything because it would give a bad image. But at the same time I just want to be with him for five minutes': Urška Žigart quoted in Bontinck, J-G., 'Tour de France femmes : «Tadej est relax, drôle, blagueur»... Urska Zigart, la fiancée de Pogačar, se confie', *Le Parisien*, 29 July 2022

182 'I know what he has to sacrifice for it. Getting to the top is one thing. Staying at the top is much harder. Everyone looks at you and expects only the best. You should not underestimate that pressure': Urška Žigart quoted in 'The love, grief and ambition in the life of Urška Žigart', www.aginsurance-soudal.com, 10 March 2025

182 'It feels like I need to do something, not just to sit on my sofa and enjoy the success because that's not the point ...': Tadej Pogačar quoted in Wagner, K., 'The losses driving Tadej Pogačar', *CyclingTips* originally, now *Velo*, https://velo.outsideonline.com/road/road-culture/the-losses-driving-tadej-pogacar/, 12 October 2022

186 'The greatest art always returns you to the vulnerability of the human situation': Francis Bacon quoted in Sylvester, D., *The Brutality of Fact: interviews with Francis Bacon*, Thames & Hudson, 2016

188 'I think he trusts a lot in his own abilities. So he's not really afraid of anything. Sometimes, I can get a bit stressed, like "...': Mikkel Bjerg passages quoted in McGrath, A., 'What's it like to work for Tadej Pogačar', *Escape Collective*, 7 August 2023. https://escapecollective.com/what-its-like-to-work-for-tadej-pogacar/

189 'The home trainer is good, but it's not enough. He lost three weeks of training and he could only do three good weeks in June': Iñigo San Millán quoted in Scherrer, G., 'Pour l'entraîneur de Pogačar, « cela ressemble à un gros échec mais en réalité, c'est une énorme performance »', *L'Équipe*, 20 July 2023

190 'You can never underestimate him ...': Arthur van Dongen quoted in 'How Jonas Vingegaard (again) won the Tour de France | All-In: The Trilogy' film, Amazon Prime Video, 2024

193 'We waited for quite some time to hug him. His masseur was shedding thick tears. Tadej told us he was okay. He was comforting us, not us comforting him': Mirko Pogačar quoted in Grčman, L., quoting the Pogačars' speech on stage at the Slovenian Athlete of the Year ceremony in 2023, Aleteia, 20 December 2023

195 'Maybe it's just too much for my body going full gas all year. Today, I probably paid the price': Tadej Pogačar interviewed by Eurosport/GCN, 'Tadej Pogačar - Interview at the finish - Glasgow UCI World Championships ITT 2023', Cycling Pro Net YouTube channel, 11 August 2023. https://www.youtube.com/watch?v=XQNtXw6J5EE

197 'He's exceptional ... also assimilates nutrition better': Javier Sola quoted in Arribas, C., 'Javier Sola: "Pogačar está tocado con la varita', *El Pais*, 3 May 2024

198 'It [interval training] increases capillarisation of muscle. It increases mitochondrial mass, increases lactate...': Jeroen Swart quoted in interview with Fran Reyes, 'Sierra Alpha' episode [Podcast], *KM0 for Friends of the Cycling Podcast*, 2 May 2024:

201 'They were missing that optimal cycle between training and recovery, adaptation and improving ...': Jeroen Swart quoted in Moseley, D., 'Inside UAE Team Emirates: SA Dr Jeroen Swart's Winning Formula', *Bicycling*, 14 July 2025: https://www.bicycling.co.za/pro-cycling/inside-uae-team-emirates-sa-dr-jeroen-swarts-winning-formula/

202 'Everyone can see how effortlessly he rides and lives. But no matter how funny, jovial and instinctive he comes across, there's always a plan behind it. He knows exactly what he's doing': Stijn Quanten in Rodiers, R., Scheeln, D., 'De successen van Pogačar werden in januari ook al in België opgestart: "Niemand herkende Tadej en Urska met hun mutsen"', *Het Nieuwsblad*, 20 July 2024: https://www.nieuwsblad.be/sport/wielrennen/wegwielrennen/de-successen-van-pogacar-werden-in-januari-ook-al-in-belgie-opgestart-niemand-herkende-tadej-en-urska-met-hun-mutsen/26374987.html

202 'That was a surprise. You think you're at the limit, but you don't actually know where the limit is': Jeroen Swart quoted in Moseley, D., 'Inside UAE Team Emirates: SA Dr Jeroen Swart's Winning Formula', *Bicycling*, 14 July 2025

205 'These guys are not your friends. They are going to cut your throat whenever they have the opportunity. And you need to remember, the day when they're on their knees, that you need to do the same thing': Allan Peiper quoted in self-written essay for *The Road Book 2020*, Boulting, Ned, *The Road Book Almanack*, 2020

205 'He wasn't sure of himself [last year]. I think this is why this year they've done everything they could so that he went confident into all races, and not doubting himself': Urška Žigart speaking to Sammy Neyrinck, 'In gesprek met Urska Zigart: "Voor mij hoeft Tadej niks te doen om speciaal te zijn"', *Sporza*, 24 July 2024

209 'I did some pretty good numbers ... later in the race': Ben O'Connor quoted in McGrath, A., 'Il mago di Oz', *Alvento*, issue 34, 2024

211 'He's riding in a different world. He could win by five minutes or a minute, our group didn't seem to be bothered ...' – Tadej Pogačar moves out of sight at the Giro d'Italia', *Cyclingnews*, 20 May 2024. https://www.cyclingnews.com/features/hes-riding-in-a-different-world-tadej-pogacar-moves-out-of-sight-at-the-giro-ditalia/

211 'You can really hear that he means it, it's really from his heart. So it's really easy to then say, "OK, I'll do the same tomorrow to get the same acknowledgement from him ... nice space to be in': Mikkel Bjerg passages quoted in McGrath, A., 'What's it like to work for Tadej Pogačar', *Escape Collective*, 7 August 2023

215 'Fuck you, man': Tadej Pogačar quoted in Netflix, Tour de France: Unchained, Box to Box Films and Quad, season 3, released 2 July 2025

215 'not having the balls': Remco Evenepoel quote to ITV Sport, 2024 Tour de France after stage 9.

216 'I get so many messages, every single interview with you guys [the media], everybody saying don't waste energy. But I think I will never change ...' Tadej Pogačar after stage 14 of the 2024 Tour de France to several media, including ITV, ITV Cycling, posted 13 July 2024. https://www.facebook.com/watch/?v=893998569212281

216 'Our nutritionist is super angry, as we're not allowed to eat those': Tadej Pogačar in winner's speech on Tour de France podium, 21 July 2024

217 'The first Tour was the hardest to win because I only won it on the last day. But I think this one ...:': Tadej Pogačar quoted in Hautbois, Y., 'Tadej Pogačar, triple vainqueur du Tour de France : « Celui-ci est le plus grand »', *L'Équipe*, 21 July 2024

218 'A cannibal? He eats human flesh. I eat sweets at the finish and gels and bars on the bike': Tadej Pogačar, 'Tadej Pogačar grapt: "Een kannibaal? Ik? Die eet mensenvlees, ik eet snoepjes"', *Sporza*, 19 July 2024https://sporza.be/nl/2024/07/19/tadej-pogacar-grapt-een-kannibaal-ik-die-eet-mensenvlees-ik~1721402379803/

219 'It's not the main reason, but for sure it didn't help. I think she deserves her spot. She's the double national champion in road race and time trial': Tadej Pogačar, 'Tourwinnaar Pogačar in Surhuisterveen: 'Ben mentaal uitgeput, wil relaxen, naar het strand", NOS, 23 July 2024

222 'The guy in front always has an advantage. At the World Championships, Pogačar told me: "They'll look at each other, let's go." He was right': Pavel Sivakov quoted in interview with Gaudot, C., 'Pavel Sivakov : "Quand on bosse pour Tadej Pogačar, c'est toujours lui qui gagne"', Eurosport.fr, 15 October 2024. https://www.eurosport.fr/cyclisme/pavel-sivakov-quand-on-bosse-pour-tadej-pogacar-cest-toujours-lui-qui-gagne_sto20045206/story.shtml

222 'In the last hour or two hours, I went through all the emotions possible. I just couldn't give up, for everything that happened or will happen. I pushed through': Tadej Pogačar quoted in interview with Anders Mielke for Eurosport, shown on Cycling Pro Net YouTube channel, 'Tadej Pogačar - Interview at the finish - World Championships Road Race (Zürich) 2024', 29 September 2024 https://www.youtube.com/watch?v=SrZaWPnD0Zc

223 'I cannot believe what just happened. After this kind of season, I put a lot of pressure on myself today': Tadej Pogačar quoted in post-race interview with Sébastian Piquet for UCI, televised on Eurosport.

226 'Milan–San Remo is the one that is going to send me to my grave… I'm getting so close but so far, it's unbelievable': Tadej Pogačar, #318 – Cycling phenom and Tour de France champion Tadej Pogačar reveals his training strategies, on-bike nutrition, and future aspirations [Podcast], *The Peter Attia Drive*, 23 September 2024

226 'It is like a sudoku where you can't make an error. If you slip up, the damage is done and it's goodbye hopes': Filippo Ganna quoted in Scognamiglio, C., 'Ganna si scalda: "La Sanremo è un suoduku senza errori", *La Gazzetta dello Sport*, 22 March 2025

230 'It's better we take a risk. Because otherwise, if we lose one more guy for nothing, this plan is caput': Tadej Pogačar quoted in 'Milano-Sanremo 2025 | Behind the scenes' video, UAE Team Emirates YouTube channel

231 'It was no secret what he was going to do, but knowing it and following it are two different things': Michael Matthews, quoted in Giuliani, S., Farrand, S., "We didn't come here for fourth' - Michael Matthews frozen out of Milan-San Remo podium', *Cyclingnews*, 23 March 2025, https://www.cyclingnews.com/news/we-didnt-come-here-for-fourth-michael-matthews-frozen-out-of-milan-san-remo-podium/

232 'I would prefer the Poggio to be 5 km long at 10 per cent, but it is what it is. It's a really hard race for me to make...': Tadej Pogačar to Eurosport post-race, quoted in 'Tadej Pogačar - Interview at the finish - Milano-Sanremo 2025', Cycling Pro Net YouTube channel

236 'Counting down the years until retirement': Tadej Pogacar quoted in 'Pogačar se je spočil in razkril karte, nato pa še dobil svoj kriterij', RTV Slovenija, 9 August 2025

237 'It's not getting easier. The older I'm getting, the less of the kid there is in me. ..."and enjoy the moment': Tadej Pogačar to ITV Sport, 'Goodbye from ITV Sport', 27 July 2025 https://www.youtube.com/live/RUzzYvk3GaM?t=330s

242 'I have a contract until 2030. That will be your year': Pogačar to Healy, EF Pro Cycling and TNT Sports Cycling, https://www.instagram.com/p/DI9DArsgW9s/

243 'I hate riders who want to lay down the law under the pretext that they are stronger or in big teams. That's a detestable attitude': Thomas Voeckler to France Télévisions on air, 22 July 2025

247 'I've seen some [of my] highlights but not full races because I don't know how much fun it is to watch a rider ride 50 km alone': Tadej Pogačar, 'Paperon Pogačar: contratto a vita da 50 milioni in 6 stagioni. Ed è anche maglia oro', *La Gazzetta dello Sport*, November 5 2024. https://www.gazzetta.it/Ciclismo/05-11-2024/pogacar-il-contratto-con-uae-emirates-le-cifre-e-la-clausola.shtml

247 'I honestly don't like the comparisons with other people. Especially with Eddy Merckx and cyclists from that era when ...': Pogačar to numerous media at Festival dello Sport, 13 October 2024, https://www.youtube.com/watch?v=e45Qz8iyDWU&t=7s

248 'It's obvious that he is now above me. Deep down, I already thought as much ...': Eddy Merckx quoted in Le Gars, P., '« C'est évident que Tadej Pogačar est au-dessus de moi » : l'hommage d'Eddy Merckx au nouveau champion du monde', *L'Équipe*, 29 September 2024

248 'I was born under a lucky star to get this chance, this opportunity ... some other thing to make us happy': Pogačar to numerous media at Festival dello Sport, 13 October 2024, https://www.youtube.com/watch?v=e45Qz8iyDWU&t=7s

249 'I want to have fun while making history. It will be a game until I start struggling. As long as I feel good every day on the bike, as long as I don't have any p...': Tadej Pogačar quoted in Roos, A., 'Tadej Pogačar : « Je veux être le meilleur de l'histoire »', *L'Équipe*, 15 March 2024

249 'He doesn't want to leave, he's part of the country. What he's doing for Abu Dhabi is worth more than the races he wins. Pogačar is proud of that': Mauro Gianetti quoted in 'Paperon Pogačar: contratto a vita da 50 milioni in 6 stagioni. Ed è anche maglia oro', *La Gazzetta dello Sport*, 5 November 2024

250 'I don't think I'll stop right away, but I don't see myself continuing for too long either. The Los Angeles Olympic Games [in 2028] are one of my goals, which takes me to three years from now. Then I might start thinking about retirement, we'll see': Tadej Pogačar quoted in Hautbois, Y., 'Tadej Pogačar fait le bilan après son quatrième sacre sur le Tour de France : « Je ne pense pas arrêter tout de suite mais... »', *L'Équipe*, 27 July 2025